## Praise for *Implementing Lean Software Development*

"This book offers a wealth of advice for any organization that wishes to succeed at the software development game. It will help you to realize the value of adopting a product mindset to software development to recognize the inherent wastage and risk in traditional software development practices. Mary has hit another one out of the park."

—Scott Ambler, practice leader, Agile modeling

"This remarkable book combines practical advice, ready-to-use techniques, and a deep understanding of why this is the right way to develop software. I have seen software teams transformed by the ideas in this book."

—Mike Cohn, author of *Agile Estimating and Planning*

"As a lean practitioner myself, I have loved and used their first book for years. When this second book came out, I was delighted that it was even better. If you are interested in how lean principles can be useful for software development organizations, this is the book you are looking for. The Poppendiecks offer a beautiful blend of history, theory, and practice."

—Alan Shalloway, coauthor of *Design Patterns Explained*

"I've enjoyed reading the book very much. I feel it might even be better than the first lean book by Tom and Mary, while that one was already exceptionally good! Mary especially has a lot of knowledge related to lean techniques in product development and manufacturing. It's rare that these techniques are actually translated to software. This is something no other book does well (except their first book)."

—Bas Vodde

"The new book by Mary and Tom Poppendieck provides a well-written and comprehensive introduction to lean principles and selected practices for software managers and engineers. It illustrates the application of the values and practices with well-suited success stories. I enjoyed reading it."

—Roman Pichler

"In *Implementing Lean Software Development*, the Poppendiecks explore more deeply the themes they introduced in *Lean Software Development*. They begin with a compelling history of lean thinking, then move to key areas such as value, waste, and people. Each chapter includes exercises to help you apply key points. If you want a better understanding of how lean ideas can work with software, this book is for you."

—Bill Wake, independent consultant

# Implementing Lean
# Software Development

# *The Addison-Wesley Signature Series*

**The Addison-Wesley Signature Series** provides readers with practical and authoritative information on the latest trends in modern technology for computer professionals. The series is based on one simple premise: great books come from great authors. Books in the series are personally chosen by expert advisors, world-class authors in their own right. These experts are proud to put their signatures on the covers, and their signatures ensure that these thought leaders have worked closely with authors to define topic coverage, book scope, critical content, and overall uniqueness. The expert signatures also symbolize a promise to our readers: you are reading a future classic.

# THE ADDISON–WESLEY SIGNATURE SERIES
## SIGNERS: KENT BECK AND MARTIN FOWLER

**Kent Beck** has pioneered people-oriented technologies like JUnit, Extreme Programming, and patterns for software development. Kent is interested in helping teams do well by doing good — finding a style of software development that simultaneously satisfies economic, aesthetic, emotional, and practical constraints. His books focus on touching the lives of the creators and users of software.

**Martin Fowler** has been a pioneer of object technology in enterprise applications. His central concern is how to design software well. He focuses on getting to the heart of how to build enterprise software that will last well into the future. He is interested in looking behind the specifics of technologies to the patterns, practices, and principles that last for many years; these books should be usable a decade from now. Martin's criterion is that these are books he wished he could write.

## TITLES IN THE SERIES

*Implementation Patterns*
Kent Beck, ISBN 0321413091

*Test-Driven Development: By Example*
Kent Beck, ISBN 0321146530

*User Stories Applied: For Agile Software Development*
Mike Cohn, ISBN 0321205685

*Implementing Lean Software Development: From Concept to Cash*
Mary and Tom Poppendieck, ISBN 0321437381

*Refactoring Databases: Evolutionary Database Design*
Scott W. Ambler and Pramodkumar J. Sadalage, ISBN 0321293533

*Continuous Integration: Improving Software Quality and Reducing Risk*
Paul M. Duvall, with Steve Matyas and Andrew Glover, 0321336380

*Patterns of Enterprise Application Architecture*
Martin Fowler, ISBN 0321127420

*Refactoring HTML: Improving the Design of Existing Web Applications*
Elliotte Rusty Harold, ISBN 0321503635

*Beyond Software Architecture: Creating and Sustaining Winning Solutions*
Luke Hohmann, ISBN 0201775948

*Enterprise Integration Patterns: Designing, Building, and Deploying Messaging Solutions*
Gregor Hohpe and Bobby Woolf, ISBN 0321200683

*Refactoring to Patterns*
Joshua Kerievsky, ISBN 0321213351

*xUnit Test Patterns: Refactoring Test Code*
Gerard Meszaros, 0131495054

For more information, check out the series web site at www.awprofessional.com

# Implementing Lean Software Development

*From Concept to Cash*

Mary and Tom Poppendieck

**✦Addison-Wesley**

Upper Saddle River, NJ • Boston • Indianapolis • San Francisco
New York • Toronto • Montreal • London • Munich • Paris • Madrid
Capetown • Sydney • Tokyo • Singapore • Mexico City

Many of the designations used by manufacturers and sellers to distinguish their products are claimed as trademarks. Where those designations appear in this book, and Addison-Wesley was aware of a trademark claim, the designations have been printed with initial capital letters or in all capitals.

Screen Beans art is used with permission of A Bit Better Corporation. Screen Beans is a registered trademark of A Bit Better Corporation.

The authors and publisher have taken care in the preparation of this book, but make no expressed or implied warranty of any kind and assume no responsibility for errors or omissions. No liability is assumed for incidental or consequential damages in connection with or arising out of the use of the information or programs contained herein.

The publisher offers excellent discounts on this book when ordered in quantity for bulk purchases or special sales, which may include electronic versions and/or custom covers and content particular to your business, training goals, marketing focus, and branding interests. For more information, please contact:

U.S. Corporate and Government Sales
(800) 382-3419
corpsales@pearsontechgroup.com

For sales outside of the U.S., please contact:

International Sales
international@pearsoned.com

---

**This Book Is Safari Enabled**

The Safari® Enabled icon on the cover of your favorite technology book means the book is available through Safari Bookshelf. When you buy this book, you get free access to the online edition for 45 days.

Safari Bookshelf is an electronic reference library that lets you easily search thousands of technical books, find code samples, download chapters, and access technical information whenever and wherever you need it.

To gain 45-day Safari Enabled access to this book:

- Go to http://www.awprofessional.com/safarienabled
- Complete the brief registration form
- Enter the coupon code EDGG-GUQI-A1FM-GZI1-K7E3

If you have difficulty registering on Safari Bookshelf or accessing the online edition, please e-mail customer-service@safaribooksonline.com.

---

Visit us on the Web: www.awprofessional.com

*Library of Congress Cataloging-in-Publication Data*
Poppendieck, Mary.
  Implementing lean software development : from concept to cash / Mary Poppendieck, Tom Poppendieck.
    p. cm.
  Includes bibliographical references and index.
  ISBN 0-321-43738-1 (pbk. : alk. paper)
  1. Computer software—Development. 2. Production management. I. Poppendieck, Thomas David. II. Title.

  QA76.76.D47P674 2006
  005.1—dc22

                                                                      2006019698

ISBN  0-321-43738-1

Text printed in the United States on recycled paper at Courier Stoughton in Stoughton, Massachusetts.

6th   Printing     August 2008

*To our parents:*
*John and Marge Brust*
*and*
*Elmer and Ruth Poppendieck*

# Contents

# Foreword

## Jeff Sutherland

I created the first Scrum in 1993 at Easel Corporation in Burlington, Massachusetts,[1] in cooperation with our CEO, who bet his company on the team that made the first Scrum work. In 1995, I began working with Ken Schwaber, who formalized the process for worldwide deployment.[2] In four companies since Easel, I have used the self-organizing nature of Scrum to move from a Type A Scrum (winning teams) to a Type B Scrum (winning product portfolios) to a Type C Scrum (winning companies).

In 2000, I introduced Scrum to PatientKeeper, and this has proven to be an excellent vehicle for lean development. Over the years we have shortened cycle times to exactly what customers need: one week for critical items, one month for minor enhancements, and three months for significant new products. The three-month releases are accumulations of one-month Sprints, and every Sprint is a release.

At PatientKeeper the entire company runs as a Scrum and inspects, adapts, self-organizes, and changes every Monday when we have our MetaScrum meeting.[3] The Product Owner runs this meeting, and all company stakeholders are present, including the CEO. Lean concepts are carefully examined here, and Sprints are started, stopped, or changed only in this meeting. The whole company, including affected customers, can be reset in one afternoon with decisions made during the weekly MetaScrum.

---

1. Sutherland, J., "Agile Development: Lessons Learned from the First Scrum," Cutter Agile Project Management Advisory Service: Executive Update, 2004, 5(20): pp. 1–4.
2. Schwaber, K., "Scrum Development Process," in *OOPSLA Business Object Design and Implementation Workshop*, J. Sutherland, et al., editors. 1997, Springer: London.
3. Sutherland, J., "Future of Scrum: Parallel Pipelining of Sprints in Complex Projects," in *AGILE 2005 Conference*. 2005. Denver, Colorado: IEEE.

We have a chief Product Owner with a team that gets the Product Backlog "ready." We have a chief ScrumMaster, who runs a 15-minute daily Scrum of Scrums. What did teams do yesterday, what will they do today, and what are the impediments to delivery? We manage 45 releases of software per year into large, mission-critical enterprises using these short meetings and using an automated system that tracks the state of concurrent Sprint backlogs. Dates are committed to customers before the start of a Sprint, and thousands of Web users and hundreds of physicians with PDAs go live at the end of every Sprint. For PatientKeeper, concept (Product Backlog) to cash (product in production) occurs in one-month intervals. We have had to eliminate waste everywhere—before, during, and after the implementation process.

In 1993, lean product development was not well understood in any industry. Scrum was the first concrete implementation of lean thinking to software development that allowed organizations of all types and sizes to start up lean teams in a couple of days using a standard pattern that was easily understood. What was hard was explaining why and how to implement the pattern to generate continuous quality and productivity improvement.

Today, the writing and courses from Mary and Tom Poppendieck provide a proven set of principles that organizations can use to adapt tools, techniques, and methods to their own specific unique contexts and capabilities. Now we can explain how to use Scrum to lean out software development. In addition to my company, PatientKeeper, I use the procedures and processes outlined in this book to teach practitioners worldwide how to optimize Scrum.

Lean software development views all agile methods as valid, proven applications of lean thinking to software. It also goes beyond agile, providing a broader perspective that enables agile methods to thrive. First, it looks along the whole value chain, from concept to cash and tries to address all the waste and delays that happen before and after the coders contribute their part. Second, it establishes a management context to extend, nourish, and leverage agile software practices. Third, it provides a proven set of principles that each organization can use to adapt tools, techniques, and methods to their own specific unique contexts and capabilities.

Every chapter in this book illustrates a set of principles that can be implemented to build more productive teams. If you want to be like Toyota, where productivity is consistently four times that of its competitors and quality is twelve times better, these practices are essential. If you execute well on the principles in this book, resistance by your competition is futile, and winning in your market is certain. The return on investment in practices outlined in this book can be very high.

To create the lean "secret sauce" for your company, we have found you must systematically implement this accumulated lean wisdom. In short, you must deeply understand the Japanese concepts of Muri, Mura, and Muda. Mary and Tom unfold them as the seven lean principles and the seven wastes of software development to help you easily understand how they work and know what to do.

Muri relates to properly loading a system and Mura relates to never stressing a person, system, or process. Yet many managers want to load developers at 110 percent. They desperately want to create a greater sense of "urgency" so developers will "work harder." They want to micromanage teams, which stifles self-organization. These ill-conceived notions often introduce wait time, churn, death marches, burnout, and failed projects.

When I ask technical managers whether they load the CPU on their laptop to 110 percent they laugh and say, "Of course not. My computer would stop running!" Yet by overloading teams, projects are often late, software is brittle and hard to maintain, and things gradually get worse, not better. One needs to understand that Toyota and Scrum use a pull system that avoids stress (Mura) and eliminates bottlenecks (Muri). The developers take what they need off the Product Backlog just in time. They choose only Product Backlog that is ready to take into a Sprint, and they never take more than they can get done in a Sprint. They go faster by surfacing impediments and working with management to eliminate waste (Muda). By removing waste, they have less work to do. Productivity goes up, and they have time to deliver quality software and focus on exactly what the customers need.

So by understanding loading (Muri) and avoiding stress (Mura) you shorten cycle time. This leans out the environment causing impediments that create waste (Muda) to be highly visible. When you eliminate these impediments, your teams move faster, do more with less, increase quality, and move the product right into the sweet spot for the customer.

I recommend you keep the Poppendiecks' books on your desk and use them regularly to help with systematic and continuous implementation of lean principles. Practice hard, and you will rapidly double productivity by using lean development to do less by avoiding waste, and then double it again by working smarter by eliminating impediments. By going four times faster in the right way, your quality will improve by a factor of twelve like Toyota.

—Jeff Sutherland, Ph.D.
Chief Technology Officer, PatientKeeper
Certified ScrumMaster Trainer
Inventor of the Scrum Development Process
July 2006

# Foreword

## *Kent Beck*

Software development is a chain with many links, and improving overall effectiveness requires looking at the whole chain. This book is for people involved in software development—not just programmers, but also managers, sponsors, customers, testers, and designers. The principles presented here eventually affect everyone connected to the development of software. This book speaks to those of you who are ready to look at the big picture of development.

For ideas to have impact, they must be grounded in both theory and experience. By translating well-proven ideas from lean manufacturing, this book presents theory and practice and applies them to software development. Many of the fundamental problems with manufacturing are also problems with software development: dealing with uncertainty and change, continuously improving processes, and delivering value to customers.

What does this book offer you? First, a wide variety of theories that provide alternative ways of thinking about how software development can be improved. Second, a set of stories about the application of these theories to real projects. Third, provocative questions to help you apply the theories and the lessons in the stories to your unique situation.

Mary is uniquely qualified to present this material. She experienced lean manufacturing firsthand, helping rescue a plant from being shut down by transforming its operations. She's also experienced software development as a programmer and a manager. I once shared a seminar with Mary, and it was a treat to see the force and confidence with which she presents her material. I can hear that same direct voice in her writing here.

If you've read the Poppendiecks' precursor book, *Lean Software Development*, this book offers new guidance towards its implementation. It reiterates the theory in the previous volume, but always with an eye towards applying the ideas in real situations. The result is a readable and practical guide to ideas that have the potential to help you transform your development.

This is a book for doers, doers who want their actions aligned with where they can do the most good. If you are such a person, I recommend this book to you as a source of ideas and energy for positive change.

—Kent Beck
Three Rivers Institute
July 2006

# Preface

## The Sequel

*Lean* was an idea borrowed from the 1990s when we wrote the book *Lean Software Development: An Agile Toolkit* in 2003. We had observed that break-through ideas from manufacturing and logistics often take a decade or two before they are adapted to provide suitable guidance for development efforts. So we decided it was not too late to use well-proven lean concepts from the 1980s and 1990s to help us explain why agile methods are a very effective approach to software development.

The strategy worked. The book *Lean Software Development* presents a set of thinking tools based on lean thinking that leaders continue to find useful for understanding agile software development. The book has been purchased by many a developer who gave it to his or her manager to read, and many managers have distributed multiple copies of the book to colleagues in support of a transition to lean/agile software development.

Meanwhile, something unexpected happened to *lean*. In the last couple of years lean initiatives have experienced a resurgence in popularity. The word *lean* was originally popularized in the early 1990s to characterize the Japanese approach to automobile manufacturing.[1] In recent years, Honda and Toyota have been doing increasingly well in the North American auto market, while Detroit automakers are restructuring. For example, Toyota's profits rose from more than $8 billion in the fiscal year ending March 31, 2003, to more than $10 billion in 2004, $11 billion in 2005, and $12 billion in 2006. Many com-

---

1. James Womack, Daniel Jones, and Daniel Roos, *The Machine That Changed the World*, Rawson Associates, 1990.

panies have taken a second look at *lean* to try to understand what's behind such steady and sustained success.

Lean initiatives seldom start in the software development or product development area of a company, but over time, successful lean initiatives make their way from manufacturing or logistics to development departments. However, lean practices from manufacturing and other operational areas do not adapt easily to a development environment, so lean initiatives have a tendency to stall when they reach software development. While the underlying lean principles remain valid, it is usually inappropriate to apply operational practices and measurements to a development environment. When lean initiatives stall in software development areas, many companies have discovered that the book *Lean Software Development* gives them a good foundation for thinking about how to modify their approach and adapt lean ideas to a development organization.

The benefits of lean and agile software development have become widely known and appreciated in the last few years, and many organizations are changing the way they develop software. We have traveled around the world visiting organizations as they implement these new approaches, and we have learned a lot from our interaction with people working hard to change the way they develop software. As our knowledge has grown, so has the demand for more information on implementing lean software development. We realized that a new book would allow us to share what we've learned with many more people than we can contact personally. Therefore we have summarized our experiences in this book, *Implementing Lean Software Development: From Concept to Cash.*

This book is not a cookbook for implementing lean software development. Like our last book, it is a set of thinking tools about how to go about adapting lean principles to your world. We start this book where the last book left off and go deeper into the issues and problems that people encounter when trying to implement lean and agile software development. You might consider this book a sequel to *Lean Software Development.* Instead of repeating what is in that book, we take a different perspective. We assume the reader is convinced that lean software development is a good idea, and focus on the essential elements of a successful implementation. We look at key aspects of implementation and discuss what is important, what isn't, and why. Our objective is to help organizations get started down the path toward more effective software development.

The first chapter of this book reviews the history of *lean*, and the second chapter reviews the seven principles of lean software development presented in *Lean Software Development.* These are followed by chapters on *value, waste, speed, people, knowledge, quality, partners,* and the *journey* ahead. Each of these eight chapters begins with a story that illustrates how one organization dealt with the issue at hand. This is followed by a discussion of key topics we have found to be important, along with short stories that illustrate the topic, and answers to typical questions we often hear. Each chapter ends with a set of exercises that helps you explore the topics more deeply.

## Acknowledgments

We would like to thank everyone who has attended our talks and classes and invited us into their companies, especially those who have shared experiences and asked penetrating questions. In this book we share the knowledge that we have gained from all of you.

Many thanks to Jeff Sutherland and Kent Beck for their kind forewords, and thanks to our editor, Greg Doench, project editor, Tyrrell Albaugh, and especially our copy editor, Nancy Hendryx. Particular thanks goes to those who have contributed ideas and stories to the book: Jill Aden, Brad Appleton, Ralph Bohnet, Mike Cohn, Bent Jensen, Brian Marick, Clare Crawford-Mason, Ryan Martens, Gerard Meszaros, Lynn Miller, Kent Schnaith, Ian Shimmings, Joel Spolsky, Jeff Sutherland, Nancy Van Schooenderwoert, Bill Wake, Werner Wild, and our friend and operations manager, who prefers to remain anonymous.

We thank everyone who read the first draft and contributed suggestions, particularly Glen Alleman, Brad Appleton, Daniel Brolund, Bob Corrick, Allan Kelly, Kent Schnaith, Dave Simpson, Alan Shalloway, and Willem van den Ende. We thank reviewers Yi Lv, Roman Pichler, Bill Wake, and especially Bas Vodde for his extensive and insightful comments. A particularly heartfelt thanks goes to Mike Cohn, who reviewed both drafts of the book, keeping up with us under a tight deadline while he was very busy. His comments and suggestions have truly helped make this a better book.

—Mary and Tom Poppendieck
July 2006

# Chapter 1

# History

## Interchangeable Parts

Paris, France, July 1785. It was 18 months after the end of the Revolutionary War in America, and four years before the start of the French Revolution. The need for weapons was on everyone's mind when Honoré Blanc invited high-ranking military men and diplomats to his gunsmith shop in Paris. He had taken apart 50 firing mechanisms (called "locks") and placed the pieces in boxes. The astonished visitors took random parts from the bins, assembled them into locks, and added them to muskets. They found that the parts fit together perfectly. For the first time it seemed possible to make guns out of interchangeable parts.

Thomas Jefferson, a diplomat in Paris at the time, was at the demonstration. The future United States president saw a way to address a big problem in his fledgling country. The United States was facing a shortage of weapons to defend itself and expand its boundaries. If interchangeable parts could be easily produced, then relatively unskilled workers could assemble a lot of guns at low cost, a real boon to the start-up country that had neither the money to buy guns nor the craftsmen to make them.

The challenge of creating a manufacturing process precise enough to make interchangeable parts for guns was taken up by Eli Whitney, who had recently patented the cotton gin. In 1798 Whitney was awarded a government contract to make 10,000 guns in two years. Ten years and several cost overruns later he finally delivered the guns, and even then the parts were not fully interchangeable. Nevertheless, Whitney is considered a central figure in developing the "American system of manufacture," a manufacturing system in which semi-skilled workers use machine tools and precise jigs to make standardized parts that are then assembled into products.

During the 1800s the United States grew dramatically as an industrial power, with much of the credit given to the new manufacturing system. Meanwhile in Europe there was strong resistance to replacing craft production. In France,

Honoré Blanc's work was terminated by a government that feared losing its control over manufacturing if unregulated workers could assemble a musket. In England, the inventors of machines that automated both spinning and weaving were attacked by angry crowds who feared losing their jobs. But in America, labor was scarce and there were few craft traditions, so the new industrial model of interchangeable parts took root and flourished.

## Interchangeable People

Detroit, USA, January 1914. Henry Ford raised wages of workers from $2.40 for a nine-hour day to $5 for an eight-hour day as he began assembly line production of the Model T. The press suggested that he was crazy, but it was a shrewd move. Ford had taken more than 85 percent of the labor out of a car, so he could well afford to double wages. He had already dropped the price of the car dramatically. Now he drove up wages and shortened work hours to help create a middle class with the time and money to buy automobiles.

It used to take more than 12 hours to assemble an automobile; now it took about 90 minutes. What happened to all of the time? Ford managers applied the ideas of efficiency expert Frederick Winslow Taylor as they designed the production line jobs. Taylor believed that most fixed wage workers spent their time trying to figure out how to work slowly, since being efficient brought no extra pay and could threaten jobs. His approach was to divide the assembly line work into very small steps, and time the workers to uncover the "one best way" to do each step.

Work on the assembly line was boring, repetitive, and tightly controlled. The workers were shown exactly how to do their job and told how much time they had to complete it. They could be trained in ten minutes, and they could be replaced in ten minutes. Like the interchangeable parts of a century earlier, interchangeable workers were at the center of a new industrial model: mass production.

High wages were supposed to make up for the lack of variety and autonomy, and for a while they did. And for a while, things went very well for Ford. Sales soared, and Ford owned the market. But after a while the Model T grew old and an increasingly prosperous middle class wanted to trade in their old cars for more stylish sedans. Ford was slow to respond, because his production system was most efficient when making only one kind of car. Meanwhile at General Motors, Alfred P. Sloan had created an organization structured to produce multiple models aimed at segmented markets. As the demand for variety and complexity grew, Ford's production system grew unwieldy.

Also as time passed workers began to feel trapped in untenable working conditions. They had become accustomed to a high standard of living and were unable to find comparable salaries elsewhere. The widespread labor unrest in the United States in the 1930s is often attributed to a system which held little respect for workers and regarded them as interchangeable.

## The Toyodas

Kariya, Japan, February 1927. Toyoda Automatic Loom Works held a workshop for textile engineers to showcase the company's new loom. First the visitors saw how Toyoda looms were manufactured with high precision tools, and then they were taken on a tour of the experimental spinning and weaving facility where 520 of the Toyoda looms were in operation. The looms were a wonder to behold; they ran at a blazingly fast 240 picks per minute and were operated by only 20 weavers. Anticipating a law abolishing nighttime labor, the machines were fully automatic and could run unattended all night. When a shuttle flying across the loom was just about out of thread, a new shuttle replaced it in a smooth, reliable exchange. If even one of the hundreds of warp threads broke or the weft thread ran out, the loom immediately stopped and signaled a weaver to fix the problem.

If you want to understand the Toyota[1] Production System, it is important to appreciate just how difficult it was to develop and manufacture the "perfect loom." Sakichi Toyoda built his first power loom in 1896 and invented an automated shuttle changing device in 1903. A test was set up to compare 50 Toyoda shuttle changing looms with a similar number of simple power looms from Europe. The results were disappointing. These early Toyoda looms were complex, low precision machines that were balky and difficult to maintain.

Sakichi Toyoda recruited technically competent employees and hired an American engineer, Charles A. Francis, to bring the American system of manufacture to his company. Francis redesigned the manufacturing equipment and built a machine tool shop to produce it. He developed standard specifications, produced standardized gauges and jigs, and reorganized the manufacturing line. At the same time, Sakichi Toyoda designed wider all-iron looms, and by 1909 he had patented a superior automated shuttle-change mechanism. Over the next decade, as war distracted Europe and America, looms designed by Sakichi Toyoda sold very well.

---

1. The "d" in the Toyoda family name was changed to a "t" when the Toyota Motor Company was established. The Japanese characters are similar, but Toyota takes two less brush strokes than Toyoda.

Although Sakichi Toyoda readily adopted high precision interchangeable parts, the loom manufacturing business had no room for interchangeable people. Automatic looms are complex, high precision machines, very sensitive to changes in materials and a challenge to keep running smoothly. Thus, highly skilled weavers were needed to set up and keep 25 or 30 machines running at once. If running a loom required skill, the design and manufacture of automated looms was even more demanding. Sakichi Toyoda had a reputation for hiring some of the most capable engineers being trained at Japanese universities. He kept his development team intact even as he started new companies, and he depended on them to carry on research in loom design and manufacture.

In 1921 Sakichi Toyoda's son Kiichiro joined his father's company and focused on advancing loom automation. In 1924 they jointly filed a patent for an improved automatic shuttle-change mechanism. The research team also developed methods to detect problems and stop the loom, so that looms could run unattended at night. Kiichiro Toyoda oversaw the building and start-up of a factory to produce the new looms, and set up 520 of them in the Toyoda experimental weaving factory. After he proudly showed off these "perfect looms," orders for the automated looms poured in. Kiichiro used the profits to start up an automotive business. He toured Detroit and spent years learning how to build engines. Toyota's first production car hit the market in 1936, but manufacturing was soon interrupted by war.

# The Toyota Production System

Koromo, Japan, October 1949. Passenger car production restrictions were lifted in post-war Japan. In 1945, Kiichiro Toyoda had challenged his company to "catch up with America," but it was clear that Toyota could not catch up by adopting America's mass production model. Mass production meant making thousands of identical parts to gain economies of scale, but materials were scarce, orders were spotty, and variety was in demand. Economies of scale were simply not available.

Kiichiro Toyoda's vision was that all parts for assembly should arrive at the assembly line "Just-in-Time" for their use. This was not to be accomplished by warehousing parts; parts should be made just before they are needed. It took time to make this vision a reality, but in 1962, a decade after Kiichiro Toyoda's death, his company adopted the Toyota Production System companywide.

## Taiichi Ohno

Taiichi Ohno was a machine shop manager who responded to Kiichiro Toyoda's challenge and vision by developing what came to be known as the Toyota Production System. He studied Ford's production system and gained insight from the way American supermarkets handled inventory. To this he added his knowledge of spinning and weaving and the insights of the workers he supervised. It took years of experimentation to gradually develop the Toyota Production System, a process that Ohno considered never-ending. He spread the ideas across the company as he was given increasingly broad areas of responsibility.

In his book, *Toyota Production System*,[2] Ohno calls the Toyota Production System "a system for the absolute elimination of waste." He explains that the system rests on two pillars: Just-in-Time flow and autonomation (also called Jidoka).

### *Just-in-Time Flow*

It is important to note that Just-in-Time flow went completely against all conventional wisdom of the time. Resistance to Ohno's efforts was tremendous, and he succeeded because he was backed by Eiji Toyoda, who held various senior management positions in the company after his cousin Kiichiro left in 1950. Both Toyodas had brilliantly perceived that the game to be played was not economies of scale, but conquering complexity. Economies of scale will reduce costs about 15 percent to 25 percent per unit when volume doubles. But costs go up by 20 percent to 35 percent every time variety doubles.[3] Just-in-Time flow drives out major contributors to the cost of variety. In fact, it is the only industrial model we have that effectively manages complexity.[4]

### *Autonomation (Jidoka)*

Toyoda automated looms could operate without weavers present because the looms detected when anything went wrong and shut down automatically. Autonomation, or its Japanese name Jidoka, means that work is organized so that the slightest abnormality is immediately detected, work stops, and the cause of the problem is remedied before work resumes. Another name for this critical concept, and one that is perhaps easier to remember, is "stop-the-line."

---

2. This section is based on Taiichi Ohno's book, *Toyota Production System: Beyond Large-Scale Production*, Productivity Press, written in Japanese in 1978 and translated into English in 1988. It is an excellent book, very readable and highly recommended even today.
3. George Stalk, "Time—The Next Source of Competitive Advantage," *Harvard Business Review*, July 1988.
4. See "Lean or Six Sigma," by Freddy Balle and Michael Balle, available at www.lean.org/library/leanorsigma.pdf.

Ohno called autonomation "automation with a human touch." He pointed out how the related word "autonomic" brings to mind another way to look at this concept. Our bodies have an autonomic nervous system that governs reflexes such as breathing, heartbeat, and digestion. If we touch something hot, our autonomic nerves cause us to withdraw our hand without waiting for the brain to send a message. Autonomation means the organization has reflexes in place that will respond instantly and correctly to events without having to go to the brain for instructions.[5]

## Shigeo Shingo

Shigeo Shingo was a consultant who helped Ohno implement the Toyota Production System at Toyota, and later helped companies around the world understand and implement the system. Those of us who implemented Just-in-Time manufacturing in the early '80s fondly remember the "Green Book,"[6] the first book on Just-in-Time published in English. It was not a good translation, and the material is heavy and technical, but it is a stunningly insightful book.

Shingo covers two major themes in the book: nonstock production and zero inspection. A careful look shows that these are actually the engineering equivalent of Ohno's pillars of the Toyota Production System.

### Nonstock Production

Just-in-Time flow means eliminating the stockpiles of in-process inventory that used to be made in the name of economies of scale. The focus is on making everything in small batches, and in order to do this, it is necessary to be able to changeover a machine from making one part to making a different part very quickly. In software development, one way to look at set-up time is to consider the time it takes to deploy software. Some organizations take weeks and months to deploy new software, and because of this they put as many features into a release as possible. This gives them a large batch of testing, training, and integration work to do for each release. On the other hand, I expect the antivirus software on my computer to be updated with a well-tested release within hours after a new threat is discovered. The change will be small, so integration and training are generally not a concern.

### Zero Inspection

The idea behind autonomation is that a system must be designed to be mistake-proof. There should not be someone looking for a machine to break or testing

---

5. Taiichi Ohno, Ibid., p. 46.
6. Shigeo Shingo, *Study of 'Toyota' Production System*, Productivity Press, 1981.

product to see if it is good. A properly mistake-proofed system will not need inspection. My video cable is an example of mistake-proofing. I can't plug a monitor cable into a computer or video projector upside down because the cable and plug are keyed. So I don't need someone to inspect that I plugged the cable in correctly, because it's impossible to get it wrong. Mistake-proofing assumes that any mistake that can be made will eventually be made, so take the time at the start to make the mistake impossible.

## Just-in-Time

The Toyota Production System was largely ignored, even in Japan, until the oil crisis of 1973, because companies were growing quickly and they could sell everything they made. But the economic slowdown triggered by the oil crisis sorted out excellent companies from mediocre ones, and Toyota emerged from the crisis quickly. The Toyota Production System was studied by other Japanese companies and many of its features were adopted. Within a decade America and Europe began to feel serious competition from Japan. For example, I (Mary) was working in a video cassette plant in the early '80s when Japanese competitors entered the market with dramatically low pricing. Investigation showed that the Japanese companies were using a new approach called Just-in-Time, so my plant studied and adopted Just-in-Time to remain competitive.

The picture that we used at our plant to depict Just-in-Time manufacturing is shown in Figure 1.1.

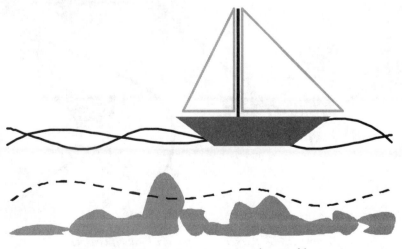

**Figure 1.1**  *Lower inventory to surface problems*

Inventory is the water level in a stream, and when the water level is high, a lot of big rocks lurking under the water are hidden. If you lower the water level, the big rocks begin to surface. At that point, you have to clear the rock out of the way, or your boat will crash into them. As the big rocks are removed, you can lower inventory level some more, find more rocks, clear them out of the stream, and keep on going until there are just pebbles left.

Why not just keep the inventory high and ignore the rocks? Well, the rocks are things like defects that creep into the product without being detected, processes that drift out of control, finished goods that people aren't going to buy before the shelf life expires, an inventory tracking system that keeps on losing track of inventory—things like that. The rocks are hidden waste that is costing you a lot of money—you just don't know it unless you lower the inventory level.

A key lesson from our Just-in-Time initiative was that we had to stop trying to maximize local efficiencies. We had a lot of expensive machines, so we thought we should run them each at maximum productivity. But that only increased our inventory, because a pile of inventory built up at the input to each machine to keep it running, and at the output from each machine as it merrily produced product that had nowhere to go. When we implemented Just-in-Time, the piles of inventory disappeared, and we were surprised to discover that the overall performance of the plant actually *increased* when we did not try to run our machines at maximum utilization (see Figure 1.2).

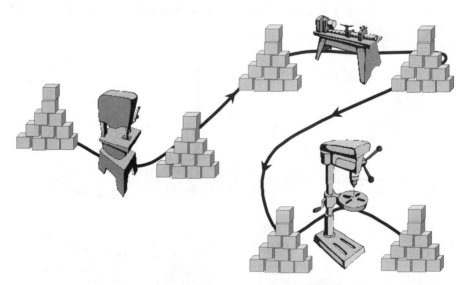

**Figure 1.2** *Stop trying to maximize local efficiencies.*

## Stop-the-Line and Safety Consciousness

One Just-in-Time practice that was easy to adopt was a stop-the-line culture. Our video tape plant made tape out of some rather volatile materials, so we had an aggressive safety program in place. Through our safety program we already knew that it was important to investigate even the smallest accident, because small accidents will eventually turn into big accidents if they are ignored.

The book *Managing the Unexpected* [7] by Weick and Sutcliffe shows that organizations like our plant create an environment where people pay attention to safety by maintaining a state of *mindfulness.* According to the authors, mindfulness has five characteristics:

1. **Preoccupation with Failure**
   We spent a lot of time thinking about what could go wrong and being prepared.

2. **Reluctance to Simplify**
   We had a large, complex plant, so safety was a large, complex issue.

3. **Sensitivity to Operations**
   Every manager in the plant was expected to spend time working on the line.

4. **Commitment to Learn from Mistakes**
   Even the smallest incident was investigated to determine how to prevent it from ever happening again.

5. **Deference to Expertise**
   Every manager knew that the people doing the work were the ones who *really* understood how the plant worked.

It was a small step to turn our safety culture into a stop-the-line culture. We added to our preoccupation with accidents a preoccupation with defects. Every step of every operation was mistake-proofed as we focused on eliminating the need for after-the-fact inspection. Whenever a defect occurred, the work team stopped producing product and looked for the root cause of the problem. If defective material made it through a process undetected, we studied the process to find out how to keep that from happening again. When I say "we" I refer to our production workers, because they were the ones who designed the process in the first place.

—Mary Poppendieck

---

7. Karl E. Weick and Kathleen M. Sutcliffe, *Managing the Unexpected: Assuring High Performance in an Age of Complexity,* Jossey-Bass, 2001.

**Figure 1.3**   *Coffee cups simulating inventory carts with kanban cards*

When we decided to move our plant to Just-in-Time, there were few consultants around to tell us what to do, so we had to figure it out ourselves. We created a simulation by covering a huge conference table with a big sheet of brown paper, then drawing the plant processes on the paper. We made "kanban cards" by writing various inventory types on strips cut from index cards. We put an inventory strip into a coffee cup and—viola!—that cup became a cart full of the indicated inventory. (See Figure 1.3.) Then we printed a week's packing orders and simulated a pull system by attempting to fill the orders, using the cups and the big sheet of paper like a game board. When a cup of inventory was packed, the inventory strip (kanban card) was moved to the previous process, which used it as a signal to make more of that material.[8]

With this manual simulation we showed the concept of a pull system to the production managers, then the general supervisors, then the shift supervisors. Finally, the shift supervisors ran through the simulation with every worker in their area. Each work area was asked to figure out the details of how to make this new pull system work in their environment. It took some months of detailed preparation, but finally everything was ready. We held our collective breath as we changed the whole plant over to a pull system in one weekend. Computerized scheduling was turned off, its place taken by manual scheduling

---

8. This scheduling approach is called Kanban, and the token showing what each process should make is called a kanban card.

via kanban cards. Our Just-in-Time system was an immediate and smashing success, largely because the details were designed by the workers, who therefore knew how to iron out the small glitches and continually improve the process.

## Lean

In 1990 the book *The Machine That Changed the World*[9] gave a new name to what had previously been called Just-in-Time or the Toyota Production System. From then on, Toyota's approach to manufacturing would become known as **Lean Production**. During the next few years, many companies attempted to adopt Lean Production, but it proved remarkably difficult. Like all new industrial models, resistance from those invested in the old model was fierce.

Many people found Lean counterintuitive and lacked a deep motivation to change long established habits. Quite often companies implemented only part of the system, perhaps trying Just-in-Time without its partner, stop-the-line. They missed the point that, "The truly lean plant...*transfers the maximum number of tasks and responsibilities to those workers actually adding value to the car on the line, and it has in place a system for detecting defects that quickly traces every problem, once discovered, to its ultimate source."*[10]

Despite the challenges faced when implementing a counterintuitive new paradigm, many lean initiatives have been immensely successful, creating truly lean businesses, which have invariably flourished. Lean thinking has moved from manufacturing to other operational areas as diverse as order processing, retail sales, and aircraft maintenance. Lean principles have also been extended to the supply chain, to product development, and to software development. See Figure 1.4.

### Lean Manufacturing/Lean Operations

Today lean manufacturing sets the standard for discipline, efficiency, and effectiveness. In fact, using lean principles in manufacturing often creates a significant competitive advantage that can be surprisingly difficult to copy. For example, Dell Computer's make-to-order system routinely delivers a "custom-built" computer in a few days, a feat which is not easily copied by competitors unwilling to give up their distribution systems. Lean has moved into nonmanufacturing operations as well. Southwest Airlines focuses on transporting custom-

---

9. James Womack, Daniel Jones, and Daniel Roos, *The Machine That Changed the World*, Rawson Associates, 1990.
10. Ibid., p. 99. Italics are from original text.

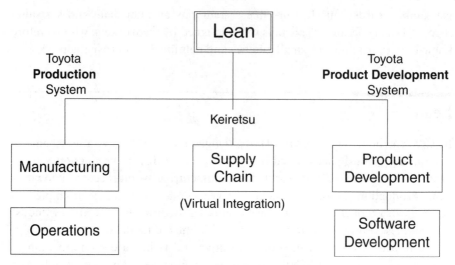

**Figure 1.4**   *The lean family tree*

ers directly from point A to point B in relatively small planes, while competitors can't easily abandon their large-batch oriented hub-and-spoke systems. A few industries, such as rapid package delivery, have been structured based on lean principles, and in those industries, only companies with lean operations can survive.

## Lean Supply Chain

When lean production practices reach the plant walls, they have to be extended to suppliers, because mass production and lean manufacturing do not work well together. Toyota realized this early, and helped its suppliers adopt the Toyota Production System. Peter Drucker estimated that Toyota's supplier network, which Drucker calls a Keiretsu, gives it a 25 percent to 30 percent cost advantage relative to its peers.[11] When Toyota moved to the United States in the late 1980s, it established a similar supplier network. Remarkably, US automotive suppliers often have lean sections of their plants dedicated to supplying Toyota, while the rest of the plant has to be run the "traditional" way because other automotive companies cannot deal with a lean supplier.[12] A lean supply chain is

---

11. Peter Drucker, *Management Challenges for the 21st Century*, Harper Business, 2001, p. 33.
12. See Jeffrey Dyer, *Collaborative Advantage: Winning Through Extended Enterprise Supplier Networks*, Oxford University Press, 2000.

also essential to Dell, since it assembles parts designed and manufactured by other companies. Through "virtual integration," Dell treats its partners as if they are inside the company, exchanging information freely so that the entire supply chain can remain lean.

In lean supply chains, companies have learned how to work across company boundaries in a seamless manner, and individual companies understand that their best interests are aligned with the best interests of the entire supply chain. For organizations involved in developing software across company boundaries, supply chain management provides a well-tested model of how separate companies might formulate and administer lean contractual relationships.

## Lean Product Development

"The real differential between Toyota and other vehicle manufacturers is not the Toyota Production System. It's the Toyota Product Development System," says Kosaku Yamada, chief engineer for the Lexus ES 300.[13] Product development is quite different than operations, and techniques that are successful in operations are often inappropriate for development work. Yet the landmark book *Product Development Performance*[14] by Clark and Fujimoto shows that effective product development has much in common with lean manufacturing. Table 1.1 summarizes the similarities described by Clark and Fujimoto.

If any company can extract the essence of the Toyota Production System and properly apply it to product development, Toyota would be the top candidate. So there was no surprise when it became apparent in the late 1990s that Toyota has a unique and highly successful approach to product development. Toyota's approach is both counterintuitive and insightful. There is little attempt to use the manufacturing-specific practices of the Toyota Production System in product development, but the underlying principles clearly come from the same heritage.

The product coming out of a development process can be brilliant or mundane. It might have an elegant design and hit the market exactly right, or it might fall short of both customer and revenue expectations. Toyota products tend to routinely fall in the first category. Observers attribute this to the leadership of a chief engineer, responsible for the business success of the product, who has both a keen grasp of what the market will value and the technical capability

---

13. Gary S. Vasilash, "Engaging the ES 300," *Automotive Design and Production*, September, 2001.
14. Kim B. Clark and Takahiro Fujimoto, *Product Development Performance: Strategy, Organization, and Management in the World Auto Industry*, Harvard Business School Press, 1991.

**Table 1.1** *Similarities between Lean Manufacturing and Effective Product Development*[15]

| Lean Manufacturing | Lean Development |
| --- | --- |
| Frequent set-up changes | Frequent product changes (software releases) |
| Short manufacturing throughput time | Short development time |
| Reduced work-in-process inventory between manufacturing steps | Reduced information inventory between development steps |
| Frequent transfer of small batches of parts between manufacturing steps | Frequent transfer of preliminary information between development steps |
| Reduced inventory requires slack resources and more information flow between steps | Reduced development time requires slack resources and information flow between stages |
| Adaptability to changes in volume, product mix, and product design | Adaptability to changes in product design, schedule, and cost targets |
| Broad task assignments for production workers gives higher productivity | Broad task assignments for engineers (developers) gives higher productivity |
| Focus on quick problem solving and continuous process improvement | Focus on frequent incremental innovation and continuous product and process improvement |
| Simultaneous improvement in quality, delivery time, and manufacturing productivity | Simultaneous improvement in quality, development time, and development productivity |

to oversee the systems design. In the book *The Toyota Way*,[16] Jeffrey Liker recounts the stories of the development of the Lexus and the Prius, emphasizing how these breakthrough designs were brought to market in record time under the leadership of two brilliant chief engineers.

Product development is a knowledge creation process. Toyota's Product Development System creates knowledge through broad exploration of design spaces, hands-on experimentation with multiple prototypes, and regular inte-

---

15. Adapted from Kim B. Clark and Takahiro Fujimoto, *Product Development Performance*, p. 172.
16. Jeffrey Liker, *The Toyota Way: 14 Management Principles from the World's Greatest Manufacturer*, McGraw Hill, 2004.

gration meetings at which the emerging design is evaluated and decisions are made based on as much detailed information as possible. The tacit knowledge gained during both development and production is condensed into concise and useful one-page summaries that effectively make the knowledge explicit. Generating and preserving knowledge for future use is *the* hallmark of the Toyota Product Development System.

The National Center for Manufacturing Sciences (NCMS) conducted a multi-year study of the Toyota Product Development System, and the findings are summarized by Michael Kennedy in the book *Product Development for the Lean Enterprise*.[17] In this book Kennedy identifies four cornerstone elements of the Toyota Product Development System (see Figure 1.5).

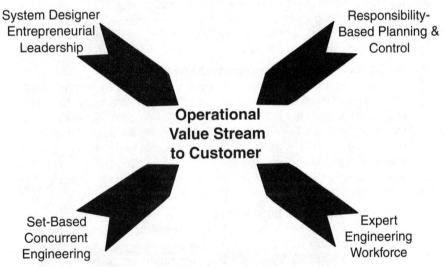

## Knowledge-Based Engineering
## (The Lean Development System)

System Designer
Entrepreneurial
Leadership

Responsibility-
Based Planning &
Control

**Operational
Value Stream
to Customer**

Set-Based
Concurrent
Engineering

Expert
Engineering
Workforce

*An operational value stream emerges from the
interaction of four cornerstone elements.*

**Figure 1.5**   *Cornerstone elements of the Toyota Product Development System*[18]

17. Michael Kennedy, *Product Development for the Lean Enterprise: Why Toyota's System Is Four Times More Productive and How You Can Implement It*, Oaklea Press, 2003.
18. This figure is from Michael Kennedy, Ibid., p. 120. Used with permission.

### The Toyota Product Development System

The Toyota Product Development System has four cornerstone elements:

1. **System Design by an Entrepreneurial Leader**
   The chief engineer at Toyota owns responsibility for the business success of the product. He is a very experienced engineer, fully capable of creating the system-level design of the vehicle. But he is also responsible for developing a deep understanding of the target market and creating a vehicle that will delight the customers. The chief engineer creates a vision of the new product which he transmits to the development team and refreshes frequently by talking to the engineers making day-to-day decisions. He defends the vision when necessary and arbitrates tradeoffs if disagreements arise. He sets the schedule and modifies the process so everything is pulled together on time.

2. **Expert Engineering Workforce**
   From the days of Sakichi Toyoda, the Toyoda and Toyota companies have always had top notch technical people designing their technically sophisticated products. It takes years for an engineer to really become an expert in a particular area, and at Toyota, engineers are not moved around or motivated to move into management before they truly master their field. Managers are teachers who have become masters in the area they supervise; they train new engineers and move them from apprentice to journeyman to master engineer.

3. **Responsibility-Based Planning and Control**
   The chief engineer sets the vehicle development schedule, which consists of key synchronization points about two or three months apart. Engineers know what is expected at the next synchronization point, and they deliver the expected results without being tracked. If engineers need information to do their job, they are expected to "pull" it from its source. Recently, Toyota chief engineers have pioneered the practice of an "Oobeya" or large room where team members may work, and the whole team meets regularly. The Oobeya contains big visible charts to show issues and status.

4. **Set-Based Concurrent Engineering**
   Set-based engineering means exploring multiple design spaces and converging on an optimal solution by gradually narrowing options. What does this mean in practice? It means being very careful not to make decisions until they absolutely must be made and working hard to maintain options so that decisions can be made as late as possible with the most amount of information possible. The paradox of set-based design is that this approach to creating knowledge builds redundancy into the development approach, which might appear to be a waste. However, when looking at the whole system, set-based design allows the development team to arrive at a more optimal solution much faster than an approach that closes off options quickly for the sake of being "decisive."[19]

---

19. For more on set-based engineering, see Chapter 7.

## Lean Software Development

Software development is a form of product development. In fact, much of the software you use was probably purchased as a product. Software that is not developed as a standalone product may be embedded in hardware, or it may be the essence of a game or a search capability. Some software, including much custom software, is developed as part of a business process. Customers don't buy the software we develop. They buy games or word processors or search capability or a hardware device or a business process. In this sense, most useful software is embedded in something larger than its code base.

It is the product, the activity, or the process in which software is embedded that is the real product under development. The software development is just a subset of the overall product development process. So in a very real sense, we can call software development a subset of product development. And thus, if we want to understand lean software development, we would do well to discover what constitutes excellent product development.

The Toyota Production System and the Toyota Product Development System stem from the same underlying principles. The first step in implementing lean software development is to understand these underlying principles, which will be discussed in the next chapter.

---

# Try This

1. Go to the Toyota Web site, and view the videos on Jidoka (www.toyota.co.jp/en/vision/production_system/video.html[20]). The videos on Just-in-Time and the Toyota Production System are also worth viewing.

2. Do you have a tendency to work in batches? If you had to mail 100 letters, how would you go about folding the letters, stuffing the envelopes, adding address labels and stamps? Would you process one envelope at a time, or would you perform each step in a batch? Why? Try timing both ways and see which is faster. If you have children, ask them how they would approach the problem.

---

20. This was a newly published Web site as of April, 2006. The page can also be reached by going to www.toyota.co.jp/en/ and following this sequence: Top Page > Company > Vision & Philosophy > Toyota Production System > Video Introducing the Toyota Production System.

3. Table 1.1 lists similarities between manufacturing and product development. Discuss this table with your team, one line at a time. Does it make sense in your world to think of partially done work as inventory? Do the other analogies make sense? Analogies are a double-edged sword. Where might the analogies between manufacturing and product development lead you astray?

4. Work-arounds: You have an organization of intelligent people. Do these people make it their job to work around problems, or are problems considered a trigger to stop-the-line and find the root cause? Make a list of the Top 10 problems that occurred in your group in the last week. List after each problem the way it was resolved. Rank each problem on a scale of 0–5. The rank of 5 means that you are confident that the cause of the problem has been identified and eliminated and it is unlikely to occur again. The rank of 0 means that there is no doubt the problem will crop up again. What is your total score?

5. If people in your organization instinctively work around problems, they have the *wrong reflexes*! Brainstorm what it will take to develop a culture that does not tolerate abnormalities, whether it is a broken build or a miscommunication, a failed installation or code that is not robust enough to hold up in production. Have a "stop-the-line" committee investigate the ideas and choose the best candidate to get started. In the one chosen area, switch from a work-around culture to a stop-the-line culture. Be sure reflexive stop-the-line habits are developed! Repeat.

# Chapter 2

# Principles

## Principles and Practices

Principles are underlying truths that don't change over time or space, while practices are the application of principles to a particular situation. Practices can and should differ as you move from one environment to the next, and they also change as a situation evolves.

Let's say that you want to change your software development practices because they aren't working very well, but it's not clear what new practices you should adopt. In other words, you would like to move away from something, but it's not clear where you are heading. As you look for a new approach to software development, is it better to spend your time understanding principles or studying practices?

There is a learn-by-doing approach: Adopt a coherent set of practices with confidence that this will eventually lead to understanding of the principles behind them. Then there is an understand-before-doing approach: Understand the underlying principles, and use them to develop practices for specific situations. We observe that the best results come from combining the two approaches. Copying practices without understanding the underlying principles has a long history of mediocre results. But when the underlying principles are understood, it is useful to copy practices that work for similar organizations and modify them to fit your environment. This can provide a jump-start to implementing the principles.

For example, when Mary's video tape plant implemented Just-in-Time, it was not possible to simply copy Toyota's practices because her plant was a process plant, not an assembly plant. The management team had to think carefully about what Just-in-Time meant in their world. They decided to use the Toyota Kanban system and implement pull scheduling, which were specific practices. But they knew that inventory reduction alone was not enough to achieve breakthrough cost reduction, so they developed unique approaches to engage production workers and create a stop-the-line culture. This combination of understanding principles and adapting practices led to dramatic success.

Many companies copied Toyota's Kanban system during the 1990s with mediocre results. Those companies didn't see lean as a management system aimed at eliminating waste. We suspect that many companies with Kanban systems left plenty of waste in their value streams. Similarly, many companies will implement some of the agile software development practices discussed later in this book, but if they don't recognize waste and manage the value stream so as to eliminate it, if they don't possess a deep respect for their workers and partners, results may be similarly mediocre.

## Software Development

Lean practices from manufacturing and supply chain management don't translate easily to software development, because both software and development are individually quite different than operations and logistics. Let's take a look at each of these words—software and development—and analyze just where their uniqueness lies.

### Software

Embedded software is the part of a product that is expected to change. If it didn't need to change, then it might as well be hardware. Enterprise software is the part of a business process that bears the brunt of its complexity. If there is a messy calculation or complicated information flow, software gets assigned the job. Software gets the user interaction jobs, the last minute jobs, the "figure it out in the future" jobs. Because of this, almost everything we know about good software architecture has to do with making software easy to change.[1] And that's not a surprise because well over half of all software is developed after first release to production.[2]

---

1. For example, in the article "Quality With a Name," Jim Shore defines a high-quality software architecture this way: "A good software design minimizes the time required to create, modify, and maintain the software while achieving acceptable run-time performance." See: www.jamesshore.com/Articles/Quality-With-a-Name.html

2. The percentage of software lifecycle cost attributed to "maintenance" ranges between 40 percent and 90 percent. See Kajko-Mattsson, Mira, Ulf Westblom, Stefan Forssander, Gunnar Andersson, Mats Medin, Sari Ebarasi, Tord Fahlgren, Sven-Erik Johansson, Stefan Törnquist, and Margareta Holmgren, "Taxonomy of Problem Management Activities." Proceedings of the Fifth European Conference on Software Maintenance and Reengineering, March 2001, 1–10.

As time goes on, modifying production software tends to get more difficult and expensive. Changes add complexity, and complexity usually calcifies the code base, making it brittle and easy to break. Far too often companies are startled to discover that their software investment has turned into a tangle of unmanageable code. But this doesn't have to happen. The best software products have been around for a decade or more, and every useful product of that age has been changed regularly over its lifetime. These products have architectures and development processes that build change tolerance into the code. All code worthy of the name software should be designed and built with change tolerance in mind.

## Development

Development is the process of transforming ideas into products. There are two schools of thought about how go about this transformation: We might call one the deterministic school of thought and the second the empirical school of thought. The deterministic school starts by creating a complete product definition, and then creates a realization of that definition. The empirical school starts with a high-level product concept and then establishes well-defined feedback loops that adjust activities so as to create an optimal interpretation of the concept.

The Toyota Product Development System sits squarely in the empirical school, starting with a vehicle concept rather than a definition and empirically fleshing out the concept into a product throughout the development process. For example, the product concept of the Prius did not mention a hybrid engine; it set a fuel economy target of 20 kilometers per liter (47.5 miles per gallon). The Prius product concept also called for a roomy cabin for passengers, but did not set vehicle dimensions. Only during development did the team settle on the hybrid engine, barely out of the research lab, as the best way to achieve the aggressive fuel economy target.[3]

We believe that any development process that deals with a changing environment should be an empirical process, because it provides the best known approach for adapting to change. As we noted above, software by its very nature should be designed to adapt to change both during initial development and over its lifecycle. Thus, software development should be an empirical process.

---

3. Jeffrey Liker, *The Toyota Way*, McGraw-Hill, 2004. See Chapter 6 on the development of the Prius.

## What Is This Thing Called "Waterfall?"

I didn't run into the term "waterfall" until 1999 when I started working on a government project. I had been a (very good) programmer in the 1970s, writing software that controlled machines. This might be called embedded software today, but in those days the computers were hardly small enough to be embedded. I worked on some large projects that involved building and starting up complex process lines to make tape.[4] My colleagues on these projects were engineers with years of experience developing large, complex tape-making lines. The projects were managed by seasoned experts, who knew how to get approval for an overall budget and schedule, then turn things over to the experts to adapt the plan as needed to deliver a working line. Everyone was well aware of the fact that while budget and schedule were important, the overriding goal was to deliver a line that made excellent product. And we always did.

When I became the information systems manager of a video cassette plant, I used the approach I had learned as an engineer to manage the development of new software, always keeping in mind that my department's primary job was to support production. Later I moved into product development, where we used a rigorous but very adaptable stage-gate process to commercialize new products.

Thus, I managed to escape working with the waterfall methodology until I bumped into it in 1999 on that government project. I was puzzled by the waterfall approach because I couldn't understand how it could possibly work; and as a matter of fact, it didn't work. As I compared my experience working on complex, successful projects to the prescribed waterfall approach which failed on a relatively small project, I decided to write a book about what really works.[5] In that book we outlined seven principles of software development, which are summarized below.

—Mary Poppendieck

---

4. The equipment needed for making tape bears some resemblance to the automated looms manufactured by Toyoda Automatic Loom in the 1920s.
5. Mary and Tom Poppendieck, *Lean Software Development: An Agile Toolkit*, Addison-Wesley, 2003.

# The Seven Principles of Lean Software Development

In this section we summarize the seven principles of software development that formed the core of our previous book. Some readers may notice that the wording of some principles has changed a bit, but the intent remains the same. After each principle we add a prevailing myth, which makes the principle counterintuitive for those who believe the myth.

## Principle 1: Eliminate Waste

Taiichi Ohno called the Toyota Production System a management system for "the absolute elimination of waste."[6] When asked how it worked, he said, "All we are doing is looking at the timeline from the moment a customer gives us an order to the point when we collect the cash. And we are reducing that timeline by removing the nonvalue-added wastes."[7] In a nutshell, that's what Lean Production is all about. In Lean Software Development the goal of eliminating waste is the same, but the start and end of the timeline may be modified. You start the timeline clock when you receive an order to address a customer need (whatever that means in your organization) and stop it when software is deployed that addresses the need. Lean Software Development focuses on reducing that timeline by removing all nonvalue-adding wastes.

To eliminate waste, you first have to recognize it. Since waste is anything that does not add value, the first step to eliminating waste is to develop a keen sense of what value really is. There is no substitute for developing a deep understanding of what customers will actually value once they start using the software. In our industry, value has a habit of changing because, quite often, customers don't really know what they want. In addition, once they see new software in action, their idea of what they want will invariably shift. Nevertheless, great software development organizations develop a deep sense of customer value and continually delight their customers. Think of Google; it regularly and repeatedly delights customers around the world.

Once you have a good understanding of value, the next step is to develop a capability to really see waste. Waste is anything that interferes with giving customers what they value at the time and place where it will provide the most value. Anything we do that does not add customer value is waste, and any delay that keeps customers from getting value when they want it is also waste.

---

6. Taiichi Ohno, *Toyota Production System: Beyond Large Scale Production*, Productivity Press, 1988, p. 4.
7. Ibid., p. ix.

In manufacturing, inventory is waste. Inventory has to be handled, moved, stored, tracked, and retrieved. Not only does this take time and effort, but it also adds complexity—a large cost multiplier. Inventory gets lost, grows obsolete, hides quality problems, and ties up money. So one goal in manufacturing is to carry as little inventory as possible.

The inventory of software development is partially done work. Partially done software has all of the evils of manufacturing inventory: It gets lost, grows obsolete, hides quality problems, and ties up money. Moreover, much of the risk of software development lies in partially done work.

A big form of waste in software development is "churn." In our classes, we've often encountered "requirements churn" in the 30 percent to 50 percent range, and we've seen many test-and-fix cycles that take twice as long as the initial development time. We've found that software development churn is always associated with large inventories of partially done work. When requirements are specified long before coding, of course they change. When testing occurs long after coding, test-and-fix churn is inevitable. Unfortunately, these types of churn are often just a precursor to the ever larger churn created by delayed (aka big-bang) integration.

But far and away the biggest source of waste in software development is extra features. Only about 20 percent of the features and functions in typical custom software are used regularly. Something like two-thirds of the features and functions in typical custom software are rarely used.[8] We are not talking about the necessary safety or security features. We are talking about features that really weren't needed in the first place. There is a *huge* cost to developing extra features in a software system. They add complexity to the code base that will drive up its cost at an alarming rate, making it more and more expensive to maintain, dramatically reducing its useful life.

### Myth: Early Specification Reduces Waste

The reason we develop all of this extra code lies in a game we play with our customers. We set up the rules:

> Will you, valued customer, please give us a list of everything you want the software to do? We will write it down and ask you to sign off on the result. After that, if you want changes or additions, you will have to go through an arduous process

---

8. When Jim Johnson, chairman of the Standish Group reported these ratios at XP 2002 in Sardinia, they came from a limited study. Since then we have asked almost every group we address if these numbers match their experience, particularly if they are developing custom software. The response has always confirmed that these numbers, if not precisely correct, are in the right ballpark.

called "change management" to get a change approved. So you had better think of everything you want right now, because we have to know about all of it at the beginning in order to develop good software.

Is it any wonder that our customers throw everything, including the kitchen sink, into their list of requirements? Far too often the game of scope control has the opposite effect—it creates scope bloat. Just as Taiichi Ohno called overproduction the worst waste in manufacturing, unused features are the worst kind of waste in software development. Every bit of code that is there and not needed creates complexity that will plague the code base for the rest of its life. Unused code still requires unnecessary testing, documentation, and support. It will do its share of making the code base brittle and difficult to understand and change as time goes on. The cost of complexity in code dominates all other costs, and extra features that turn out to be unnecessary are one of the biggest killers of software productivity.

We need a process that allows us to develop the 20 percent of the code that will deliver 80 percent of the value, and only then go on to develop the next most important features. We should never establish scope with a list of everything that a system might possibly need, especially if the list comes from customers who don't really know what they want.

## Principle 2: Build Quality In

"We need more discipline around here, not less," skeptical managers often tell us. Lean Software Development is very disciplined, we always respond. It's just that you look at discipline a bit differently. Your goal is to build quality into the code from the start, not test it in later. You don't focus on putting defects into a tracking system; you avoid creating defects in the first place. It takes a highly disciplined organization to do that.

▼──────────────────────────────────────▼

### Defect Queues

We were visiting an organization that was certified at CMM Level 4 and on the verge of reaching CMM Level 5. We were impressed with the people and the discipline; we were not surprised that their products were doing very well.

But something bothered us. Recently their release cycle time had slowed down from six weeks to four months, and they asked us to help them figure out why. We sketched the release cycle timeline on a board, and at the end of the cycle we found a four-week testing period. "It's no wonder you can't release in six weeks. You take four weeks to test your product!" I said.

"I know. We should automate testing," the quality manager replied, "but that seems rather simplistic." I agreed. This was a top-notch organization. There was probably more to this problem than automated testing would resolve.

"Let's do a Pareto analysis[9] of the four weeks of testing," I suggested. "What do you do during the four weeks that takes the most time?"

"Fix the defects," was the immediate response.

"Oh, so you're not really testing during the four weeks, you're fixing defects!" I said. "It's not fair to call that testing. What if there were no defects to fix—*then* how long would testing take?"

"Oh, maybe two or three days," came the answer.

"So, if you could do testing in two or three days, *then* could you move your releases back to every six weeks?" I asked.

"Definitely," was the immediate reply.

"Well, it seems that you are testing too late in your process. You really should be finding these defects much sooner," I suggested.

"Oh, but we are!" he said. "They're in our defect tracking system."

"You mean you know about these defects, but you're not doing anything about them until the end?" I asked, astonished.

"Yes," came the sheepish reply.

"OK, you know what you have to do," I said. "Don't record the defects when you find them, just fix them! Get your final testing down to a couple of days by setting the expectation that the code should work when final verification begins." I had no doubt that this very competent organization would be able to meet this goal once the team decided that it was important.

—Mary Poppendieck

---

9. A Pareto analysis is an application of the "vital few and trivial many" rule, also called the "80/20" rule, first popularized by quality guru J.M. Juran. The analysis proceeds thus: Divide a problem into categories, find the biggest category, look for the root cause of the problem creating that category, and fix it. Once the cause of the biggest problem is eliminated, it's time to repeat the cycle with another Pareto analysis on the remaining problems. Chapter 7 contains a more detailed example of a team using this technique.

According to Shigeo Shingo, there are two kinds of inspection: inspection after defects occur and inspection to prevent defects.[10] If you really want quality, you don't inspect after the fact, you control conditions so as not to allow defects in the first place. If this is not possible, then you inspect the product after each small step, so that defects are caught immediately after they occur. When a defect is found, you stop-the-line, find its cause, and fix it immediately.

Defect tracking systems are queues of partially done work, queues of rework if you will. Too often we think that just because a defect is in a queue, it's OK, we won't lose track of it. But in the lean paradigm, queues are collection points for waste. The goal is to have no defects in the queue, in fact, the ultimate goal is to eliminate the defect tracking queue altogether. If you find this impossible to imagine, consider Nancy Van Schooenderwoert's experience on a three-year project that developed complex and often-changing embedded software.[11] Over the three-year period there were a total of 51 defects after unit testing with a maximum of two defects open at once. Who needs a defect tracking system for two defects?

Today we have the tools to keep most defects out of code as it is being developed. A group of developers using test-driven-development writes unit tests and acceptance tests before they write the associated code. They integrate both code and tests into the system as often as possible—every hour or so—and run a test harness to see that no defects have been introduced. If the tests don't pass, they do not add new code until the problem is fixed or the failing code is backed out. At the end of the day, a longer and more complete test harness is run. Every weekend the system is attached to an even more comprehensive test harness. Organizations using this process report incredibly low defect rates, as well as very short timeframes to find the cause of defects that are discovered.

10. See Shigeo Shingo, *Study of 'Toyota' Production System*, Productivity Press, 1981, Chapter 2.3.
11. Nancy Van Schooenderwoert and Ron Morsicato, "Taming the Embedded Tiger— Agile Test Techniques for Embedded Software," Proceedings, Agile Development Conference, Salt Lake City, June, 2004, and Nancy Van Schooenderwoert, "Embedded Agile Project by the Numbers with Newbies," Proceedings, Agile 2006 Conference, Minneapolis, July 2006.

## Productivity Soared[12]

Test-driven development (TDD) is an amazingly effective approach to improving code quality. In February 2004 I introduced the technique to a company that was struggling with quality issues. Although none of the code (which was written in Java) was more than five years old, they already considered this to be a legacy application. On average there were ten defects reported per every thousand lines of noncomment source statements (NCSS) in the six months following release.

The poor quality of the company's software was affecting its reputation, customer satisfaction, and its ability to add new features in a timely manner.

To correct these problems the team began using the Scrum[13] agile development process and soon afterwards adopted TDD. Following the adoption of TDD the number of defects reported dropped to less than three per thousand lines of code. Even this 70 percent reduction in defects understates the improvement because the team didn't track whether a reported defect was caused by code written before or after TDD. That is, some of the defects being reported were still the result of code written before TDD was adopted. Conservatively, the team probably achieved an 80 percent to 90 percent improvement.

The improved quality paid dividends in more than one way. Because the team spent so much less time tracking down bugs (both in the debugger during development and afterward when a user reported a bug) productivity soared. Prior to adopting TDD the team completed an average of seven function points per person-month. After adopting TDD they completed an average of 23 function points per person-month. The team was over three times more productive with far fewer defects.

—Mike Cohn, President, Mountain Goat Software

### Myth: The Job of Testing Is to Find Defects

The job of tests, and the people that develop and runs tests, is to *prevent* defects, not to find them. A quality assurance organization should champion processes that build quality into the code from the start rather than test quality

---

12. Thanks to Mike Cohn for sharing his experience. Used with permission.
13. Scrum is a well-known iterative development methodology. See Ken Schwaber and Mike Beedle, *Agile Software Development with SCRUM*, Prentice Hall, 2001, and Ken Schwaber, *Agile Project Management with Scrum*, Microsoft, 2004.

in later. This is not to say that verification is unnecessary. Final verification is a good idea. It's just that finding defects should be the exception, not the rule, during verification. If verification routinely triggers test-and-fix cycles, then the development process is defective.

In Mary's plant, common wisdom held that 80 percent of the defects that seemed to be caused by people making mistakes were actually caused by a system that allowed the mistakes to happen. Therefore, the vast majority of defects were actually management problems. The slogan, "Do it right the first time," was the rallying cry for doing away with after-the-fact inspection. It meant mistake-proofing each manufacturing step so that it was easy to avoid creating defects.

When we use the slogan "Do it right the first time," in software development, it should mean that we use test-driven development and continuous integration to be sure the code behaves exactly as intended at that point in time. Unfortunately, the slogan has been used to imply something very different. "Do it right the first time," has been interpreted to mean that once code is written, it should never have to be changed. This interpretation encourages developers to use some of the worst known practices for the design and development of complex systems. It is a dangerous myth to think that software should not have to be changed once it is written.

Let's revisit the best opportunity for eliminating waste in software development: *Write less code*. In order to write less code, we need to find the 20 percent of the code that will provide 80 percent of the value and write that first. Then we add more features, stopping when the value of the next feature set is less than its cost. When we add new features, we have to keep the code simple and clean, or complexity will soon overwhelm us. So we refactor the design to take the new capability into account, keep the code base simple, and get rid of software's worst enemy: duplication. This means that we should routinely expect to change existing code.

## Principle 3: Create Knowledge

One of the puzzling aspects of "waterfall" development is the idea that knowledge, in the form of "requirements," exists prior to and separate from coding. Software development is a knowledge-creating process. While an overall architectural concept will be sketched out prior to coding, the validation of that architecture comes as the code is being written. In practice, the detailed design of software always occurs during coding, even if a detailed design document was written ahead of time. An early design cannot fully anticipate the complexity encountered during implementation, nor can it take into account the ongoing feedback that comes from actually building the software. Worse, early detailed designs are not amenable to feedback from stakeholders and customers. A development process focused on creating knowledge will expect the design to evolve during coding and will not waste time locking it down prematurely.

Alan MacCormack, a professor at Harvard Business School, spends his time studying how organizations learn. A while back, when he was studying software development practices, a company asked him to evaluate two of its projects—a "good" project and a "bad" project.[14] The "good" project was run by-the-book. It had an optimized design, and the resulting system was very close to the initial specification. The "bad" project underwent constant change as the development team struggled to understand and respond to changes in the market.

When the projects were evaluated using MacCormack's criteria, the "good" project scored poorly in quality, productivity, and market acceptance while the "bad" project was a market success. It's not surprising that the team that learned from the market throughout development created a better product. The real eye-opener was that the company's managers thought that learning about the market and building a product to satisfy it was "bad."

MacCormack has identified four practices that lead to successful software development:[15]

1. Early release of a minimum feature set to customers for evaluation and feedback

2. Daily builds and rapid feedback from integration tests

3. A team and/or leader with the experience and instincts to make good decisions

4. A modular architecture that supports the ability to easily add new features

Companies that have exhibited long-term excellence in product development share a common trait: They generate new knowledge through disciplined experimentation and codify that knowledge concisely to make it accessible to the

---

14. This story is told in "Creating a Fast and Flexible Process: Research Suggests Keys to Success" by Alan MacCormack, at www.roundtable.com/MRTIndex/FFPD/ART-maccormack.html and at www.agiledevelopmentconference.com/ 2003/files/ AlanAgileSoftwareJun03.ppt.

15. In addition to the above article, see also Alan MacCormack, "Product-Development Practices That Work: How Internet Companies Build Software," *MIT Sloan Management Review*, Winter 2001, Vol. 40 number 2.

larger organization. Not only do these companies capture explicit data, they find ways to make tacit knowledge explicit and make it part of the organizational knowledge base.[16] These companies realize that while learning about the product under development is important, codifying the knowledge for use in future products is essential.

It is important to have a development process that encourages systematic learning throughout the development cycle, but we also need to systematically improve that development process. Sometimes in the search for "standard" processes we have locked our processes up in documentation that makes it difficult for development teams to continually improve their own processes. A lean organization knows that it must constantly improve its processes because in a complex environment there will always be problems. Every abnormality should trigger a search for the root cause, experiments to find the best way to remedy the problem, and a change in process to keep it from resurfacing. Process improvement efforts should be the responsibility of development teams, and every team should set aside time to work on process improvement on a regular basis.

### Myth: Predictions Create Predictability

Predictable outcomes are one of the key expectations that the marketplace imposes on companies and their senior management, and these expectations eventually flow down to software development. Unfortunately, software development has a notorious reputation for being unpredictable, so there is a great deal of pressure to make it more predictable. The paradox is that in our zeal to improve the predictability of software development, we have institutionalized practices that have had the opposite effect. We create a plan, and then we act on that plan as if it embodies an accurate prediction of the future. Because we assume that our predictions are fact, we tend to make early decisions that lock us into a course of action that is difficult to change. Thus, we lose our capability to respond to change when our predictions turn out to be inaccurate. The solution to this problem, it would seem, is to make more accurate predictions.

We forget that the predictions of the future are always going to be inaccurate if they are 1) complex, 2) detailed, 3) about the distant future, or 4) about an uncertain environment. No amount of trying to make these kinds of predictions more accurate is going to do much good. There are, however, well-proven ways to create reliable outcomes even if we cannot start with accurate predictions.

---

16. See Ikujiro Nonaka and Hirotaka Takeuchi in *The Knowledge Creating Company: How Japanese Companies Create the Dynamics of Innovation*, Oxford University Press, 1995, p. 225.

The idea is to stop acting as if our predictions of the future are fact rather than forecast. Instead, we need to reduce our response time so we can respond correctly to events as they unfold.

In order to increase the predictability of outcomes, we need to decrease the amount of speculation that goes into making decisions. Decisions that are based on facts, rather than forecasts, produce the most predictable results. As a control engineer, Mary knows that an empirical control system—one based on feedback—delivers more predictable results than a deterministic control system. Fundamentally, an organization that has a well-developed ability to wait for events to occur and then respond quickly and correctly will deliver far more predictable outcomes than an organization that attempts to predict the future.

## Principle 4: Defer Commitment

Emergency responders are trained to deal with challenging, unpredictable, and often dangerous situations. They are taught to assess a challenging situation and decide how long they can wait before they must make critical decisions. Having set a timebox for such a decision, they learn to wait until the end of the timebox before they commit to action, because that is when they will have the most information.

We should apply the same logic to the irreversible decisions that need to be made during the course of software development: Schedule irreversible decisions for the last responsible moment, that is, the last chance to make the decision before it is too late. This is not to say that all decisions should be deferred. First and foremost, we should try to make most decisions reversible, so they can be made and then easily changed. One of the more useful goals of iterative development is to move from "analysis paralysis" to getting something concrete accomplished. But while we are developing the early features of a system, we should avoid making decisions that will lock in a critical design decision that will be difficult to change. A software system doesn't need complete flexibility, but it does need to maintain options at the points where change is likely to occur. A team and/or leader with experience in the domain and the technology will have developed good instincts and will know where to maintain options.

Many people like to get tough decisions out of the way, to address risks head-on, to reduce the number of unknowns. However, in the face of uncertainty especially when it is accompanied by complexity, the more successful approach is to tackle tough problems by experimenting with various solutions, leaving critical options open until a decision must be made. In fact, many of the best software design strategies are specifically aimed at leaving options open so that irreversible decisions can be made as late as possible.

### Myth: Planning Is Commitment

"In preparing for battle I have always found that plans are useless, but planning is indispensable." Dwight Eisenhower's famous quote gives us good perspective on the difference between planning and commitment. Planning is an important learning exercise, it is critical in developing the right reflexes in an organization, and it is necessary for establishing the high-level architectural design of a complex system.

Plans, on the other hand, are overrated. Listen to Taiichi Ohno:[17]

> Plans change very easily. Worldly affairs do not always go according to plan and orders have to change rapidly in response to change in circumstances. If one sticks to the idea that once set, a plan should not be changed, a business cannot exist for long.

> It is said that the sturdier the human spine, the more easily it bends. This elasticity is important. If something goes wrong and the backbone is placed in a cast, this vital area gets stiff and stops functioning. Sticking to a plan once it is set up is like putting the human body in a cast. It is not healthy.

Barry Boehm and Richard Turner[18] coined the term "plan-driven methods" to describe software development approaches that are based on the expectation that a plan is a commitment. They define a capable plan-driven process as one that has "the inherent capability ... to produce planned results."[19] They further note that plan-driven methods originated in the government contracting world.[20] Indeed, it is a challenge to administer contracts in the arms-length manner required by government organizations without creating a detailed plan that is regarded as a commitment.

But in the commercial world, wise businesses (such as Toyota) realize that sticking to a detailed plan is not healthy, and measuring process capability against ones ability to do so is measuring the wrong thing. Let's not succumb to the myth that planning is the same thing as making a commitment. We should plan thoughtfully and commit sparingly.

---

17. Taiichi Ohno, *Toyota Production System: Beyond Large Scale Production*, Productivity Press, 1988, p. 46.
18. See Barry Boehm and Richard Turner, *Balancing Agility and Discipline: A Guide for the Perplexed*, Addison-Wesley, 2004.
19. Ibid., p. 12.
20. Ibid., p. 10.

## Principle 5: Deliver Fast

When our children were so little that their chins were at table level when they sat in a chair, we could always find a couple of thick Sears catalogs in any house we visited and use them as a booster seat. Everyone loved to page through the catalogs, and we often ordered from them. Delivery took two or three weeks, so we didn't bother to order things we could get in local stores. Somewhere in the middle of the 1980s, a mail order company in Maine called L.L. Bean decided to compete with Sears on the basis of time. Its goal was to ship every order within 24 hours after the order arrived. This was such an amazing concept that other companies used to tour the L.L. Bean distribution center to see how the company did it.

It didn't take long for two- to three-week delivery times to seem awfully slow. The venerable Sears catalog, approaching its 100th birthday, was unable to compete and closed up shop in 1993. L.L. Bean had much lower costs, partly because it didn't have to incur the expense of tracking unfilled orders. Think about it: If we ordered a yellow shirt from Sears, we could call up a week or two later and say, "Guess what, I've changed my mind. Can you make that a blue shirt?" And they would change the order. But if we called L.L. Bean with the same request, they would say, "Have you looked on your doorstep? It should be arriving today."

*The moral of this story is that we need to figure out how to deliver software so fast that our customers don't have time to change their minds.*

FedEx pretty much invented overnight shipping. Southwest pioneered rapid turnaround at airline gates. Both companies have maintained leadership in their respective industry even after widespread imitation. Dell created a speed-based assemble-to-order model that has proven remarkably difficult to imitate. Toyota was able to bring the revolutionary hybrid Prius to market in 15 months, a product development speed that few automobile companies can begin to approach.

Companies that compete on the basis of time often have a significant cost advantage over their competitors: They have eliminated a huge amount of waste, and waste costs money. In addition, they have extremely low defect rates. Repeatable and reliable speed is impossible without superb quality. Furthermore they develop a deep customer understanding. They are so fast that they can afford take an experimental approach to product development, trying new ideas and learning what works.

## Myth: Haste Makes Waste

In the software development industry, it has long been thought that in order to get high quality you have to, "slow down and be careful." But when an industry imposes a compromise like that on its customers, the company that breaks the compromise stands to gain a significant competitive advantage.[21] Google and PatientKeeper, featured later in this book, are just two of many companies that deliver software very fast and with high quality. Software development organizations that continue to believe speed and quality are incompatible face the prospect of going the way of the Sears catalog in the not-too-distant future.

Caution: Don't equate high speed with hacking. They are worlds apart. A fast-moving development team must have excellent reflexes and a disciplined, stop-the-line culture. The reason for this is clear: You can't sustain high speed unless you build quality in.

In a quest for discipline, many organizations develop detailed process plans, standardized work products, workflow documentation, and specific job descriptions. This is often done by a staff group that trains workers in the process and monitors conformance. The goal is to achieve a standardized, repeatable process which, among other things, makes it easy to move people between projects.[22] But a process designed to create interchangeable people will not produce the kind of people that are essential to make fast, flexible processes work.

If you want to go fast, you need engaged, thinking people who can be trusted to make good decisions and help each other out. In fast-moving organizations, the work is structured so that the people doing the work know what to do without being told and are expected to solve problems and adapt to changes without permission. Lean organizations work to standards, but these standards exist because they embody the best current knowledge about how to do a job. They form a baseline against which workers are expected to experiment to find better ways to do their job. Lean standards exist to be challenged and improved.[23]

There are two ways to achieve high quality. You can slow down and be careful, or you can develop people who continually improve their processes, build quality into their product, and develop the capability to repeatedly and reliably respond to their customers many times faster than their competitors.

---

21. George Stalk and Rob Lachenauer, *Hardball: Are You Playing to Play or Playing to Win*, Harvard Business School Press, 2004.
22. See Barry Boehm and Richard Turner, *Balancing Agility and Discipline: A Guide for the Perplexed*, Addison-Wesley, 2004, pp. 11–12.
23. See Jim Shook "Bringing the Toyota Production System to the United States" in *Becoming Lean*, Jeffrey Liker, editor, Productivity Press, 2004, pp. 59–60.

## Principle 6: Respect People

When Joel Spolsky was fresh out of college and a new employee at Microsoft, he was tasked with developing the macro language strategy for Excel. He spent some time learning what customers might want macros to do and wrote a spec. Much to his surprise, an applications architecture group got wind of the spec and asked to review it. Joel thought they might have some good advice for him, but he found that the small group knew even less about macros than he did—even with four Ph.D.'s and a high-profile boss (a friend of Bill Gates, who was something like employee number 6). Despite a superficial idea of how customers might use macros, the app architecture group thought it was their job to determine how macros should be implemented. Joel's managers made it clear that the decisions were his, and his programming team backed him up. But the app architecture group wasn't happy about that, and their boss called a big meeting to complain about how Joel was messing up the macro strategy.

If Microsoft were an ordinary company, you can imagine how this scenario might play out: The app architecture group gets its way, and Joel either acquiesces or leaves. But that is not what happened. The day after the big meeting, a senior vice president checked in with Joel in the cafeteria and asked, "How's it going with the app architecture group?" Joel said everything was fine, of course. But the next day Joel heard via the grapevine that the app architecture group had been disbanded. He was impressed. "At Microsoft," says Joel, "if you're the Program Manager working on the Excel macro strategy, even if you've been at the company for less than six months, it doesn't matter—you are the *GOD* of the Excel macro strategy, and nobody, not even employee number 6, is allowed to get in your way. Period." [24]

*Joel's story shows what Piniciple 6: Respect People means in software development from the point of view of the people doing the work.*

It's noteworthy that three of the four cornerstones of the Toyota Product Development System in Figure 1.5[25] concern the people involved in the product development process. Looking at these three cornerstones gives us a broader idea of what respecting people means:

---

24. Joel Spolsky, "Two Stories, " http://www.joelonsoftware.com/articles/twostories.html. Used with permission.
25. Michael Kennedy, *Product Development for the Lean Enterprise: Why Toyota's System Is Four Times More Productive and How You Can Implement It*, Oaklea Press, 2003, p. 120. Used with permission.

1. **Entrepreneurial Leader:** People like to work on successful products, and highly successful products can usually be traced to excellent leaders. A company that respects its people develops good leaders and makes sure that teams have the kind of leadership that fosters engaged, thinking people and focuses their efforts on creating a great product.

2. **Expert Technical Workforce:** Any company that expects to maintain a competitive advantage in a specific area must develop and nurture technical expertise in that area. Companies that buy all the expertise they need will find that their competitors can buy it also. Companies that see no need for expertise will find that they have no sustainable competitive advantage. Wise companies make sure that appropriate technical expertise is nurtured and teams are staffed with the needed expertise to accomplish their goals.

3. **Responsibility-Based Planning and Control:** Respecting people means that teams are given general plans and reasonable goals and are trusted to self-organize to meet the goals. Respect means that instead of telling people what to do and how to do it, you develop a reflexive organization where people use their heads and figure this out for themselves.

### Myth: There Is One Best Way

The book *Cheaper by the Dozen*[26] is a very funny, true story about a family of 12 children whose father is an efficiency expert. Since Mary grew up the fourth child in a family of 11 children, she eagerly read this book as a child. What escaped Mary until she re-read the book recently is that *Cheaper by the Dozen* gives us a unique perspective into the origins of scientific management. The father of the dozen, Frank Gilbreth, was a world-renowned consultant who insisted that there is always "one best way" to do everything. Reading between the lines, you can guess from Gilbreth's regimented household that most workers would not want to be on the receiving end of one of his efficiency efforts. But if Frank Gilbreth had a humorous lack of respect for people, then his colleague Frederick Winslow Taylor exhibited a barely masked distain for "laborers" in his writings.

After Frank Gilbreth's early death, his wife and partner, Lillian Gilbreth, took over the business and became one of the foremost industrial engineers of

---

26. Frank B. Gilbreth Jr. and Ernestine Gilbreth Carey, *Cheaper by the Dozen*, T.Y. Crowell Co., 1948. The movie by the same name is quite a departure from the book.

her time. She moved away from the idea of "one best way" both in raising her family[27] and in her professional work, where she focused on worker motivation.

But the damage was done. The task of finding and institutionalizing the "one best way" to do every job was handed over to industrial engineers in most American industries. Forerunners of the so-called process police, these industrial engineers often created standards without really understanding the work and enforced them without entertaining the possibility that there may be a better way.

There is no such thing as "one best way." There is no process that cannot be improved. To prove this to yourself, simply spend some time quietly watching people doing their work. After a while you will notice many things that could be improved. Processes should be improved by the work team doing the job. They need the time, the charter, and the guidance to tackle their problems, one at a time, biggest problem first. This never-ending continuous improvement process should be found in every software development organization.

## Principle 7: Optimize the Whole

Software development is legendary for its tendency to suboptimize.

- **Vicious Circle No. 1 (of course, this would never happen at your company):**
  - ○ A customer wants some new features, "yesterday."
  - ○ Developers hear: Get it done fast, at all costs!
  - ○ Result: Sloppy changes are made to the code base.
  - ○ Result: Complexity of the code base increases.
  - ○ Result: Number of defects in the code base increases.
  - ○ Result: There is an exponential increase in time to add features.

- **Vicious Circle No. 2 (and this wouldn't happen at your company either):**
  - ○ Testing is overloaded with work.
  - ○ Result: Testing occurs long after coding.
  - ○ Result: Developers don't get immediate feedback.
  - ○ Result: Developers create more defects.

---

27. See the sequel, Frank B. Gilbreth Jr. and Ernestine Gilbreth Carey, *Belles on Their Toes*, T.Y. Crowell Co., 1950.

o Result: Testing has more work. Systems have more defects.

o Result: Feedback to developers is delayed further. Repeat cycle.

A lean organization optimizes the whole value stream, from the time it receives an order to address a customer need until software is deployed and the need is addressed. If an organization focuses on optimizing something less than the entire value stream, we can just about guarantee that the overall value stream will suffer. We have seen this many times in value stream maps from our classes: Almost every time we spot a big delay, there is a handoff of responsibility from one department to the next, with no one responsible for shepherding the customers' concerns across the gap.

Organizations usually think that they are optimizing the whole; after all, everyone knows that suboptimization is bad, so no one wants to admit to it. Yet in surprisingly many cases, suboptimization is institutionalized in the measurement system. Consider the case of Fujitsu.[28] In 2001, Fujitsu took over the help desk of BMI, a UK airline. It analyzed the calls it received from BMI employees and found that 26 percent of the calls were for malfunctioning printers at airline check-in counters. Fujitsu measured how long the printers were down and totaled up the cost to BMI. Then Fujitsu prepared a business case and convinced BMI management to replace the printers with more robust machines. Fujitsu continued to uncover and attack the root causes of calls to the help desk, so that after 18 months, total calls were down 40 percent.

This seems like a good story, but there is something wrong. Most help desks get paid based on the number of calls handled. By reducing calls 40 percent, Fujitsu was reducing its revenue by the same amount! As it happens, Fujitsu's results were so dramatic that it was able to renegotiate its revenue agreement with BMI so that it got paid on "potential" calls rather than actual calls. Under the new agreement, Fujitsu had a financial incentive to continue to really help BMI solve its business problems.

*This story points out that outsourced call centers working under the traditional revenue model have no incentive to find and resolve the causes of customer problems.*

Crossing organizational boundaries is expensive. Peter Drucker noted that a company that maintains a single management system throughout the value stream will see a 25 percent to 30 percent cost advantage over competitors.[29]

---

28. James P. Womack and Daniel T. Jones, *Lean Consumption: How Companies and Customers Can Create Value and Wealth Together*, Free Press, 2005, pp. 58–63.

29. Peter Drucker, *Management Challenges for the 21st Century*, Harper Business, 1999, p. 33.

Thus, there's a sizable amount of savings to be gained from structuring contracts, outsourcing agreements, and cross-functional interactions with correct incentives that make sure everyone is focused on optimizing the whole.

### Myth: Optimize By Decomposition

Alfred P. Sloan invented an organizational structure designed to deal with complexity: He created decentralized divisions and used financial metrics to judge the managers' performance. This was a great improvement over Ford's hands-on control; it helped General Motors produce a variety of cars and overtake Ford as the market leader. Ever since, companies have been working to find the right metrics to manage performance.

While Sloan's use of metrics to manage complexity was brilliant, the concept can easily be carried too far. People have a tendency to decompose complex situations into small pieces, probably a legacy from the efficiency experts who divided jobs into miniscule tasks. After decomposition, each piece is measured and each measurement is optimized. You would expect that when all of the individual measurements are optimized, then the overall system would be optimized too. But you would be wrong. If you break a value stream into silos and optimize them separately, experience has shown that the overall system will almost certainly be suboptimized.

We can't measure everything, and because we have to limit our measurements, some things invariably fall between the cracks.[30] For example, we tend to measure project performance based on cost, schedule, and scope targets. But these measurements don't take quality and customer satisfaction into account. If a conflict arises, they lose out. So what should be done? The decomposition approach would add two more measurements, so now we measure cost, schedule, scope, quality, and customer satisfaction. Voila! We have turned the iron triangle into an iron pentagon.

When a measurement system has too many measurements the real goal of the effort gets lost among too many surrogates, and there is no guidance for making tradeoffs among them. The solution is to "*Measure UP*" that is, raise the measurement one level and *decrease* the number of measurements. Find a higher-level measurement that will drive the right results for the lower level metrics *and* establish a basis for making trade-offs. In the example of project metrics above, instead of adding two more measurements we should use a single measurement—the one thing that that really matters. Return on investment

---

30. A great book on this topic is Rob Austin's *Measuring and Managing Performance in Organizations*, Dorset House, 1996.

(ROI) is a possible candidate for projects. Profit and loss models work well for products.[31] If we optimize the one thing that really matters, the other numbers will take care of themselves.

## Used Cars[32]

The ROI exercises in our classes are popular because they help people think about how to make tradeoff decisions that really satisfy customers. In one class, Ian and his group produced an ROI for a used vehicle remarketing company. It showed that reducing the vehicle inventory time from five days to four gave a very impressive financial return.

The story behind the ROI was even more interesting. Ian had just learned about Scrum when he was assigned to replace a very old computer system at the used vehicle remarketing company. He told his customer that his team would develop software in one-month increments, and if the customer was not happy after any increment, the engagement could be canceled.

"You told him *what*?" Ian's management was not happy. There was a hint that if Ian lost the engagement at the used vehicle remarketing company he might not have further work at the consulting firm. So Ian became very dedicated to finding a way to delight his customer every month.

By asking around, Ian found out that reducing vehicle inventory time would have positive financial impact, and in our class he got some practice in quantifying that impact. He went to his customer and got some real data, which he plugged into a simple financial model. The results helped both Ian and his customer focus development each month on the most valuable features.

After a few months, Ian wrote to tell us that his customer was so pleased with the results that his consulting firm was going to receive quite a bit more business, and his managers were delighted. Today Ian's managers have embraced agile software development, and the company considers itself one of the top agile companies in the United Kingdom.

—Mary Poppendieck

---

31. See Mary and Tom Poppendieck, *Lean Software Development: An Agile Toolkit*, Addison-Wesley, 2003, pp. 83–92.
32. Thanks to Ian Shimmings for letting us use this story.

## Try This

1.  Which one of the seven myths seems especially poignant in your situation? Why?

    Early specification reduces waste
    The job of testing is to find defects
    Predictions create predictability
    Planning is commitment
    Haste makes waste
    There is one best way
    Optimize by decomposition

2.  When should the value stream timeline start in your organization? What does it mean to "receive an order" in your environment? Some companies start the timeline for product development when a product concept is approved for development (the order comes from the approval process). Others start the timeline from the time marketing recognizes a customer need and requests a new feature. What works best for you?

3.  Churn: In your organization,

    a.  What percentage of requirements change after they are documented?

    b.  What percentage of development time is spent in "test and fix" or "hardening" activities at the end of a development cycle?

    c.  What might you do to reduce these percentages?

4.  People: How much training do first-line supervisors receive about how to lead their departments? What kinds of items receive emphasis on their appraisals? How much training do first-line project managers receive about how to lead their teams? What kinds of items receive emphasis on their appraisals? Is there a difference? Why?

5.  Measurements: Have everyone in your organization list on a sheet of paper the key performance measurements they believe they are evaluated against. Then compile all of the measurements into a single list, perhaps anonymously. How many measurements are on the list? Are they the right ones? Are any key measurements missing? Can you think of ways to "Measure UP?"

# Chapter 3

# Value

## Lean Solutions

In the book *Lean Solutions* James Womack and Daniel Jones start out by noting that they themselves are customers with problems to solve, and they are quite annoyed with the amount of hassle that is involved in being a consumer these days. From their vantage point as customers, they have this message for those of us who provide them with goods and services:[1]

- "Solve my problem completely."
- "Don't waste my time."
- "Provide exactly what I want."
- "Deliver value exactly where I want it."
- "Supply value exactly when I want it.
- "Reduce the number of decisions I must make to solve my problems."

Let's take a look at a company that seems to have gotten this message several years ago.

## Google

*Google may be the only company in the world whose stated goal is to have users leave its Web site as quickly as possible.*[2]

In 1999 Google joined the crowded field of search engines with the lofty goal of making the world's information accessible to everyone. The company decided

---

1. James Womack and Daniel Jones, *Lean Solutions: How Companies and Customers Can Create Value and Wealth Together*, Free Press, 2005, p. 15.
2. From the Google Web site, www.google.com/corporate/tenthings.html.

that in order to do this, it needed to focus on two things: 1) provide more relevant search results than anyone else, and 2) provide a truly engaging user experience. The strategy worked. In the last issue of 1999, *PC Magazine* awarded Google a technical excellence award in Web applications. As *PC Magazine* said, "It doesn't take many visits to Google to get hooked. And who can avoid getting hooked on a search engine that consistently returns good results?"[3] The award drew attention to Google and started its meteoric climb to the top of the search engine industry.

Google's corporate philosophy, published on its Web site, begins with these four points:[4]

1. Focus on the user and all else will follow.

2. It's best to do one thing really, really well.

3. Democracy on the Web works.

4. Fast is better than slow.

In its early days, Google resisted strong pressure to compromise on the user experience—pop-up and banner ads, all the rage at the time, were strictly banned because users found them annoying. Google has always been fanatical about speed. Any noticeable delay in responding to a search request would waste users' time. While most of their competitors were creating portals, Google kept its home page extremely simple: one logo, 30 small words, and a single search box with a couple of buttons. Google didn't want to distract users with extra features.

Finally, Google was really, really good at finding relevant search results, and it got better over time. The founders had developed a unique way of ranking search results—they tallied the number of "votes" for a page, that is, the number and importance of references to the page. The page with the most votes won. As time went on, Google continually refined its ability to have people vote on pages and ranked them accordingly.

Google applies the same four principles in its product development process:

1. **Value—Focus on the user and all else will follow:** Development teams are encouraged to develop products with a "laser like focus" on users. Once the product becomes popular, company officials are expected to figure out how to make a profit.[5]

---

3. *PC Magazine*, December 14, 1999, p. 104.
4. From the Google Web site, www.google.com/corporate/tenthings.html.
5. "Google's Missing Piece," by David A. Vise, *Washington Post*, February 10, 2005, p. E05.

2. **Excellence—It's best to do one thing really, really well:** Google is like its search engine, built to be extraordinarily good at what it does. Its deep technical bench gives it the flexibility to experiment and try many things at once.[6]

3. **Democracy—Democracy on the Web works:** New ideas gain traction at Google by attracting a critical mass of enthusiastic people willing to work on them. Products gain stature by getting listed on the Google Labs site and attracting user attention.

4. **Speed—Fast is better than slow:** At Google, things that would take years at other companies happen very quickly...on the order of days or weeks.[7]

Consider Google's approach to adding maps to its repertoire of capabilities. In March 2004 Google launched a beta version of Google Local, a tool to restrict a search to a geographic area. In October of the same year, Google acquired the company Keyhole, giving it access to detailed, worldwide, satellite imagery. In February 2005 Google added mapping capability to Google Local. In April 2005 it added satellite imagery just six months after acquiring Keyhole. Two months later, Google Earth was launched, packaging satellite images, maps, and local searches in an innovative and engaging desktop interface that imitates a globe and streams data from the Internet.

Google focuses on its strategic vision: Organize the world's information, and make it universally accessible and useful. To support that vision, Google develops both internal tools and Web-based products that involve a mix of sophisticated algorithms, complex hardware, and well-designed software. Products and tools are developed quickly and incrementally by small teams that include product management, design, engineering, testing, launch, and continuing engineering. Teams are encouraged to release products before they are fully refined in order to get feedback from users. Google's software has a reputation for elegant design and high quality, and it invariably delights users.

By all measures, Google is a very successful organization (as of this writing), and more importantly, its products have changed the way the world works. Google continually introduces new products despite the fact that it doesn't have a long-term product map and it expects technical staff to spend 20 percent of their time on their own projects. The company decides what products to work on much the same way it ranks search results: priority is based on the interest of development teams and number of users attracted to the product.

---

6. "How Google Grows...and Grows...and Grows," by Keith H. Hammonds, *Fast Company*, Issue 69, April 2003, p. 74.

7. From http://video.google.com/videoplay?docid=-8618166999532839788.

We believe that Google has been successful because it gives users exactly the information they want, when and where they want it, with no hassle, and no wasted time or annoying ads. Google is easy enough for a small child to use. And it solves the whole problem—checks spelling, translates languages, converts units, contains a dictionary, calculator, and maps—the very definition of a "lean solution."

## From Concept to Cash

Let's take a walk through the product development timeline of Google's first offering and see how it worked.

### Concept

In 1996, Larry Page and Sergey Brin joined forces to address a problem they shared—searching the Internet. They were graduate students in computer science at Stanford University, doing research into data mining, so they decided to try some data mining on the Internet. Two years later they published the paper that laid out in quite a bit of detail the product concept behind Google.[8]

Coming up with a brilliant product concept is the start of innovation. This can be a long process of research, or it can be a stroke of insight. Companies can create conditions for innovation, but there is no magic formula for coming up with great insights. However, a flash of insight is hardly enough: "Innovation is 5 percent inspiration and 95 percent perspiration."[9] The problem in most companies is that people with inspiration do not have the time or charter to pursue it. Companies that routinely turn inspiration into innovation create time and space for people and teams with good ideas to incubate those ideas and turn them into a product concept.

### Feasibility

Google, like Dell, started up in a dorm room. When the first Google interface was brought up on the Stanford University Web site, the data mining PCs were in Page's room. Just like Michael Dell, Page and Brin soon left school to start a business. The worst that could happen was that they would have to go back and complete their degrees. Google was founded in late 1998, but for almost a year the new company's product was labeled "beta," while Page and Brin

8. Sergey Brin and Lawrence Page, "The Anatomy of a Large-Scale Hypertextual Web Search Engine," Computer Networks and ISDN Systems, 30(1–7):107–117, April 1998.
9. This quote is from Thomas Edison.

explored the feasibility of the product. Google began to get media attention, traffic grew, and Page and Brin secured a round of financing. Finally the beta label was removed and the research project turned into the foundation of a real product.

The feasibility stage of product development is important, because it provides space for experimentation. Note that the feasibility stage is not a paper study. Concepts are fine, but there is nothing quite like checking things out in the real world.

## Handspreads

The thing I remember most about the feasibility stage at 3M was the handspreads. Handspreads were samples of new products or parts of new products that were produced with the most rudimentary hand-operated equipment in a lab. But rudimentary equipment aside, these handmade samples were very good renditions of the eventual product.

We would go through a lot of these handmade samples, each one carefully labeled so we could tie results back to each sample's properties. We did all sorts of things to test the samples—maybe we'd do destructive testing, or maybe we'd put them out to weather in the sun, or maybe run them by customers.

To me, the feasibility stage means running lots and lots of experiments to find out what really works—in the field—under real conditions and with real customers.

—Mary Poppendieck

This is also the time for systems design, a critically important discipline that many companies seem to do without. What are the major features of the business process, the key modules of the hardware? What interfaces will the system have, and how will they interact? How will the software architecture support the product? What are the key constraints of the system, and how will they be addressed? An excellent systems design is the foundation of an excellent product. It should neither be done by amateurs nor by arms-length experts. Rather, it should be done by seasoned designers who know the systems design will evolve as the product emerges and who know how to make sure that evolution is taken into account so it can proceed smoothly.

*Pilot*

Google started with a page rank system based on Web references. As soon as it went live, the scientists started collecting data on everything they could think of: which results were used and which were not, what kind of phrases were used to find particular results, what kind of misspellings were the most common, how fast results were returned, how fast people responded, and so on. Google continuously tuned its ranking system and hardware and software architecture based on this extensive data analysis. It developed tools to facilitate the development of applications capable of accessing its vast data structures. It developed many trial applications and put them in Google Labs so users could vote with their attention and improve them with their feedback. And it experimented widely to discover a way to bring in advertising revenue that users would find useful instead of distracting.

No one expects fully formed products to emerge from the feasibility stage of product development. All that feasibility proves is that the product "could" work. At that point the real learning of product development begins. Good product development is composed of discovery cycles of trial and learning that increasingly refine the design of the product. The objective is not to complete the product but to get it to a point where a set of capabilities can be tested in a pilot. Through a series of increasingly complete pilots the product emerges.

The pilot stage of software development is more likely to involve actual release to customers than the equivalent stage in hardware development, although as we will see in Chapter 8, the Polaris submarine produced a series of working submarines, starting three years into a nine-year program. Even if a hardware pilot is not released to customers, it's a good idea to plan hardware pilots that integrate embedded software as early in the development program as possible.

Releasing software to customers during the pilot stage is almost always beneficial, as long as the systems design was done well during the feasibility stage. Of course, early release is not always practical. Embedded software, for example, can't really be released before the hardware. Games cannot be released in a partially done state, even to reviewers, because first impressions are almost everything in the game world, and shelf life is very short. But in most situations, we would be strongly biased in favor of evaluating software with alpha and beta releases. In particular, in legacy conversion projects you never know how your software will work until it is running on the real (usually messy) database with real users, at least in a mirrored environment.

*Cash*

Google eventually started making a lot of money—money generated by the value it provides to its advertisers and users. Google had to experiment and learn for a good while before it figured out how to take the hassle out of advertising and make ads as relevant as search results. Google is not without competition, and to keep the cash flowing, it will have to continue to provide extraordinary value to its users.

## Delighted Customers

In 1984, Dr. Noriaki Kano of Tokyo Rika University published a landmark paper on "attractive quality."[10] In it, he presented the Kano model, a tool to help clarify how to create great products that delight customers (see Figure 3.1).

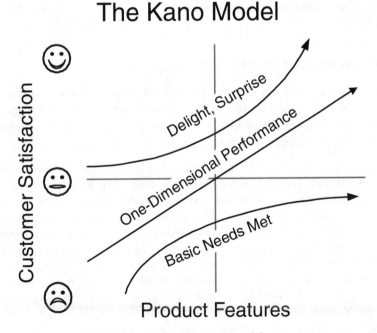

Figure 3.1    *The Kano model*

---

10.  Kano Noriaki, Nobuhiko Seraku, Fumio Takahashi, and Shinichi Tsuji: "Attractive Quality and Must-Be Quality," Hinshitsu. *The Journal of the Japanese Society for Quality Control*, April 1984, pp. 39–48.

The Kano model shows that just to get in the door, you have to meet customers' basic needs. After that, there are two areas for differentiation: 1) increase performance by adding features, or 2) discover needs that customers aren't even aware of and delight them by meeting these needs. Kano noted that increasing performance gives linear results—customer satisfaction is increased in direct proportion to the increased performance. To get an exponential increase in satisfaction, you need to discover and meet unmet needs and thus surprise and delight customers. Kano said that great products do not come from simply listening to what customers ask for, but from developing a deep understanding of the customer's world, discovering unmet needs, and surprising customers by catering to these needs. This is the way to create delighted customers.

Google seems to be very good at delighting customers. As we travel around the world giving talks and classes, we usually ask the question: How many people in the room really *like* Google? Invariably, just about everyone raises their hand, and then we hear about an amazing number of ways in which people use Google products. Our son regularly sends us pointers to unique new Google features. Our granddaughter routinely uses Google to do elementary school research.

## Deep Customer Understanding

"Great software grows out of a mind-meld between a person who really understands the business and a person who really understands the technology," Tom was telling an interviewer. Suddenly the reporter's eyes lit up. "I understand!" he exclaimed, and then he interrupted the interview to tell us this story:

> It was the late '90s when every newspaper suddenly had to have a Web site. All of the other newspapers hired an outside firm to design their Web sites. We hired a programmer instead, and I worked with him. It was difficult at first for me to understand what he was talking about, but after a while I began to see what a Web site might be able to do for us. I was a business person interacting with a technical person, and we learned together what was desirable and what was possible. Eventually this led to something really valuable. We decided to offer access to our content for an increased subscription fee, even though our competitors were giving away access to their content. A *very* large percent of our subscribers signed up to pay the higher rate. Right now, every one of the newspapers similar to ours is struggling financially. On the other hand, we are *very* profitable.

There's plenty of average software in the world, but occasionally some truly innovative software catches our attention. And we want to know "How do they do that?" or more accurately, "How can *we* do that?"

## Focus on the Job

In 1982, 30-year-old Scott Cook was wondering the same thing.[11] The IBM PC had just been introduced, and Cook was one of a host of entrepreneurs trying to invent software products to sell to PC owners. Cook had an advantage over his peers. He had spent five years in brand management at Procter & Gamble, where he acquired a playbook for creating and selling products that would change people's lives. So he did what any good P&G brand manager would do. He started by finding a job that needed to be done for which no optimal tool yet existed. He noticed his wife's frustration with managing the family finances and decided that financial management software could provide a better tool to get that job done. Cook wasn't alone in this discovery. By the time he had founded Intuit and introduced Quicken in 1983, it had no fewer than 46 competitors.

At P&G Cook had learned to deal with competition by thoroughly understanding the job that people need to do, what was wrong with current tools, and exactly what it meant to do the job better. He started by methodically researching how people currently managed their finances. He learned that most people did only three things: pay bills, maintain their check register, and periodically total and review their expenditures. And he discovered that they found these jobs unpleasant and wanted to complete them as fast as possible. So Quicken was designed from the beginning to do three—and only three—jobs faster than they could be done manually. By shifting his view of the competition to paper and pencil, Cook could not only ignore existing software competitors, he changed the basis of competition.

The P&G playbook included research throughout the product lifecycle. Cook found that competing financial software was laden with features and took hours to install. Cook decided to create a program so simple that a PC novice could install it and be writing checks in fifteen minutes. Then he more or less invented usability testing so that Quicken 1.0 could be tested and simplified until it met this goal. Meanwhile, the same tests confirmed that it took experienced PC users up to five hours to write their first check on the feature-laden competing products.

Because having a better tool is not enough, Intuit's research extended to packaging and pricing. The people who have a job to do must clearly understand that there is a better tool for the job. Finally, Intuit continued to improve the tool, making sure that it maintained its position as the best tool for the job.

---

11. From *Inside Intuit* by Suzanne Taylor and Kathy Schroeder, Harvard Business School Press, 2003.

Cook contends that value is created by *focusing on the job that needs to be done and improving the product so that it does the job better than any alternative.* [12]

## My Customers

When I was developing process control systems, there was no question who my customers were—the production workers controlling the line—and the job they were trying to do—make tape. If our system did not help them do that job, they would ignore the system and make tape without it. Our mandate was clear: If the production workers don't use your system, it's your fault. You haven't understood the job that needs to be done.

—Mary Poppendieck

## The Customer-Focused Organization

How are great products conceived and developed? In 1991, Clark and Fujimoto's book *Product Development Performance*[13] presented strong evidence that great products are the result of excellent, detailed information flow. The customers' perception of the product is determined by the quality of the flow of information between the marketplace and the development team. The technical integrity of the product is determined by the quality of the information flow among upstream and downstream technical team members. There are two steps you can take to facilitate this information flow: 1) provide leadership, and 2) empower a complete team.

### Leadership

We have long observed that successful development efforts are highly correlated with the existence of a champion—a person who deeply understands the customers' job and the technology that will surprise and delight those customers A champion has the responsibility for making key product decisions and the

---

12. Clayton Christensen, Scott Cook, and Taddy Hall, "Marketing Malpractice: The Cause and the Cure," *Harvard Business Review*, December, 2005.
13. Kim Clark and Takahiro Fujimoto, *Product Development Performance*, Harvard Business School, 1991.

accountability for the results of those decisions. Martin Cagan of the Silicon Valley Product Group says:[14]

> Behind every great product there is a person with great empathy for the customer, insight into what is possible, and the ability to see what is essential and what is incidental. This person has a deep understanding of the customer as well as her own teams' capabilities. She operates from a strong basis of knowledge and confidence. She thinks in terms of delivering superior value to the marketplace, and she defines good products that can be executed with a strong effort. This person may have the title of product manager or may happen to be anyone on the product team from an engineer to a company founder—the key is that this role must exist and the responsibilities carried out by someone with the skills and talents the tasks demand.

When we see struggling development programs, we usually observe that the champion role does not exist. There are several different models for implementing the role of champion. The best models clarify who has responsibility and accountability for the success of the product.

### The Chief Engineer

At Toyota, a chief engineer is held responsible for the business success of a vehicle family. This leader is a seasoned engineer with an in-depth knowledge of vehicle design. With the assistance of a small staff, he develops a deep understanding of the target customers and what they will value. He looks at marketing research, talks to dealers, and goes to places frequented by his target customer base to watch and ask questions. He checks with advanced development, styling, and production engineering. He gets input from finance and direction from senior management. In the end, however, it is the chief engineer who personally integrates this information, decides what customers will value, writes the product concept, and directs its development. [15]

Consider the Sienna. The first version of the Toyota minivan didn't sell particularly well. When Chief Engineer Yuji Yokoya set out to improve the vehicle, he knew he needed more than focus groups and voice-of-the-customer data. So

---

14. "Behind Every Great Product—The Role of the Product Manager," by Martin Cagan, Silicon Valley Product Group; white paper downloaded from www.svproduct.com. February 7, 2006. Used with permission.
15. Information in this paragraph is from Chapter 7 of Durward Kenneth Sobek II's "Principles That Shape Product Development Systems: A Toyota-Chrysler Comparison," a dissertation submitted in partial fulfillment of the requirements for the degree of Doctor of Philosophy (Industrial and Operations Engineering) at the University of Michigan, 1997.

he followed Toyota tradition of genchi-genbutsu, or "go, see, and confirm." He drove a minivan—usually a Sienna—for 85,000 km (53,000 miles) through every state in the United States, every province in Canada, and every estado in Mexico. He usually traveled with a key member of the design team, including John Jula, a good-sized engineer who would redesign the seats. As he traveled, Yokoya came to understand what Sienna customers would value: more space, comfortable front seats for parents, a back designed for kids, and family pricing. The resulting 2004 Sienna more than doubled the minivan's sales and raised the Sienna to the top of a crowded pack.

We recently bought a Sienna minivan. We seriously considered other vehicles, but we found the foot space in the front passenger seat of competing minivans to be cramped. We drive our minivan for days when we are on vacation, so front seat comfort is really important to us. When we test-drove a Sienna, we could tell that John Jula was thinking of us when he designed the front passenger seat of that car.

The chief engineer approach has the advantage of integrating a lot of information in the mind of a single, responsible individual. In addition, the entrepreneurial spirit that ownership creates has a long history of bringing brilliant innovations to the marketplace. Teams love to follow great leaders, because great leaders help make whole teams successful.

Most Open Source projects have a "Strong Project Leader" (or Chief Engineer).[16] These Open Source projects start out with the vision of one individual, and even when many volunteers are working on the project, all code is reviewed and "committed" by the project leader or hand-picked assistants.

The chief engineer approach is not a panacea. It is possible for someone with the title of chief engineer to focus on control rather than leveraging the diverse capabilities of the entire team. This is not a problem in Open Source projects, because it is impossible for Open Source project leaders to attract volunteer developers unless they are "leaders" in the best sense of the word. However, it can be a problem in companies that do not have good training grounds for chief engineers or in companies that believe a chief engineer should focus on task management rather than integrating knowledge.

Many successful software companies were founded by an entrepreneur who combined technical capability with a clear insight into an unfilled market need. eBay is a good example. In effect, these companies were started by chief engineers. Unfortunately, we have seen many successful chief engineers who founded companies become unsuccessful CEOs as their companies grow. They

---

16. See Eric S. Raymond, "The Cathedral and the Bazaar," www.catb.org/~esr/writings/cathedral-bazaar/cathedral-bazaar/, 2000.

neglect to create new chief engineers to replace themselves, often turning over the job of defining customer value to a marketing department. After five or ten years, these companies often falter as competitors take over the initial market and there is no chief engineer to envision the future and lead teams to create great follow-on products.

### Leadership Team

The goal of development is to fill some need that has thus far gone unfilled, either because a new technology makes it possible to fill the need, the need was not recognized, or some combination of the two. Sometimes the best way to bring these two ideas together is to have two leaders, one with a deep market understanding and the other as a technical lead. At Intuit, for example, the practice of pairing a product marketing expert with a technical expert started with the founders. Scott Cook created the market vision for Quicken while Tom Proulx led technical development.[17]

When there is a third critical piece of the equation—manufacturing for example—it makes sense to have three leaders for a product development effort. Honda uses a sales, engineering, and development—or SED—system in which leaders from sales, production engineering, and development work as a team to come to key product decisions. Above the SED leadership team, Honda also has a Large Project Leader (LPL), whose role is similar to the Toyota chief engineer.

It is important to provide leadership at the most critical points of a product. For example, at Alias (now part of Autodesk), a Toronto company that makes 3-D graphics products, the user experience is a critical feature of every product. Therefore, two interaction designers are assigned to as many teams as possible with full responsibility for customer research, interaction design, and usability testing.[18] A lot of customer feedback is solicited through contextual inquiry, interviews, surveys, and usability testing. But the interaction designer is expected to integrate that input with a deep understanding of the job the software is trying to accomplish, and design a product that will accomplish the job in a superb manner.

Members of a leadership team must be "joined at the hip" so to speak, creating a unified direction for the entire development team.

---

17. See Suzanne Taylor and Kathy Schroeder, *Inside Intuit*, Harvard Business School Press, 2003.
18. Lynn Miller, director of user interface development, Autodesk, Toronto, "Case Study of Customer Input for a Successful Product," Experience Report, Agile 2005.

### Shared Leadership

The Chrysler NS minivan platform (Caravan/Voyager/Town and Country) was an instant hit when it was introduced in 1996. It redefined the minivan concept by adding a driver's side passenger door and received *Motor Trend's* Car of the Year award. In fact, we owned a 1997 Chrysler Town and Country minivan for eight years. This car was not developed by a chief engineer but by a team of experts, who worked together to come to a common understanding of what customers would value. The team conducted extensive market research, did detailed quality function deployment (QFD) analysis, and even developed usability experiments to help make specific decisions. The team was dedicated and colocated, and it spent a lot of time (usually one day a week) reviewing status, educating each other, and solving problems. The team leader's primary job was to manage the development process, fostering cooperation and team building, pushing for consensus decisions, and keeping the team on the right path.[19]

Although it does not bring clarity to who has responsibility and accountability for decisions, the shared leadership approach can work for moderate-sized software development projects. In the Open Source community, Apache is a good example of a shared leadership approach.[20]

### Who's Responsible?

Good marketing and technical leadership does not preclude an involved team that goes on customer calls together, asks questions from various perspectives, and develops a shared view of customer value. Mary's product development experience was at 3M, where conventional wisdom says that every new product needs a "champion." The champion is usually a technical expert who has found an unmet market need and developed the technology to get the job done. But a champion cannot be successful unless she or he works with a cross-functional team that, in effect, forms a mini business unit to commercialize the new product. The team works together to clarify market needs and determine key product features. This combination of a champion and a team with members from all important business functions has served 3M for decades, generating incredible growth through the introduction of thousands of new products every year.

At 3M, the development team generally comes to a consensus on key decisions, but in the end, the champion is responsible for the product and breaks any deadlocks. Similarly, at Toyota the basic principle is, "Teamwork is the key

---

19.  Sobek, Ibid. Sobek personally observed this team in action and reported on it in his thesis.
20.  See Roy T. Fielding, "Shared Leadership in the Apache Project," *Communications of the ACM*, April 1999.

to getting high quality work done, but some individual always needs to be responsible."[21] In "Who Has the D? How Clear Decision Roles Enhance Organizational Performance" Paul Rogers and Marcia Blenko argue that good decision making is the hallmark of high-performing organizations and clarity of the decision-making roles is fundamental to making good, timely decisions.[22]

## Assigning a Decision Maker

I was the champion for several new products at 3M. I found it to be a very challenging and rewarding role.

Disagreements naturally arose during our weekly product development team meetings, because different functions have different perspectives. Sometimes I wondered if quality ever wanted to release a product to the market or if marketing appreciated that developing a product was hard work. I noticed that the disagreements often focused not on the merits of the decision, but on who got to decide.

Therefore I found it very helpful to appoint a decision maker. I chose the function most appropriate to make the decision on the table—quality would approve final release, marketing would decide which shows we would be in, development would decide if a technical feature was easy or difficult, and so on.

I found that once I appointed a decision maker, the tenor of the discussion immediately changed. Team members started lobbying the decision maker to see their point of view. The decision maker changed his or her viewpoint to be more inclusive of others. And the subsequent discussion usually focused on the merits of the decision, not on who got to make it.

—Mary Poppendieck

## Complete Teams

Complete products are developed by complete teams. When Intuit executives decided to develop Quicken Rental Property Manager, they established a development team led by a brand champion that included everyone necessary to put

---

21. James Morgan and Jeffrey Liker, *The Toyota Product Development System: Integrating People, Process, and Technology*, Productivity Press, 2006, p. 103.
22. Paul Rogers and Marcia Blenko, "Who Has the D? How Clear Decision Roles Enhance Organizational Performance," *Harvard Business Review*, January 2006.

the product on the market, "not just software engineers."[23] The team members had worked together before—they were veterans of 20 years of Quicken upgrades. But this was a first for the team. A new Quicken-branded product would be developed for the first time in many years. The team's charter was to solve the customers' problem—no more and no less—while developing just enough process to accomplish the task as quickly as possible.

The development team decided that its main job was to learn—learn about the customers' job so they could develop just the right features, and learn about what kind of process would provide just enough structure without any waste. The team checked in with the management team on a regular basis to report on status, receive guidance, and get approval to continue to the next checkpoint. At each of these meetings the development team reported on what it had learned and what it planned to learn by the next checkpoint. Except for guidance received at these meetings, the team made both product and process decisions on its own.

The Quicken Rental Property Manager team began by going as a group to interview customers. Team members found that developers asked different questions than did marketing people and that everyone gained a deeper insight because of the various perspectives. They found that the development process didn't require nearly as much paperwork as before, because everyone heard the same thing from customers.

Team members were energized by the challenge and became thoroughly engaged in developing a new process and a new product. Within a year, Quicken Rental Property Manager was released to reviews that raved about its clean interface and simple setup and operation.

### Design for Operations

One of the big advances in manufacturing quality occurred when production engineers were asked to join the product design team. Every design was evaluated for ease of manufacturing before it was approved, and suddenly we began to see products that were not only easy to manufacture quickly but also easy to service. This was called design for manufacturability.

---

23. Reported by Soni Meckem at the Lean Design & Development 2005, Conference, Chicago, March, 2005.

## Design for Manufacturability

Long ago in our plant, video cassettes were assembled by hand. The plant manager asked all department heads to spend time working on the line, so I worked an occasional late-night shift assembling video cassettes. There was one screw that had a piece of plastic that got in the way of a screwdriver, so we had to use a specially-made angled screwdriver for that screw. Every time I had to reach for that special tool and fiddle to position the screw, I dreamed about getting the designers on the line to assemble a few cassettes themselves.

Later when design engineers reported to me, I always required that their designs be reviewed by manufacturing before they were finalized. At first the designers found this puzzling, but in no time they gained a healthy respect for the reality of manufacturing. Soon they were bringing their drawings to the manufacturing supervisor for his comments every couple of days. Needless to say, the new designs were easy to assemble.

—Mary Poppendieck

In software development, the equivalent of design for manufacturability is design for operations. Some of the more underrepresented functions on software development teams are computer operations, networking, maintenance, and customer support. Every development team should have members who will challenge the team to consider what kinds of problems arise when software is actually being used in production and what capabilities are necessary to both avoid and recover from those problems.

## Everything That Can Possibly Go Wrong Eventually Will Go Wrong

A friend and former developer, who is now an operations manager, has a favorite saying for developers to keep in mind: "Everything that can possibly go wrong eventually *will* go wrong in production, and we need ways to find and contain the problem and then recover from it." Recently he wrote to describe his latest problem.

"A company 'XZY' is rolling out new releases of their software basically every week. These releases tend to be feature complete and not exhibit too many regression bugs. The main problem is that the software is unstable either over time or under load. When it passes functional testing in QA, it is often unready for the demands of production."

I suggested a root cause analysis of the cause of each failure. Turns out, he was way ahead of me.

"Thorough postmortem analysis is absolutely a part of every single problem response. What we are finding is not a single, recurring failure, but a pattern of failures that are all ultimately related to unsafe coding practices. The application developers at XZY find new ways to crash the site nearly every week."

Unfortunately, the development team no longer felt responsible for the software and was uninterested in the results of the failure analysis.

—Mary Poppendieck

# Custom Development

Just because software is being developed for a one-of-a-kind application does not excuse an organization from the obligation of creating value and delighting customers. The objective is still to create software that will deliver outstanding value to the organization that is paying for it. In fact, the need for leadership and complete teams is perhaps more important for custom development than for product offerings, because the absence of competitive pressure can weaken the intense customer focus that is the core competency of successful software product companies.

## From Projects to Products

Custom software is often developed as a project, but we believe that product development provides a more useful model. One of the interesting things about projects is that they tend to be funded all at once at the beginning of the project (see Figure 3.2). Once funding is allocated, the question naturally arises, "What are we going to get for that investment, and when will it be done?" The answers to these questions are regarded as a commitment—after all, money has been allocated—so the success of the project is measured based on whether or not the cost, schedule, and scope commitments are met.

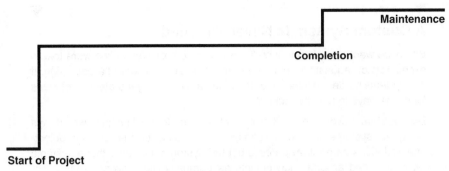

**Figure 3.2**   *Typical project funding profile*

Products, on the other hand, are typically funded incrementally (see Figure 3.3). This incremental funding is a clear signal to all that the scope is expected to evolve as knowledge is gained. The success of product development is generally measured based on the market share and profitability that the product eventually achieves.

There are other differences between projects and products. Projects have a beginning and (apparently) an end. Products, on the other hand, have a beginning and (hopefully) no end. Software is much more like a product than a project, because most good software lives on and changes for a long time. As we noted in Chapter 2, well over half of all software is developed after first release to production.

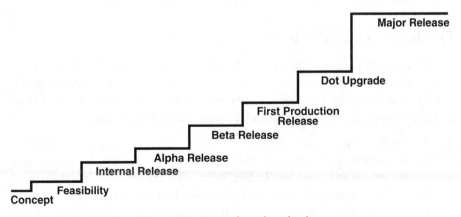

**Figure 3.3**   *Typical product funding*

## A Custom System Is Never Finished

When we went to a plant to install a process control system, we were told to expect lots of requests for changes—and this was considered a good sign. If our systems made a difference to the plant, they would generate a lot of ideas for better ways to use the technology.

Because we never expected a control system to be finished, we always designed systems that were configurable. Some of the original object-oriented ideas came from process control systems, because these systems were designed around such objects as pumps, rollers, ovens, and so on. Since a tape line was constantly making different products, the control system had to allow an operator to change the speed, pressure, and temperature of these objects very easily.

Even with configurable systems, we always liked to come away from an installation with a long list of changes and additional features that the plant operators wanted. This was the highest form of compliment.

—Mary Poppendieck

Projects tend to be staffed with a new team for each project. Products tend to be developed by intact teams that continue to support it over time. Software would be better off supported by an intact team, because the knowledge of the customer, the code, and the domain are difficult to transfer, while most software has a long useful lifespan of upgrades and improvements.

## IT—Business Collaboration

In the *McKinsey Quarterly* report "When IT's Customers Are External,"[24] Simon MacGibbon and coauthors propose that business-facing areas of an IT department should be run like a software company. They point out that software companies differ in three ways from internal IT departments:

1.  Software companies do research to really understand what the market wants, so they can come out with products that will sell. If they do this poorly, they won't last long. In fact, software companies update their market research continually, always looking for better ways to serve the market. Because they can't demand that their customers get involved in the

---

24.  "When IT's Customers Are External," by Simon P. MacGibbon, Jeffrey R. Schumacher, and Ranjit S. Tinaikar, *McKinsey Quarterly*, Q1 2006.

system design, software companies devise all manner of advisory panels and focus groups to discover firsthand what customers really need. Too often IT departments skip the marketing step assuming that someone else has done the market research and are surprised when their products don't meet the business needs.

2. Software companies sell to highly competitive markets, so they have to keep their costs in line. They design products that are simple enough that they can develop and maintain them cost-effectively, while making sure the feature sets provide their customers a compelling reason to buy the software. Too often IT departments assume that a list of business requirements are all essential features of the system, even if very expensive features are involved. They have little incentive to perform the same cost/benefit balancing act that software companies must play to stay in business.

3. Software companies realize that if customers are not successful with their products the company will not have a sustainable business, so it looks for every opportunity to help customers be successful, creating a broader revenue base for themselves while ensuring their products are successful in the marketplace over the long run. Too often IT departments feel that success with the systems they deliver is the responsibility of the business unit. While it is true, as we discuss below, that business units ought to be accountable for the success of software development efforts commissioned by their business, it is also true that the IT department is not successful unless its products contribute to the success of the business.

Many IT departments use the project model for software development, but the project model comes from the contracting industry, where trust is not part of the contract. In order to create healthy IT–business collaborations, we suggest that a product model be adopted, because the incentives built into this model are much more likely to produce a collaborative relationship. When IT is inside a company, there is no reason, really, to set up the we-they model for doing business that projects were designed to deal with. In particular, you do not need to fix scope at the beginning, you do not need customer sign-offs, you do not need to monitor detailed scope to schedule, and you do not need to do everything that your customers say is important. Instead, you need to work in collaboration with your business partner to deliver the most business value in the shortest amount of time for the lowest cost, help them to use the system effectively, and continue to deliver more and better features over time.

## Everything Else Failed

I struck up a conversation with the chief information officer of a large financial holding company at a conference. He was an electrical engineer by training, who had been asked to take over IT and "fix it."

"That was well over three years ago, and you have to understand, I failed." He said. "I tried the CMM thing and I tried the PMI thing, and after two years I got frustrated and went back to my old job.

"But after another year they asked me to try again, so this time I did things differently. I split the organization in half: operations and development. Then I divided the development group into six product teams. Each product team has to sell its products to the businesses, and they are measured on how much profit they generate compared to cost.

"It's only been six months, but so far it has been immensely successful. Don't know why I didn't think of it earlier."

—Mary Poppendieck

### *Accountability*

IT departments inside large companies have traditionally been separate organizations from the businesses they support. This is usually because the company desires a standard information infrastructure and because technical expertise can be more easily developed when experts are in the same organization. However, it has led to lack of clarity about who is responsible for the results of software development activities and, quite often, a lack of clarity about how to measure those results.

The problem of accountability is not unique to IT organizations. It occurs any time people on the same team work for different organizations with different ways of measuring performance. For example, an organization developing embedded software might be managed separately from the hardware development department. A consulting firm working for a business clearly has a separate management structure from its client.

It is not particularly effective to subdivide the effort along organizational lines and then have one part of the development team give "requirements" to the other part of the team. This approach has a tendency to obscure the overall business objective of the joint venture, and has a long history of generating suboptimal results. It is far more effective for members of a complete cross-functional team to share responsibility for achieving the business results that justified the funding of their work.

But in the end, there should be a single point of responsibility for the overall business results of an IT investment. We believe that this accountability should rest with the business funding the effort. When business leaders manage IT investments with the same rigor they bring to running their business, these investments will be more likely to produce significant business results.[25]

## Try This

1. Use the Kano model to analyze a current development effort. Make a list of features and capabilities—at a high level—and put them on an index card or Post-it Note. Use a large sheet to make the Kano model, and mount it on the wall. Next, attach the cards or notes to the appropriate area of the Kano model. How many features fall in the category of "delighters"? What percentage of features are "delighters"?

2. In Chapter 10 we describe a single number that is a good measurement of customer satisfaction, called a "net promoter score." Compute the net promoter score for your customers. Create a simple survey that asks your customers how likely they are to recommend your product or service to a colleague on a scale of 0–10. What percentage of responses are 9s and 10s? This is your promoter percentage. What percentage of responses are 0–6s? This is your detractor percentage. Subtract the detractor percentage from the promoter percentage. Is the net score positive or negative?

3. Make a list of all the programs or projects that are currently active. For each effort, write down the name of the current leader or leaders. How many leaders does each effort have? Have you written down someone who provides both a market and technical leadership for each effort? Is there any correlation between how well a project is doing and its market/technical leadership (or lack thereof)?

4. Complete Teams: Do you have operations people on your team? Is someone from tech support regularly consulted when designing new features? Are testers involved in development right from the start? When do technical writers get involved? Are customers or customer proxies treated as full team members?

25. See "Who's Accountable for IT?" by Dan Lohmeyer, Sofya Pogreb, and Scott Robinson, *McKinsey Quarterly*, December 7, 2004.

5. Projects / Products: Are development efforts funded incrementally or all at once? What are the success criteria of a development effort? Are teams kept intact or do people regularly move to new teams? Do teams maintain the code they develop? Who is accountable for the business results of the money allocated to software development?

# Chapter 4

# Waste

## Write Less Code

If we were to look for the root cause of waste in software development, a really good candidate would be complexity. Complexity calcifies our code and causes it to turn brittle and break. In *Conquering Complexity in Your Business*, Michael George suggests that complexity is like cholesterol: It clogs up the arteries of an organization; it is "the silent killer of profits and growth.[1] The prescription for complexity in software development is simple: *Write Less Code!*

Let's take a look at how a multibillion Euro company has gone about doing just that.

### Zara

When Madonna gave a series of concerts in Spain recently, the outfit she wore at her first concert could be spotted on teens in the audience at her last concert. The Madonna look-alike outfits were purchased at Zara, a rapidly growing fashion clothing chain. Zara's strategy is to be a fast follower, betting that it's more profitable to develop the fashions its customers ask for than to push new designs onto the market. In the rapidly changing world of fashion, a fast follower has to be very fast—Zara can go from concept to cash in two weeks; entirely new lines might take a month.

Zara accounts for perhaps 70 percent of the sales of Inditex, a clothing company located in western Spain with over €5 billion in annual sales. Zara competes fiercely with Stockholm-based H&M, Venice-based Benetton, and San

---

1. Michael George and Stephen Wilson, *Conquering Complexity in Your Business: How Wal-Mart, Toyota, and Other Top Companies Are Breaking Through the Ceiling on Profits and Growth*, McGraw-Hill, 2004.

Francisco-based Gap and posts some of the healthiest profits in its industry. It has close to 900 stores as of this writing, about three-quarters of them in Europe, and is expanding rapidly.

Instead of hiring high-profile designers to create new products for each selling season, Zara hires the best graduates from design schools and has them work with store managers to create the garments that customers are looking for. Zara launches 11,000 new items a year, compared to its competitors' 2,000 to 4,000.[2] Zara stores are lightly stocked. Orders are sent to headquarters twice a week, and the clothes arrive two or three days later—on hangers, priced, and ready to sell. Zara eschews economies of scale and manufactures in small lots, usually in cooperatives in western Spain. It operates well below capacity so as to be able to maintain its ability to fill orders twice a week even during peak demand.[3]

Zara gets more revenue for its efforts than its competitors: It sells 85 percent of its stock at full price, compared to an industry average of 60 percent to 70 percent. Unsold items account for less than 10 percent of sales compared to an industry average of 17 percent to 20 percent.[4] Zara also spends less money than its competitors: Zara's parent company, Inditex, spends about 0.3 percent of sales on advertising compared to a 3 percent to 4 percent industry average. And it spends perhaps 0.5 percent of sales on IT compared to an industry average of about 2 percent.[5]

Stop. Let's go over that one again. A €5 billion company spends 0.5 percent of sales on IT? Indeed, Inditex's IT staff of about 50 people develops all of its applications. Stores use PDAs and a modem to transmit sales totals and new orders to headquarters. Instead of a CRM system, designers are expected to talk to store managers. And with such low inventories, an ERP system would be overkill. Interestingly, the CEO who orchestrated this minimalist approach is a former IT manager.[6]

---

2. Data from "Inditex: The Future of Fast Fashion," *The Economist*, June 18, 2005.
3. Kasra Ferdows, Michael A. Lewis, and Jose A.D. Machuca, "Rapid-Fire Fulfillment," *Harvard Business Review*, November 2004.
4. From "Rapid Fire Fulfillment," Ibid.
5. Andrew McAfee, "Do You Have Too Much IT?" *MIT-Sloan Management Review*, Spring 2004.
6. From "Do You Have Too Much IT?" Ibid.

In "Do You Have Too Much IT?"[7] Andrew McAfee lists five principles that guide Inditex's use of technology:

1. **IT is an aid to judgment not a substitute for it.** Information systems help managers sort though the data they need to make decisions, but they do not make decisions for people, or even suggest them.

2. **Computerization is standardized and targeted.** Stores and regions are not allowed to deviate from the single corporate solution, and developers *minimize* system features rather than maximize them.

3. **Technology initiatives begin from within.** Business goals always shape the company's use of technology, not vice versa. The IT department works with line managers to understand their needs, and only then do they look at available technology to find solutions.

4. **The process is the focus.** The store's PDAs are not "personal productivity devices" for managers. They support the daily cadence of sales reports and the twice-weekly cadence of orders and shipments. They enforce a consistent process across all stores.

5. **Alignment is pervasive.** It helps to have a CEO who used to be an IT manager, but business-IT alignment takes much more. The business people and technology people really understand each other's worlds. There is no we-they divide and no over-the-wall software.

## Complexity

Just about every start-up company with a single software product is nimble and can quickly respond to customers and adapt to change. But after a couple of years of success, software companies often start to slow down and become unresponsive. They have developed a complex code base, a complex array of products, and a complex organizational structure. Unless they get the complexity under control quickly at this point, it will gradually strangle the very responsiveness that gave the company its initial competitive advantage.

The cost of complexity is not linear, it is exponential, and the cost of complexity eventually comes to dominate all other costs in most software systems (see Figure 4.1). Complex code is brittle and breaks easily, making it almost impossible to change safely. Wise software development organizations place top priority on keeping the code base simple, clean, and small.

---

7. Ibid.

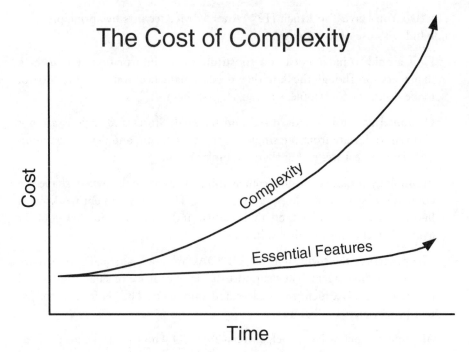

Figure 4.1    *The cost of complexity is exponential.*

### *Justify Every Feature*

The first step to controlling complexity is to aggressively limit the features and functions that make it into the code base in the first place. Every feature that gets developed should pass the hurdle of proving that it will create more economic value than its fully loaded, lifecycle cost. Loading software products with a laundry list of features is the lazy approach to marketing: We don't know what customers will value, so we put in lots of features in hopes that customers will find some things they like. But loading software with features is worse than just laziness; it's a recipe for disaster. Software is complex by nature, and unless that complexity is carefully managed, it rapidly grows out of control.

It takes courage to limit the feature set of a development effort, but it almost always pays for itself many times over. In the product world, launching a product with just the right features, no more and no less, demonstrates that the company really understands what customers want. This was Intuit's strategy when it launched QuickBooks. Intuit realized that very small businesses did not want software designed for accountants, and so it developed a product that did not even have double entry bookkeeping, something its competitors considered fundamental. Intuit understood well who its customers were and what job they were trying to do, and delivered only the capabilities that its customers were looking for.

Jeff Sutherland, CTO of PatientKeeper (a company we discuss in Chapter 5) emphasizes that developers should not develop any feature until there is a well-defined market demand. He says:[8]

> The task then is to refine the code base to better meet customer need. If that is not clear, the programmers should not write a line of code. Every line of code costs money to write and more money to support. It is better for the developers to be surfing than writing code that won't be needed. If they write code that ultimately is not used, I will be paying for that code for the life of the system, which is typically longer than my professional life. If they went surfing, they would have fun, and I would have a less expensive system and fewer headaches to maintain.

### Minimum Useful Feature Sets

Whether we are developing custom or product software, the ideal approach is to divide the software into *minimum useful feature sets*, and deploy these one set at a time, highest priority (or highest payback) first. A minimum useful feature set is one which helps customers do a useful portion of their job better. While there are environments in which an all-or-nothing approach might seem like the only way to proceed, this is rarely necessary either from a technical or from the customers' job point of view.[9] We have been conditioned to think that the large-batch, all-or-nothing approach to software development is good. It's time to recondition ourselves to think that this is the worst possible approach to good software development.

Deploying small, useful feature sets in a custom development project allows customers to start using the software much faster. When these feature sets start generating a return on investment earlier, the company can invest less money, payback the investment sooner, and, usually, generate more profit over the life of the system.[10] Technically, implementing minimum useful feature sets is not only practical, but when done correctly, the code is refactored and simplified with each new feature set. This helps minimize the complexity of the code base, thus minimizing its lifecycle cost. From a customers' viewpoint, receiving minimum useful feature sets means getting their job done sooner and finding out how they *really* would like the software to work while there is plenty of time to

---

8. Posted on object-technology@yahoogroups.com on March 11, 2003, Message 121. Used with permission.
9. Games are a notable exception.
10. See Mark Denne and Jane Cleland-Huang, *Software by Numbers: Low-Risk, High-Return Development*, Prentice Hall, 2004.

ask for changes. And from a sustainability point of view, systems implemented incrementally with minimum useful feature sets are usually easier to maintain because incremental development can be extended over the life of the system. There is nothing not to like about implementing software in minimum useful feature sets.

### Don't Automate Complexity

We are not helping our customers if we simply automate a complex or messy process; we would simply be encasing a process filled with waste in a straight jacket of software complexity. Any process that is a candidate for automation should first be clarified and simplified, possibly even removing existing automation. Only then can the process be clearly understood and the leverage points for effective automation identified.

## "Our Company Is All About Complexity"

At a recent seminar, one of the value stream maps (described later in this chapter) depicted a software ordering process rather than a software development process. As we analyzed the map, we saw that about half of all orders had to be revised, often after they had gone through an arduous customer approval process. The delay and changes caused by the error-prone process were creating a lot of unhappy customers and slow deliveries.

"So why aren't you looking for these errors earlier? Why wait so long?" I asked.

"Well, there are a lot of reasons," explained the person presenting the value stream map. "Often the problems are time related. The order was OK when it was submitted, but time passed, contracts expired, and so the pricing or the terms changed."

As we delved deeper, it was clear that the order processing group was expending heroic efforts to get the orders right, but the pricing structure was so complex that it overwhelmed them.

"Maybe you should look at your pricing structure," I suggested. "It seems extraordinarily complex to me."

"Oh, our company is all about complexity," came the immediate response. "We just revised our pricing structure, and the objective was not to make it simple; the objective was to optimize the amount of revenue we get from every customer."

I suggested that with all the problems we saw in the value stream map, the extra revenue was probably eaten up several times by the complexity.

"Not only that," someone agreed and then elaborated, "the new pricing structure is a compromise that no one likes: not customers, not order processing, not even sales."

Even though the order processing problem itself was very large and very visible, until that moment, no one had traced the underlying problem to its root cause, because no one had been conditioned to think of complexity as bad. In fact, the solution under consideration was to create a computer system to manage the complexity.

I suggested that the process needed simplification, not automation, because if they automated the current complexity they would be casting it in concrete, and that would probably prevent them from *ever* simplifying their ordering process.

*—Mary Poppendieck*

## The Seven Wastes

Everyone who has studied lean manufacturing has learned Shigeo Shingo's seven wastes of manufacturing.[11] In our previous book, we translated these seven wastes into the seven wastes of software development. In this section we revisit that translation, making a few changes presented in Table 4.1. Finding waste is not about putting waste in a category; categories help reinforce the habit of seeing waste. The real purpose of discovering and eliminating waste is to reduce costs and make our products more effective.

---

11. Shigeo Shingo, *Study of "Toyoda" Production System from an Industrial Engineering Viewpoint*, Productivity Press, 1981, Chapter 5.

**Table 4.1** *The Seven Wastes*

| Manufacturing | Software Development |
| --- | --- |
| In-Process Inventory | Partially Done Work |
| Over-Production | Extra Features |
| Extra Processing | Relearning |
| Transportation | Handoffs |
| Motion | Task Switching |
| Waiting | Delays |
| Defects | Defects |

## Partially Done Work

The inventory of software development is partially done work. The objective is to move from the start of work on a system to integrated, tested, documented, deployable code in a single, rapid flow. The only way to accomplish this is to divide work into small batches, or iterations.

---

### Examples of Partially Done Work

1. **Uncoded Documentation:** The longer design and requirements documents sit on the shelf, the more likely they will need to be changed. Development teams are often annoyed as requirements change, but from a customer perspective the real problem is that the requirements were written too soon.

2. **Unsynchronized Code:** When code is checked out to personal workspaces, or branches are created for parallel development, these workspaces and branches will almost always have to be merged back together. Workspaces and parallel code lines should be synchronized as frequently as is possible because the longer they are separate, the more difficult it will be to merge them.

3. **Untested Code:** Writing code without a way to detect defects immediately is the fastest way to build up an inventory of partially done work. When measuring how much code is done, there should be *no partial credit*. Either code is integrated, tested, and accepted, or it doesn't count.

4. **Undocumented Code:** If documentation will be needed, it should be done as the code is written. Ideally, code should be self-documenting, but user documentation, help screens, and so on may also be necessary. Just as testers belong on the development team, so do technical writers. After all, these are the people who are going to help customers get their job done. A lot of extra features can be avoided if the technical writers are constantly asking the rest of the team: "And exactly how is that is going to help our customers get their job done?"

5. **Undeployed Code:** Not every environment can deploy code as frequently as desirable, because new software can get in the way of customers getting their current jobs done. However, there should be a bias toward deploying code as soon as possible. In fact, it's often easier for users to absorb changes in small increments; less training is required and disruption can usually be minimized.

---

**We have a big inventory of documentation but we can't change that because government regulations require us to have a Software Requirements Specifications (SRS) and traceability to code.**

If you must have an SRS and traceability, then consider writing as much of the SRS as executable tests as possible. Consider using FIT (Framework for Integrated Tests) or a similar acceptance testing tool, to write specifications-by-example.[12] A tool like this can give you traceability of tests to the code for free. If you run the tests every day and save the output in your configuration management system, you will have a record of exactly which tests passed and which ones didn't at any point in time. Regulators will love this.

## Extra Features

Taiichi Ohno emphasized that overproduction—making inventory that is not needed immediately—is the worst of the seven wastes of manufacturing. Similarly, the worst of the seven wastes of software development is adding features that are not needed to get the customers' current job done. If there isn't a clear and present economic need for the feature, it *should not be developed*.

---

12. See *Fit for Developing Software: Framework for Integrated Tests*, by Rick Mugridge and Ward Cunningham, Prentice Hall, 2005. See also www.fitnesse.org. Chapter 7 begins with a case study involving FIT and Fitnesse.

**Does this mean we can't anticipate what we know has to be done?**

We are often asked this question. We offer these guidelines:

1. Use your common sense. Remember these are guidelines.

2. Focus on the customer's job. If it takes several iterations to create the software needed to do a job, features that are absolutely necessary to do that job are not extra features.

3. Be strongly biased against adding features. If there is any question about the need for a feature, it's premature. Wait.

4. Creating an architectural capability to add features later rather than sooner is good. Extracting a reusable services "framework" for the enterprise has often proven to be a good idea. Creating a speculative application framework that can be configured to do just about anything has a track record of failure. Understand the difference.

## Relearning

Recently we were participating in a panel discussion about how agile software development affects customers when someone asked, "Are there any customers in the room? We should hear the perspective of real customers." One lonely person raised his hand. He was asked, "What makes agile development challenging for you?"

"I think," he said, "that the biggest problem I have is remembering what decisions I have already made and what things I have already tried, so I tend to try them over again."

Rediscovering something we once knew and have forgotten is perhaps the best definition of "rework" in development. We know we should remember what we have learned. Nevertheless, our approach to capturing knowledge is quite often far too verbose and far less rigorous than it ought to be. The complex topic of creating and preserving knowledge will be addressed further in Chapter 7.

Another way to waste knowledge is to ignore the knowledge people bring to the workplace by failing to engage them in the development process. This is even more serious than losing track of the knowledge we have generated. It is critical to leverage the knowledge of all workers by drawing on the experience that they have built up over time.

**We have tried to document all of our design decisions as they are made. The problem is, this documentation is never looked at again.**

This is a common problem, and it is the reason many organizations have stopped documenting design decisions altogether. The knowledge gained from trying things that do not work can be the most relevant knowledge for solving your problem, but capturing that knowledge in a manner that is easy to reference later is a challenge. Start by asking: Is what you are doing right now working? If not, then don't keep on doing it. Instead, revisit your overall objectives and work with your team devise a method of preserving knowledge that will accomplish those objectives in the most efficient and effective manner. See Chapter 7 for some ideas.

## Handoffs

There's nothing quite like teaching a child how to ride a bicycle. First she has to learn balance while moving, so you run along beside her holding the bike lightly until she gets the hang of it. That's pretty tiring, so the moment she has just a bit of the feeling of balance you quickly teach her how to get started. The first time she successfully pedals away from you, it suddenly dawns on you that you have forgotten to teach her how to *stop!* A few more mishaps, and the child is on her own. A couple of hours later you are amazed at how confidently she is hurtling down the path, starting easily and stopping with brakes screeching.

Handoffs are similar to giving a bicycle to someone who doesn't know how to ride. You can give them a big instruction book on how to ride the bike, but it won't be much help. Far better that you stay and help them experience the feeling of balance that comes with gaining momentum. Then give some pointers as they practice starting, stopping, turning, going down a hill, going up a hill. Before long your colleague *knows* how to ride the bike, although she can't describe how she does it. This kind of knowledge is called tacit knowledge, and it is very difficult to hand off to other people through documentation.

When work is handed off to colleagues, a vast amount of tacit knowledge is left behind in the mind of the originator. Consider this: If each handoff leaves 50 percent of the knowledge behind (a very conservative estimate) then:

- 25 percent of the knowledge is left after two handoffs,

- 12 percent of the knowledge is left after three handoffs,

- 6 percent of the knowledge is left after four handoffs, and

- 3 percent of the knowledge is left after five handoffs.

Because tacit knowledge is so difficult to communicate, handoffs *always* result in lost knowledge; the real question is how to minimize that waste.

---

**Some Ways to Reduce the Waste of Handoffs**

1. Reduce the number of handoffs.

2. Use design-build teams (complete, cross-functional teams) so that people can teach each other how to ride.

3. Use high bandwidth communication: Documents leave virtually all tacit knowledge behind. Replace them with face-to-face discussion, direct observation, interaction with mock-ups, prototypes, and simulations.

4. Release partial or preliminary work for consideration and feedback—as soon as possible and as often as practical.

---

## Task Switching

Software development requires a lot of deep concentrated thinking in order to get one's arms around the existing complexity and correctly add the next piece of the puzzle. Switching to a different task is not only distracting, it takes time and often detracts from the results of both tasks. When knowledge workers have three or four tasks to do, they will often spend more time resetting their minds as they switch to each new task than they spend actually working on it. This task switching time is waste.

Furthermore, trying to do multiple tasks at the same time usually doesn't make sense. Assume that you have three tasks to do, tasks A, B, and C. Assume for the sake of argument that each task takes a week. If you do the tasks one at a time, then at the end of the first week, task A will be done and begin delivering value. At the end of the second week, task B will also be delivering value, and at the end of their third week, you will be done with all three tasks and a lot of value will already have been realized.

But let's say that you decide to work on all three at once, perhaps to make the customer for each task feel that their work is important to you. Figure 4.2 shows the best case outcome for this scenario. Each task is divided into eight even parts, and a minimum amount of time spent in task switching. Even with this ideal case, *none* of the tasks will be done at the end of three weeks. In addition to the wasted time needed to complete the tasks, the potential value they could have contributed by being done earlier is also wasted.

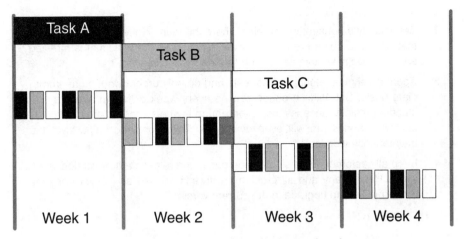

**Figure 4.2** *Switching between three one-week tasks means none of them get done in three weeks.*

**We don't want a separate maintenance team, so we have to have task switching.**

Any code that is deployed will need maintenance, and sometimes separate maintenance teams are formed so that developers can focus on development and not have to task-switch with maintenance tasks. However, we generally recommend against this, because we believe that it is best for a team to remain with its product over the product's lifecycle. Otherwise people may begin to believe that there is such a thing as "finishing" the code, which is usually a myth. Code is a living thing that will (and should!) constantly change.

Having a development team support its own code means that the development team will have to task-switch to handle support. Of course, this provides great motivation to deliver defect-free code, so the team can concentrate on new development.

Still, there will be support demands that distract developers, if for no other reason than the things customers think of as "defects" may have been "features" in the developer's mind. Here are some ways others have used to minimize disruptions caused by the need to support code:

1. Have two people rotate off the team every month or every iteration to handle all maintenance for the duration.

2.  Set aside two hours each morning where the team jointly handles all issues that developed over the last 24 hours. Then have the daily status meeting and focus on new development for the rest of the day.

3.  Aggressively triage support requests and do only urgent work on an immediate basis. Set aside a period of time every week or two to address outstanding maintenance issues. If the period is short enough, most requests can wait, and some will even disappear. This technique helps level the maintenance workload.[13]

4.  Keep all customers on a single code base, and release a new version every week. Handle any and all problems with this release and require anyone with a problem to upgrade to the current version.

## Delays

Waiting for people to be available who are working in other areas is a large cause of the waste of delay. Developers make critical decisions about every 15 minutes—and it's naive to think that all the information necessary to make these decisions is going to be found in a written document. A decision can be made quickly if the developer has a good understanding of what the code is supposed to accomplish, and if there is someone in the room who can answer any remaining questions. Lacking that, developers have three options: stop and try to find out the answer, switch to some other task, or just guess and keep on going. If the hassle factor of finding out the answer is high, the developer will take the second or third course of action. If there isn't much penalty involved, developers are likely to spend a good deal of time waiting for answers before they proceed. None of these approaches is good.

Complete, collocated teams and short iterations with regular feedback can dramatically decrease delays while increasing the quality of decisions. This is not the only approach to reducing delays, but no matter where team members are physically located, it is important to make sure that knowledge is available exactly when and where it is needed—not too soon, or it will have to be changed, and not too late, or it will have to be ignored.

---

13. We would like to thank to Bent Jensen for mentioning this approach, which he finds very useful.

**How can software take so long?**

From a customer perspective, there are bigger delays than developers waiting for answers to questions, and these can be far more problematic.

1. Waiting for me to know exactly what I want before they get going on solving my problem. How am I supposed to know?

2. Waiting for months for project approval.

3. Waiting forever to have people assigned.

4. Waiting for the assigned people to be available.

5. The annoying change approval process; they made me wait months, and they think nothing has changed in my business?

6. Waiting for the whole system to be done before I can get the key features that I really need right now.

7. Waiting for the code to pass tests—how can this take so long?

8. Waiting for that new piece of software to stop messing up my existing programs—or vice versa—who knows?

# Defects

Every code base should include a set of mistake-proofing tests that do not let defects into the code, both at the unit and acceptance test level. However, these tests can only prove that the code does what we think it should do and doesn't fail in ways that we anticipated. Somehow software still finds devious ways to fail, so testing experts who are good at exploratory testing should test the code early and often to find as many of these unexpected failures as possible. Whenever a defect is found, a test should be created so that it can never happen again. In addition, tools may be needed to test for security holes, load capability, and so on. Combinatorial test tools can also be very useful. We should attempt to find all defects as early as possible, so that when we get to final verification, we do not routinely find defects. If software routinely enters final verification with defects, then it is being produced by a defective process.

A good agile team has an extremely low defect rate, because the primary focus is on mistake-proofing the code and making defects unusual. The secondary focus is on finding defects as early as possible and looking for ways to keep that kind of defect from reoccurring.

But the real reason for moving testing to the beginning of development is deeper than mistake-proofing. Acceptance tests are best when they constitute the *design* of the product and match that design to the structure of the domain. Unit tests are best considered the *design* of the code; writing unit tests before writing code leads to simpler, more understandable, and more testable code. These tests tell us exactly and in detail how we expect the code and the ultimate product to work. As such, they also constitute the best documentation of the system, documentation that is always current because the tests must always pass.

---

**Isn't such extensive automated testing a waste?**

Shigeo Shingo says that "inspection to prevent defects" is absolutely required of any process, but that "inspection to find defects" is waste.[14] Development teams have found that preventing errors from ever being introduced and never building good code on top of bad is *always* faster in the end. Furthermore, a test harness makes it easy and safe to change code over time, multiplying the benefits. Finally, organizations that used to write extensive requirements specifications find that writing tests as executable specifications can take considerably less time than they used to spend on writing specifications and tracing them to code.

**We can't test in the customer's unique environment, so we always find defects upon installation.**

Sometimes you can't do final integration testing in a real world customer environment, so you find defects at installation. But even in this case, you should launch an improvement program which itemizes the most common instances of failure upon installation and then attacks the root causes of those instances, highest priority first, until defects at a customer site become a rarity.

Several companies we know make installation *part of the development iteration:* An iteration is not done until the software is running in production at a customer site. With this approach, the entire development team is engaged in the customer installation. Time is set aside to be able to respond to customer requests—and no attempt is made to distinguish defects from features—anything the customer wants is accommodated as far as practical.

---

14. Shingo, Ibid., p. 288.

# Mapping the Value Stream

As we mentioned in Chapter 2, Taiichi Ohno summed up the Toyota Production System thus: "All we are doing is looking at the timeline from the moment a customer gives us an order to the point when we collect the cash. And we are reducing that timeline by removing the nonvalue-added wastes."[15] The timeline that Ohno mentions can be drawn as a value stream map, a diagnostic tool frequently used in lean initiatives. We like to use the same timeline diagnostic in a development environment, but we change the start and stop points to reflect the different interaction of a customer with development.

Value stream maps always begin and end with a customer. In development, the clock starts on a value stream map when a customer places an order—exactly what this means will differ from one organization to the next. The clock stops when the solution is successfully deployed—or launched—solving the customer's problem. The value stream map is a timeline of the major events that occur from the time the clock starts until it stops.

The objective of lean is to reduce the development timeline by removing non-value-adding wastes. Value stream maps have proven remarkably effective at exposing waste, because delays in the flow are almost always a sign of significant waste. By looking for long delays (which indicate queues) and loop-backs (which indicate churn), a clear picture of the waste in the process emerges. In our classes, small teams do rough value stream maps in a half an hour. Even though these maps are rough guesses at reality, they are surprisingly useful in helping people understand the major issues in their processes.

## Preparation

### Choose a Value Stream

The first step in developing a value stream map is to decide what to map. The ideal is to map a process, not a single event, but this can be difficult in development. A good alternative is to map a single project that is representative of an "average" project or a class of projects. In choosing a value stream to map, group similar types of development together. For example, you might map how long it takes to go from product concept to launch of a medium-sized product. Or you might do a timeline for adding a high-priority new feature to an existing application.

---

15. Taiichi Ohno, *Toyota Production System: Beyond Large Scale Production*, Productivity Press, 1988, p. 6.

Most software maintenance departments already understand how to group similar types of development together. Typically they divide maintenance requests into three categories and guarantee a response time by category. For example, they may guarantee resolution of an extremely urgent problem in two hours, an important problem in one day, and a routine problem may get relegated to the next biweekly release. Software maintenance organizations with service level agreements might teach us a lesson or two about value stream maps.

### Choose When to Start and Stop the Timeline

The first question to answer is when to start the timeline. In new product development, it is typical to start the clock when a product concept is approved. However, this does not take into account the fuzzy front end of product development, so you might want to start the clock earlier, for example, when marketing recognizes the need. You should not start the product development clock any later than approval of product concept, even if your particular organization does not get involved until later. If you are working with embedded software, you should ideally start the clock with the main product not the software portion. The objective is to draw a value stream map from concept to cash: Start the timeline either when a customer need is identified or when the organization commits to developing a product, and stop the timeline when the product is launched.

When software is developed in response to customer requests, the timeline should generally be started when a request is submitted—assuming that the request is the equivalent of placing an order. Usually you would not wait to start the timeline when a feature is approved, because in most cases *the approval process should be included in the value stream.* You are looking at value from the *customers'* point of view, and customers do not care about other requests or how busy you are, they care about how long it takes for you to act on *their* request. Back up one step and see if you can start the process from the customers' perspective. How do customers place an order?

### Identify the Value Stream Owner

You can map a value stream without an owner, but you will get a lot more mileage out of value stream mapping if the exercise is led by the value stream owner. When we do value stream maps in our class there usually is no value stream owner. We find that the biggest problems always occur at organizational boundaries, where no one is responsible for the customers' request and people on each side of the boundary try to optimize their own local efficiency. It might languish in a queue before it gets approved, wait for ages to move from one function to another, or sit forever waiting for deployment. But unless there is a value stream owner responsible for the customers' request throughout the system, no one seems empowered to tackle these sources of waste.

### Keep It Simple

Value stream maps are diagnostic tools to help you find waste; all by themselves they usually don't add a lot of value. They help you put on your customers' glasses and look at your development process through their eyes. They have a tendency to change your perspective and start up useful conversations. They are a good starting point for finding and eliminating waste.

Your objective is to map maybe ten or so major steps—from customer order to customer satisfied—on one or two sheets. It is more important to go from end-to-end—from concept to cash—than to go into detail on one small area. Once you have finished the map, answer two questions:

1. How long does it take to get a product developed or to fill a customer request? (You are looking for elapsed time, not chargeable hours.)

2. What percent of that elapsed time is spent actually adding value? (This is called process cycle efficiency.[16])

We have seen many different value stream map formats, every one of them acceptable because they all generate a lot of insightful discussion about waste. You might make some notations about capacity or defect rates if that helps identify waste. Just don't lose site of the purpose of value stream maps in the process for creating them: Learn to see waste so that you can eliminate it.

## Examples

Probably the best way to understand value stream mapping is to just do it. We find that people in our classes can dive in and create useful maps with a minimum of instruction. However, the value of the maps lies not in creating them, but in diagnosing what they are telling us. So we will sketch some maps that are typical of ones we have seen in our classes and discuss their implications.[17]

---

16. See Michael George and Stephen Wilson, *Conquering Complexity in Your Business: How Wal-Mart, Toyota, and Other Top Companies Are Breaking Through the Ceiling On Profits and Growth*, McGraw-Hill, 2004, p. 29.

17. Note that the maps are always hand drawn. We are using a text editor for clarity, but we recommend flip chart paper and pens for value stream maps.

*Example 1*

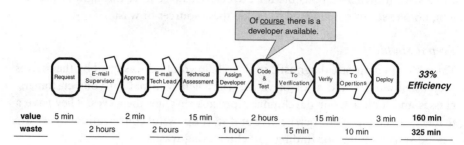

**Figure 4.3** *Value stream map of a small, high-priority feature change request—Organization A*

Example 1 (Figure 4.3) shows a value stream map of a small, high-priority feature change, and is taken from a value stream map drawn in one of our classes. The customer's request comes in by e-mail to a supervisor, who approves it in an average of two hours. It takes another two hours for a brief technical assessment, at which time it is assigned to a developer. The person describing this map to us then said: "Of course, a developer is available because this is high priority." Thus the development starts within an hour, and the two hours of work is completed promptly. It immediately goes to final verification and is rapidly deployed. Bottom line: A small, high-priority feature takes an average of eight hours from request to deployment. Two hours and forty minutes are spent actually working on the request, which is one third of the eight hours total time, giving a process cycle efficiency of 33 percent.

Many software maintenance organizations have processes similar to this. It is a very efficient process, as will be seen by comparison to the next example. But there is room for improvement, because the request waits for two hours for technical assessment. If the developer could also do this assessment, an average of two hours could be saved.

*Example 2*

Example 2 (Figure 4.4) is a value stream map for a request of about the same size as the request in Example 1; a simple feature change that takes about two hours to code and test. However, it takes more than six weeks to complete the work. From the customers' viewpoint, it takes an extra 15 minutes to write up a request because a standard form must be used that requires a lot more information. Since requests are reviewed once a week, the request waits an average of a half week before approval. Then the request waits an average of two weeks

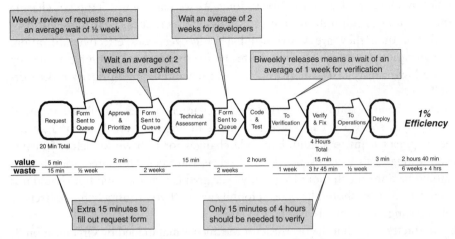

**Figure 4.4** *Value stream map of a small, high-priority feature change request—Organization B*

for one of the scarce architects, and after a technical review, it waits an average of two more weeks for developers to become available. After two hours of coding and testing, the request waits for an average of a week, because releases are scheduled for once every two weeks. Just before release there is a final verification. Even though the code was thoroughly tested when it was written, some code added to the release package in the last week has introduced a defect into the feature which went undetected until final verification. So it takes four hours to fix and retest the release, which, you will notice, is *twice* the time it took to write and test the code in the first place. Since verification only took 15 minutes in the previous example, the other three hours and forty five minutes are waste introduced by the process. Finally everything is ready to deploy, but it takes an average of another half week for the original requestor to get around to using the new feature in production.

Examples 1 and 2 are close approximations of real value stream maps that were done in the same class, so we were able to ascertain that the environments and problems were quite similar. Organization B agreed that if they had been using the process of Organization A, they could have completed their request in about a day.

There are two lessons to take away from these two examples. First, even though developers in both organizations are equally busy, Organization A was organized so that there were always some developers available to drop low-priority work to tackle high-priority requests. On the other hand, Organization B was focusing so hard on full resource utilization that the request had to wait twice in queues that were two weeks long. As we will see in Chapter 5, chasing the phantom of full utilization creates long queues that take far more effort to maintain than they are worth—and actually *decreases* effective utilization. Organization A was able to eliminate the overhead of maintaining queues by using low-priority tasks to create slack and scheduling high-priority tasks Just-in-Time.

The second lesson is that periodic releases force us to accumulate batches of undeployed software. The biweekly releases of Organization B encouraged the development team to accumulate code changes for two weeks before integration testing. This is a mistake. Even if releases are periodic, integration testing should be done much more frequently. The goal is that the final test should not find defects; they should have been found earlier. If you routinely find defects at final testing, then you are testing too late.

It's pretty clear that the overhead of the queues maintained by Organization B, as well as the wasteful big-bang integration at the end, completely overwhelmed any phantom utilization advantage of their batch-and-queue approach.

## Example 3

In Example 3 (Figure 4.5) we examine the value stream map of a fast-track project similar to one we saw in a class. Due to competitive pressure, the company was in a hurry to get features developed, so the features were divided into small projects and assigned to teams to develop. The analysts, developers, and testers worked closely together, so each team rapidly completed its task and sent their well-tested code to the quality assurance (QA) department for final verification. At this point the project teams were assigned new features, and they paid no attention to what happened next. But upon probing, we found that one person in the room knew what happened next: The QA department spent two to three *months* merging the multiple branches and resolving incompatibilities. This waste was more or less invisible, because it occurred after a handoff between geographically separate organizations, and no one seemed to be responsible for the software after it left the site for QA.

Later in the class we did an exercise where we scored the basic disciplines of the company. (See exercise 4 at the end of Chapter 8.) All four groups in the company rated their configuration management discipline as 2 or lower on a scale of 0–5. We had never seen configuration management ratings so low. It turned out that most of the developers knew the configuration management system was not capable of tracking branches correctly, but the organization was branching more aggressively than any company we've seen. As can be expected, merging the branches took far longer than the coding itself.

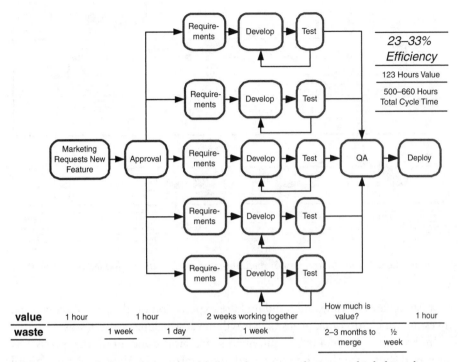

**Figure 4.5**   *Value stream map of fast-track project split into multiple branches*

In this case, the value stream owner was in the room, and when we did a future value stream map, he sketched how things were going to change. Since the branching was causing such problems, it would be abandoned and replaced with continuous integration tools, which already existed. He expected that the two to three months of integration testing could be reduced to a day or two.

### Example 4

In almost every class, we see at least one value stream map similar to Example 4 (Figure 4.6). In this map, a request makes its way to a monthly review meeting after two months of analysis and waiting, only to be rejected twice before it finally obtains approval. This is symptomatic of a long queue of waiting work, so we usually ask how long that queue really is. After all, each project in the queue has been estimated, and it's easy to total up the numbers. We find that initial queues of undone work can be *years* long. We invariably suggest that most of the work in this queue should be abandoned, and the queue size should be limited to an amount of work that the organization can reasonably expect to do in the near term future. After all, there is usually no danger of running out of work. Maintaining queues of several years of work serves no purpose other than

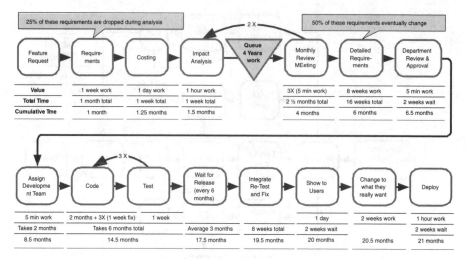

**Figure 4.6**  *Value stream map of medium-sized project in overloaded department*

to waste reviewers' time and build up false expectation on the part of requesters. Investing time estimating projects that will never get done is also a waste.

In Example 4, detailed requirements are not done until the project is approved, but once they are completed and approved by the department, there is still a two month wait before a development team is assigned. The team is not dedicated to the project, so it takes six months to complete about two months of coding. In addition, testing does not occur until after coding, so there are three cycles of testing and fixing defects. Once the feature passes its tests, it has to wait for the next release, which occurs every six months, resulting in an average wait of three months. When the tested modules are finally merged, it takes two months to fix all of the defects that occur between feature sets, since there was no continuous integration and ongoing testing as new features were added to the release.

Finally the software is ready to show to the users, a few months short of two years after they requested it. Not surprisingly, many of their requirements have changed. In fact, by the time the software is ready to release, a quarter of the high-level requirements are no longer valid, and half of the detailed requirements have changed. The development and testing teams interrupt current projects to change the code to do what the users really want, which usually takes only a couple of weeks. But when they are done the people in operations are not ready to deploy the software, so it takes about two more weeks before the feature is available in production. Twenty-one months have elapsed since the feature was requested, and we might generously say that four months of that time was spent adding value, giving a 19 percent process cycle efficiency. A less generous view of how much of the time was really spent adding value would yield a far lower process cycle efficiency.

Unfortunately, we see this kind of value stream map all the time. We hear that organizations are overloaded with work, but when we look at the value stream maps we see huge opportunities to increase the output of the organization by eliminating waste. In this example, if we just look at the churn, we see that 50 percent of the detailed requirements are changed. Requirements churn is a symptom of writing requirements too early. Requirements should be done in smaller chunks, much closer to the time they will be converted to code, preferably in the form of executable tests. In this example we also see churn in test and fix cycles, both during initial development and upon integration. This is a symptom of testing too late. Code should be tested immediately and then continuously plugged into a test harness to be sure no defects appear as other parts of the code base are changed.

Finally, we see that the six-month release cycle, which is supposed to consolidate efforts and reduce waste, only serves to introduce more waste. Features have to wait an average of three months after development to be deployed, giving them plenty of time to grow obsolete and get out of sync as new features are added. Meanwhile developers are off on other projects, so when they have to fix these problems, it takes time to get reacquainted with the code. The two week delay before deployment could also be reduced if people from operations were involved earlier in the process.

### Diagnosis

Value stream maps are a timeline of the steps from concept to launch or from feature request to deployed code. They should depict average times for the typical steps in a process. Once the map is done, the first things to look for are churn and delays. Churn indicates a timing problem. Requirements churn indicates that requirements are being detailed too soon. Test-and-fix churn indicates that tests are being developed and run too late.

Delays are usually caused by long queues, indicating that too much work has been dumped into the organization. As we will see in Chapter 5, things move through a system much faster when work is limited to the capacity of the organization to complete it. Delays can also indicate an organizational boundary: A delay occurs when work is handed off to an organization that is not ready for it. The best cure for this is to get people from the receiving organization involved well before the handoff occurs.

There are other sources of waste that will be exposed by value stream maps: failure to synchronize, an arduous approval process, lack of involvement of operations and support. But these will show up only if you map the end-to-end process from concept to cash.

## Future Value Stream Maps

Every organization we encounter has more work than it can possibly do. However, we generally find that far more work can be done, faster and with higher quality, by simply removing the enormous waste seen in most value stream maps. Toward the end of our classes we ask each group to create a future value stream map, using lean principles to redesign their process. We ask that maps depict a process that is practical for the organization to implement in a three to six month timeframe. No matter where the group started with their current value stream map, the future maps invariably shows improvements in process cycle efficiency and overall cycle time in the range of 50 percent to 500 percent.

Current value stream maps are relatively useless unless they are used to find and eliminate waste. Drawing a future value stream map is a good way to create a plan for removing the biggest wastes. However, we caution that a future map should not be an ideal map. It should show the path for immediate improvement. Pick the biggest delays or the longest queues or the worst churn and address it first. Draw a new map that shows where your organization can reasonably expect to be in three to six months with one to three key changes. Once those changes are made, it's time to draw a new current value stream map and to help pinpoint the next most important areas to address.

---

# Try This

1.  How long would it take your organization to deploy a change that involved just one single line of code? Do you deploy changes at this pace on a repeatable, reliable basis?

2.  Complexity Score: Give your organization a complexity score on a scale of 1–5, where 1 = a minimalist approach similar to Inditex, and 5 = an approach which results in maxumim complexity. What one single thing could you do to reduce your complexity score one point? (Note: A more complex approval process is not a good candidate for reducing complexity. Inditex's approach to governance and approval is as minimalist as the systems themselves.)

3.  Seven Wastes: Pick the *one* waste that is the worst offender in your organization—1) partially done work, 2) extra features, 3) relearning 4) handoffs, 5) task switching, 6) delays, 7) defects. What single thing can you do to significantly reduce that waste?

4. Hold a weekly waste clean-up hour. During the first week, start the hour by talking about one of the seven wastes. Spend the first quarter of the meeting coming to an agreement about what the waste really means in your world. Then spend the next 15 minutes brainstorming to create a list of examples of that particular waste in your development process. Pick the top five candidates and during the next week measure how much waste each one actually causes. At the next weekly meeting, look at your measurements and decide which waste is the "biggest loser" and create a plan to do something about it. Execute the plan and measure the results during the next week. At the next weekly meeting, decide if the results warrant a permanent change, and if so, make the change permanent. At the next weekly meeting, move on to the next waste and repeat the process.

5. Value stream map: If you want to draw a value stream map of your process, try it in steps:

   - Gather anyone who is interested and take an hour to draw a map—no more—and a half hour to discuss what you've learned.

   - Now take a half day to gather some data that was missing during the first exercise and encourage the involvement of a few key people who seemed to be missing. This time, take two hours to draw the map and an hour to discuss its implications.

   - Have you learned enough from these two quick experiments to know where your biggest waste is? If so, move on to doing one or two quick future value stream maps, and then start addressing the biggest waste.

# Chapter 5

# Speed

## Deliver Fast

Speed is the absence of waste.

If you diligently work to eliminate waste, you will increase the percentage of time you spend adding value during each process cycle. And you will deliver faster—probably much faster.

This fundamental lean equation works in manufacturing. It works in logistics. It works in office operations. PatientKeeper provides a good example of how this works in software development.

## PatientKeeper

Five years ago a killer application emerged in the health care industry: Give doctors access to patient information on a PDA. Today (2006) PatientKeeper appears to be winning the race to dominate this exploding market. It has overwhelmed its competition with the capability to bring new products and features to market just about every week. The company's 60 or so technical people produce more software than many organizations several times larger, and their software is certified to manage life-critical data. They don't show any sign that complexity is slowing them down even though they sell to a variety of very large health care organizations and support several platforms that integrate with multiple backend systems.

A key strategy that has kept PatientKeeper at the front of the pack is an emphasis on unprecedented speed in delivering features. For the past three years, PatientKeeper has delivered about 45 software releases a year to large health care organizations using simultaneous overlapping iterations (or Sprints) (see Figure 5.1). Every iteration ends in a live release at a customer site. Every one is delivered on time.

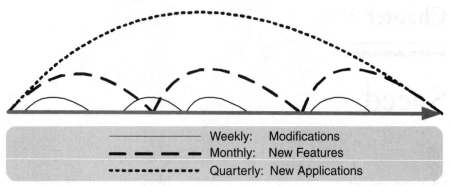

Weekly:    Modifications
Monthly:   New Features
Quarterly: New Applications

**Figure 5.1**    *Simultaneous overlapping iterations running through one set of development teams*[1]

PatientKeeper CTO Jeff Sutherland explains how this works:[2]

- All Sprints result in a production release of software.

- QA starts testing as soon as development updates the first code. They can independently kick off the build process and direct it to any QA server.

- By mid-Sprint, the install team deploys Release Candidate1into the customer's test environment. Now the customer is testing along side internal QA.

- As soon as customer starts feeding back issues, they are addressed by development along with any other issues QA finds.

- Functionality which the customers view as essential to go live continues to surprise us right until the end of the Sprint. We embrace those surprises as it makes the product better faster for all customers.

- It typically takes two or three Release Candidates to go live. All development tasks are complete, all QA issues addressed, and all customer issues completed. QA has run a regression test on the entire system.

- Everyone goes live together at the end of the Sprint. Could be a multi-hospital system with hundreds of physician PDA users and thousands of Web users. We typically take 3–5 customers live at the end of a Sprint.

- Done means all customers are live with no outstanding critical issues. Note that in this scenario, the customer and installation teams are as tightly in the loop as QA and development.

---

1. From Jeff Sutherland, "Future of Scrum: Parallel Pipelining of Sprints in Complex Projects," Research Report, Agile 2005. Used with permission.
2. Posted on Scrumdevelopment@yahoogroups.com on September 25, 2005. The fourth point is from message 9404, August 5, 2005, message 8849. Used with permission.

At PatientKeeper, product managers are responsible for deciding exactly what customers want and creating fine-grain definitions of features that are ready for coding. That means, for example, that the product manager has verified a user interface capability through prototypes and possibly focus groups, and made final, detailed decisions on how the interface will work. No attempt is made to distinguish feature requests from defects; they all go into an automated backlog. The product manager is responsible for assigning backlog items to releases.

Development teams are assigned to releases, which consist of assigned backlog items. A developer takes an item from the backlog, breaks it into tasks, and estimates each task. The estimates are entered into the system and rolled up automatically to the backlog item. At the end of each day, it takes no more than a minute for each developer to enter into the tracking system the time spent on each task and its estimated percent complete. With this data in the tracking system, anyone in the company can obtain solid information about how much more time is necessary to complete every release under development.

The rule is that all releases must be on time, so if the system shows that there is too much work, backlog items are removed from the release to match required work to the capacity of the development teams. Because the tracking system gives accurate, up-to-date information about the time to complete any collection of backlog items, tradeoffs can be accurately identified, and valid decisions can be made. Priorities are resolved at weekly meetings which are attended by all the relevant decision makers, including the CEO. Program managers implement the decisions by changing the assignment of backlog items to a release, and development teams self-organize to resolve any problems.

PatientKeeper is fast: It can deliver any application it chooses to develop in 90 days or less. It will not surprise anyone who understands lean that the company has to maintain superb quality in order to support such rapid delivery. Jeff Sutherland explains that rapid cycle time:[3]

- Increases learning tremendously.
- Eliminates buggy software because you die if you don't fix this.
- Fixes the install process because you die if you have to install 45 releases this year and install is not easy.
- Improves the upgrade process because there is a constant flow of upgrades that are mandatory. Makes upgrades easy.
- Forces implementation of sustainable pace..... You die a death of attrition without it.

---

3. Posted on Scrumdevelopment@yahoogroups.com on November 21, 2004, message 5439. Used with permission.

Although this mode of operation seems natural at PatientKeeper, it amazes outsiders. One of the keys is that everyone in the company works together in a spirit of trust, respect, commitment, and continuous improvement. Teams include product managers, developers, QA, and product support. The lead architect is the most experienced and trusted engineer in the company.

## Time: The Universal Currency

Everything that goes wrong in a process shows up as a time delay. Defects add delay. Complexity slows things down. Low productivity shows up as taking more time. Change intolerance makes things go very slowly. Building the wrong thing adds a huge delay. Too many things in process create queues and slows down the flow.

Time, specifically cycle time, is the universal lean measurement that alerts us when anything is going wrong. A capable development process is one that transforms identified customer needs into delivered customer value at a reliable, repeatable cadence, which we call cycle time. It is this cycle time that paces the organization, causes value to flow, forces quality to be built into the product, and clarifies the capacity of the organization.

A lean organization makes sure that processes are both *available* when work arrives at the process, and *capable* of doing the job expected of the process.[4] You can find out if your processes are available and capable by looking for the red flag called "expediting." Expediting happens when work arrives at a process and gets stuck in a queue, but someone thinks the work is so important that they personally "push it through." If requests are regularly pushed through the system by an "expediter," something is wrong. Either the process is not *available* when work comes in, or it is not *capable* of doing the work.

What does this mean for software development? Consider a software maintenance department that has guaranteed response times of two hours for an emergency, one day for a normal problem, and two weeks for lower priority changes. When an emergency occurs, the department can promise a two hour maximum response time and probably deliver a lot faster. When other requests arrive, it can also promise a reliable response time compatible with the type of request. Since the department has a reliable and repeatable cadence of work, it has established a predictable level of work that can be done. When this threshold is reached, routine requests are turned down or backup capacity is engaged.

---

4. See www.lean.org.

Lean organizations evaluate their operational performance by measuring the end-to-end cycle time of core business processes. The value stream maps in Chapter 4 mapped an end-to-end process that started and ended with a customer. They laid out the steps and totaled up the time from concept to launch (for products), or from customer request to deployed software. Excellent performance comes from completing this cycle with as little wasted time and effort as possible.

The best way to measure the quality of a software development process is to measure the average end-to-end cycle time of the development process. Specifically, what is the *average* time it takes to repeatedly and reliably go from concept to cash or from customer order to deployed software? The idea is not to measure one instance of this cycle time; measure the *average* time it takes your organization to go from customer need to need filled.

---

**But size varies all over the map. There is no such thing as "average" for us.**

If you can treat your work like a product, the best approach is to establish a regular release cycle—every two weeks, every six weeks, every six months—whatever is practical for you. Make it as short a period as you can possibly manage. Then determine how much work you can do in a release, and don't accept any more than that. Never delay a release because something isn't ready—take out some features and be careful not to take on so much work next release. Pretty soon you will know how much you can accept in a release.

It helps to divide work within cycles into fine-grain items the same way Patient-Keeper does. In Chapter 8 we discuss how to divide work into "stories," which are one to three days worth of development work. Over time a development team will complete these stories at a reliable, repeatable velocity—which is the demonstrated capacity of the team.

If regular releases don't make sense in your world, try—very hard—to put an upper limit on project size—six months is a good target—no more than twelve. It has been reported that for many years, Wal-Mart and Dell have limited IT projects size to approximately nine months; surely you can too.

Having set an upper limit on project size, group your projects into two or three groups: emergency, small, and large or some similar categories. Then try to reach a "service level" for each category.

**Our projects are far too big and too unique to think about cycles. They go on for years.**

No matter how big a development effort is, it gets done in small steps. We used to look at these steps sequentially and create a lot of partially done work at each step. Instead, figure out how to divide up that big effort differently. Divide it into increments of demonstrable value or minimum useful feature sets. In Chapter 8 we will show how a version of the Polaris submarine was launched just three years into a nine year development program. Surely there is a version of your system that can be demonstrated in one third of the overall development time.

Next, try to establish smaller cycles—six weeks to three months—where everything available up to that point is integrated, any existing capability is demonstrated and evaluated, and appropriate decisions are made. Then you have a cycle of no more than three months, and your goal is to deliver a repeatable amount of working software, reliably every cycle.

## Queuing Theory

Queuing theory is the study of waiting lines or queues. We certainly have queues in software development—we have lists of requests from customers and lists of defects we intend to fix. Queuing theory has a lot to offer in helping manage those lists.

### Little's Law

Little's Law states that in a stable system, the average amount of time it takes something to get through a process is equal to the number of things in the process divided by their average completion rate (see Figure 5.2).

In the last section we said that the objective of a lean development organization is to reduce the cycle time. This equation gives us a clear idea of how to do that. One way to decrease cycle time is get things done faster—increase the average completion rate. This usually means spending more money. If we don't

$$\text{Cycle Time} = \frac{\text{Things in Process}}{\text{Average Completion Rate}}$$

**Figure 5.2**   *Little's Law*

have extra money to spend, the other way to reduce cycle time is to reduce the number of things in process. This takes a lot of intellectual fortitude, but it usually doesn't require much money.[5]

## Variation and Utilization

Little's Law applies to stable systems, but there are a couple of things that make systems unstable. First there is variation—stuff happens. Variation is often dealt with by reducing the size of batches moving through the system. For example, many stores have check-out lanes for "10 items or less" to reduce the variation in checkout time for that line. Let's say you have some code to integrate into a system. If it's six weeks' worth of work, you can be sure there will be a lot of problems. But if it's only 60 minutes of work, the amount of stuff that can go wrong is limited. If you have large projects, schedule variation will be enormous. Small projects will exhibit considerably less schedule variation.

High utilization is another thing that makes systems unstable. This is obvious to anyone who has ever been caught in a traffic jam. Once the utilization of the road goes above about 80 percent, the speed of the traffic starts to slow down. Add a few more cars and pretty soon you are moving at a crawl. When operations managers see their servers running at 80 percent capacity at peak times, they know that response time is beginning to suffer, and they quickly get more servers.

Since Google was organized by a bunch of scientists studying data mining, it's not surprising that their server structure reflects a keen understanding of queuing theory. First of all, they store data in small batches. Instead of big servers with massive amounts of data on each one, Google has thousands upon thousands of small, inexpensive servers scattered around the world, connected through a very sophisticated network. The servers aren't expected to be 100 percent reliable; instead, failures are expected and detected immediately. It's not a big deal when servers fail, because data has been split into tiny pieces and stored in lots of places. So when servers fail and are automatically removed from the network, the data they held is found somewhere else and replicated once again on a working server. Users never know anything happened; they still get almost instantaneous responses.

If you have ever wondered why Google chose to dedicate 20 percent of its scientists' and engineers' time for work on their own projects, take a look at the

---

5. See Michael George and Stephen Wilson, *Conquering Complexity in Your Business: How Wal-Mart, Toyota, and Other Top Companies Are Breaking Through the Ceiling on Profits and Growth*, McGraw-Hill, 2004, p. 37.

graph in Figure 5.3. This figure shows that cycle time starts to increase at just above 80 percent utilization, and this effect is amplified by large batches (high variation). Imagine a group of scientists who study queuing theory for a living. Suppose they find themselves running a company that must place the highest priority on bringing new products to market. For them, creating 20 percent slack in the development organization would be the most logical decision in the world. It's curious that observers applaud Google for redundant servers but do not understand the concept of slack in a development organization.

Most operations managers would get fired for trying to get maximum utilization out of each server, because it's common knowledge that high utilization slows servers to a crawl. Why is it that when development managers see a report saying that 90 percent of their available hours were used last month, their reaction is, "Oh look! We have time for another project!" Clearly these managers are not applying queuing theory to the looming traffic jam in their department.

You can't escape the laws of mathematics, not even in a development organization. If you focus on driving utilization up, things will slow down. If you think that large batches of work are the path to high utilization, you will slow things down even further, and reduce utilization in the process. If, however, you assign work in small batches and concentrate on flow, you can actually achieve very good utilization—but utilization should *never* be your primary objective.

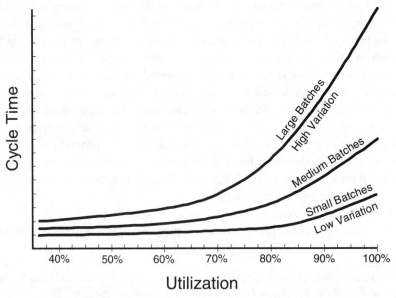

**Figure 5.3** *Queuing theory applies to development as well as traffic*

## Reducing Cycle Time

Let's agree, at least for the moment, that our objective is to reduce the average cycle time from concept to cash or from customer need to deployed software. How do we go about accomplishing this goal? Queuing theory gives us several textbook ways to reduce cycle time:

1. Even out the arrival of work

2. Minimize the number of things in process

3. Minimize the size of things in process

4. Establish a regular cadence

5. Limit work to capacity

6. Use pull scheduling

### Even Out the Arrival of Work

At the heart of every lean process is an even level of work. In a factory, for example, a monthly plan to build 10,000 widgets translates into building one widget every minute. The factory work is then paced to produce at a steady rate of one widget per minute.

The budgeting and approval processes are probably the worst offenders when it comes to creating a steady flow of development work. Requests are queued for months at a time, and large projects may wait for the annual budgeting cycle for approval. Some think that by considering all proposals at the same time, an organization can make a better choice about how to spend its budget. However, this practice creates long queues of work to be done, and if all of the work is released at the same time, it wreaks havoc on the development organization. Moreover, it means that decisions are made well out of sync with need, and by the time the projects are started, the real need in the business will probably have experienced considerable change. Tying project approvals to the budgeting cycle is generally unnecessary and usually unrealistic in all but the slowest moving businesses.

▼────────────────────────────────────────▼

## All of our work is in the first half of the year.

I was having dinner with a fairly high-level manager of a very large IT organization. They had a practice of moving developers around to different projects, and I suggested that they might want to consider assigning teams to specific business areas so they could become familiar with their customers.

"We couldn't do that," he said. "The business leaders all want their work to be done in the first half of the year, from January to June, so we try to do the background stuff they aren't interested in the second half of the year."

"Why do they want all of the work done in the first half of the year?" I asked. "Is your business seasonal?"

"No," he replied. And then after thinking for a moment, he added, "They get their budgets at the end of December, and so I suppose they want the work done as soon as possible after that."

"I know you want to be responsive to the business leaders," I said, "But you can't let them get away with that. You have to make it clear what that kind of schedule does to your ability to support them. What if you took every business leader's budget and allocated a team of people to their business based on their annual budget, then let the business leader decide how the team would spend their time throughout the year?"

"Well, that would make too much sense," he grinned. "It would mean a lot of change...." And he promised to consider it further.

—Mary Poppendieck

Queues at the beginning of the development process may seem like a good place to hold work so that it can be released to the development organization at an even pace. But those queues should be no bigger than necessary to even out the arrival of work. Often we find that work arrives at a steady pace, and if that is the case, then long queues are really unnecessary.

## Doctor's Appointments

Here in the United States, doctors stop accepting new patients when their backlog of appointments starts to grow too long. In many clinics, the waiting list for an appointment is about two months—it is not allowed to get longer, but then again, it never seemed to get any shorter either. This would be regarded as a stable system in queuing theory.

One clinic in Minnesota studied lean ideas and decided to see what would happen if they shortened the waiting time. For a while, most doctors worked an extra half day every week while the schedulers made sure that the arrival of work remained stable. Over the period of a half a year, the clinic reduced waiting times for an appointment to about two days. The clinic found that doctors still saw the same number of patients with the same mix of problems. Some doctors were surprised to find that they did not need a cushion of sixty days of appointments to keep them busy; in fact, they saw very little difference in their workload.

From a patient point of view, there was a dramatic difference—suddenly they could call up and get an appointment within a day or two. This was truly a "lean solution" for patients.

—Mary Poppendieck

---

### Minimize the Number of Things in Process

In manufacturing, people have learned that a lot of in-process-inventory just gums up the works and slows things down. Somehow we don't seem to have learned this same lesson in development. We have long release cycles and let stuff accumulate before releasing it to production. We have approval processes that dump work into an organization far beyond its capacity to respond. We have sequential processes that build up an amazing amount of unsynchronized work. We have long defect lists. Sometimes we are even proud of how many defects we've found. This partially done work is just like the inventory in manufacturing—it slows down the flow, it hides quality problems, it grows obsolete, usually pretty rapidly.

One of the less obvious offenders is the long list of customer requests that we don't have time for. Every software development organization we know of has more work to do that in can possibly accommodate, but the wise ones do not accept requests for features that they cannot hope to deliver. Why should we keep a request list short? From a customer's perspective, once something has been submitted for action, the order has been placed and our response time is being measured. Queues of work waiting for approval absorb energy every time they are estimated, reprioritized, and discussed at meetings. To-do queues often serve as buffers that insulate developers from customers; they can be used to obscure reality and they often generate unrealistic expectations.

---

**But we have such a long list of things to do, how can we pare it down?**

We generally find that long queues of work to do are unrealistic and unnecessary. Here are some ideas of how to deal with these queues.

1.  Start by asking, "How many things in this queue are we realistically never going to get around to?" Cut all of the things you'll never get to out of the queue immediately. Be honest. Just hit the delete key.

2.  So, how many items did that exercise get rid of? Half? Now take the remaining items and do a Pareto analysis on them. Rate each one on a scale of 1 to 5. The critical items will rate a 5. The unimportant items will rate a 1. Now get rid of all except those that got 4s and 5s. Just hit delete. Don't worry, if they turn out to be important, they'll come back at you.

3.  Now take the items that are left and calculate how many days, months, or years of work they represent. Will you have other things added to the list that will be more important? With that in mind, do you have the capacity to do the remaining items on the list in the near future? If not, should you add additional capacity?

4.  If your list is still unrealistically long, there is probably some purpose that it is serving beyond making effective decisions on what to do and what not to do. For example, a long list might deflect undue attention or absorb frivolous requests. Break the list into two lists, one which will serve the exterior purpose, and the other which you will keep short and work off of.

## Seven Years?

"We prioritize this list every week," the manager said.

"Do you know about how many requests there are in the list?" I asked.

"Yes, there are about 750," he said.

"Do you know how many of those you can do in, say, a month, on the average?"

"Yes, we average about nine every month," he answered. The company kept good statistics.

"Wow!" someone else said. "That's seven years of work!"

"Seven years!" the manager was astonished. "I had never looked at it that way."

"And why do you keep so many on the list if you know you will never get to them?" I asked.

"Well, our process expert said we don't want to lose track of anything. And we've gotten so we don't spend much time on the list every week."

"So you never get back to the customers and say, 'No, sorry.' And they probably keep expecting you to develop their features," I said. "Don't you want to be a bit more honest with your customers?"

"Yes, we used to tell them 'No' all the time—I was very aggressive about it when we were small and I was more involved. Customers seemed to appreciate the honesty. Maybe we should start doing that again...."

—Mary Poppendieck

*Minimize the Size of Things in Process*

The amount of unfinished work in an organization is a function of either the length of its release cycle or the size of its work packages. Keeping the release cycle short and the maximum work package size small is a difficult discipline. The natural tendency is to stretch out product releases or project durations, because the steps involved in releasing work to production seem to involve so much work. However, stretching out the time between releases is moving in exactly the wrong direction from a lean perspective. If a release seems to take a long time, don't stretch out releases. Find out what is causing all the time and address it. If something is difficult, do it more often, and you'll get a lot better at it.

## Releases Take Too Long

After a talk at a company, the QA manager came to me and said, "I don't see how we can follow your advice. We have a lot of pressure to put as many features as we can in each release, because they are so far apart."

"Why not release more often?" I asked.

"We can't possibly release more often because verification takes so long," came the immediate reply.

"Why does verification take so long?" I wondered.

"We find lots of problems in verification that have to be fixed," he said. I began to see a vicious circle.

"Can't you find most of the problems before verification?" I asked. After all, he was the QA manager.

"Verification is supposed to be independent," the QA manager replied. "If we verify the code while the developers are writing it, that would destroy our independence."

I was really surprised. There are a lot of good reasons to delay final verification. In embedded systems the hardware usually isn't ready until the end. When deploying to a customer site, you don't have access to their environment until the very last moment. But this was a new one.

"I can understand independent verification," I said, "but how is that related to long release cycles? Can't verification be independent but test a smaller amount of code?"

"Well, I'll have to think about it, but we might get too close to the developers that way." He sounded reluctant. I guessed that their long release cycles were not going to get shorter any time soon.

—Mary Poppendieck

## Oh, NOW I Get It!

We were teaching a class that had done current value stream maps and then future value stream maps. The last of the groups was presenting their future map. Suddenly someone from a different group exclaimed, "Oh, NOW I get it!" The presenter paused to see what this was all about.

"When I developed that future value stream map that I just finished presenting," he said, "I cut the release cycle to a third of its former length, and I was really frustrated that I still had a rather low process cycle efficiency. What I just realized is that I've been trying to optimize utilization with releases. The whole concept of a release is what's driving down my efficiency. If I could release as soon as a patch is ready instead of waiting for a release, the process cycle efficiency would be much better!"

The speaker was obviously proud of this blinding insight, but as he looked around he noticed that most people weren't all that impressed. Then he said kind of sheepishly, "I guess this is what you've been trying to say all morning. It just took the idea this long to sink into my head."

—Tom & Mary Poppendieck

### Establish a Regular Cadence

Iterations are the cadence of a development organization. Every couple of weeks something gets done. After a short time people begin to count on it. They can make plans based on a track record of delivery. The amount of work that can be accomplished in an iteration quickly becomes apparent; after a short time people stop arguing about it. They can commit to customers with confidence. There is a steady heartbeat that moves everything through the system at a regular pace. A regular cadence produces the same effect as line leveling in manufacturing.

What should the cadence be? One friend favors one week iterations. He finds it's just long enough to get customers with emergencies to be sure the problem is real before his team dives in and just short enough to deliver very timely work. Another friend swears by 30 days, because it gives the team time to think things through before they start coding, yet is short enough that managers can wait until the next iteration to ask for changes.

The cadence is right when work flows evenly. If there is a big flurry of activity at the end of an iteration then the iteration length is probably *too long*; shorter iterations will help to even out the workload. Cadence should be short enough that customers can wait until the end of an iteration to ask for changes, yet long enough to allow the system to stabilize. This is best understood by considering a household thermostat. If the thermostat turns on the furnace the instant the temperature falls below the temperature setting, and turns it off the instant the temperature rises above the setting, the furnace will cycle on and off too frequently for its own good. So thermostats have a lag built into them. They wait for the temperature to drop a degree or two below the setting before turning on the furnace, and they wait until the temperature goes a degree or two above the setting before turning the furnace off. This lag in response is small enough so you don't feel much difference, and big enough to keep the furnace from oscillating. Use the same concept when finding the right cadence for your situation.

## Asynchronous Cadence

One embedded software department we know of found their release schedule was getting too complicated as hardware models proliferated. So they decided to create a single version of the software that would run on all hardware models. Once they established the platform, they added technology capabilities to the software at three-week intervals. As new hardware models were developed, their engineers could look at the plan for software "technology drops" and decide which drop to pick up. A new model might wait a couple weeks for a technology drop with a feature it really needed, or the software department might be convinced to change its technology drop schedule, but only if other hardware models agreed.

By uncoupling the software from the hardware, the software department was able to establish its own cadence, and it didn't take long to discover that the new system was much more productive.

—Mary Poppendieck

### Limit Work to Capacity

Far too often we hear that the marketing department or the business unit, "Has to have it all by such-and-such a date," without regard for the development organization's capacity to deliver. Not only does this show lack of respect for the people developing the product, it also slows down development considerably. We know what happens to computer systems when we exceed their capacity—it's called thrashing.

## A Long Saturday in the Airport

We got to the Melbourne airport at 7:30 on a fine Saturday morning, plenty of time to catch our 10:00 a.m. flight to Auckland. A check-in desk had just opened up, so we put our luggage on the scale and tried to hand our tickets to the check-in agent. "Not so fast," she said. "The computers are down." As we looked around, we finally noticed the long lines everywhere.

"How long have they been down?" we asked.

"Oh, about an hour," she said.

In most US airports, each airline desk is probably accessing a different computer system, but in airports like Melbourne, there is one computer system that everyone shares. So that meant the whole airport—both domestic and international terminals—had been down for an hour.

Shortly after that the phone rang. Someone was calling to spread the word that the computers were coming back up. Throughout the airport we could see dozens of people poised at their terminals. And then, everyone began typing furiously, all at the same time. It took about 15 seconds for the system to crash again. "It's been like that for the last half hour," the agent told us. "Every ten minutes they say the system is coming up, and then it crashes again."

We could guess why: The system probably was not designed for hundreds of people to type at exactly the same time.

The computer system finally came up three hours later. We were rather late getting into Auckland.

—Mary & Tom Poppendieck

Time sometimes seems to be elastic in a development organization. People can and do work overtime, and when this happens in short bursts they can even accomplish more this way. However, sustained overtime is not sustainable. People get tired and careless at the end of a long day, and more often that not, working long hours will slow things down rather than speed things up. Sometimes an organization tries to work so far beyond its capacity that it begins to thrash. This can happen even if there appear to be enough people, if key roles are not filled and a critical area of development is stretched beyond its capacity to respond.

## A Customer Service Problem

I was visiting a company that asked me to look at its customer service process. As we drew a value stream map on the white board, we got to the point where a customer service team was on site installing software. At that point, I was told, they had a problem. "How often does this happen?" I asked.

"Every *single* time," they all agreed.

"Okay, so how does the problem get fixed?" I asked.

"It doesn't." General agreement again.

"It *doesn't*?" I had to be sure I heard that right.

"Yes, a request is made to development, but it goes into a queue. It never comes out unless it's one of our Top 3 priority customers. They're just too busy."

With what? I wondered, but instead I asked, "So what happens to the customer?"

"Well, the customer service people stay on site. They do other things. It can be weeks before they get any help."

"But you said they only get help if they are one of the Top 3," I said.

"Well, the customer eventually complains enough that they get moved up into the Top 3, and another one gets bumped out."

"It would appear to me," I said, "that you don't have a customer service problem, you have a problem delivering code that can be counted on to work at a customer site." In the ensuing discussion I could tell that this was a sore point.

"Why can't the development department focus on figuring out what is causing this and fix it?" I asked.

"Our investors are very demanding," they said. "We have a product map. We have to be developing new systems for new customers. We have to keep on adding more customers."

"But if you can't bring new customers up, why do you want them?" I asked. "It seems to me that you're thrashing."

"Yes, that's a good word," some agreed. But others didn't seem to think that the problem was such a big deal. Which, in the end, was probably the source of the problem in the first place.

—Mary Poppendieck

### Use Pull Scheduling

When a development team selects the work it will commit to for an iteration, the rule is that team members select only those (fine-grain) items they are confident that they can complete. During the first couple of iterations, they might guess wrong and select too much work. But soon they establish a team velocity, giving them the information they need to select only what is reasonable. In effect, the development team is "pulling" work from a queue. This pull mechanism limits the work expected of the team to its capacity. In the unlikely event that the team finishes ahead of time, more work can always be pulled out of the queue. Despite the fact that everyone always has work, the pull system has slack, because if emergencies arise or things go wrong, the team can adapt either by terminating the current iteration or by officially moving some items to the next iteration. Finally, since the team is working on the most important features from a customers' perspective, they are working on the right things.

## An Example of Pull Scheduling

I was visiting a medium-sized department in a large financial institution. Swen (not his real name) was responsible for business results and needed software changes to deliver them. He was very frustrated because all of his requests seemed to take forever. His frustration was matched by Karl (also not his real name), the senior manager in the IT department, who felt that Swen didn't understand how difficult his requests were or the problems he created by constantly changing his mind.

Karl insisted that each request needed to have a rough cost/benefit analysis and, if it passed, a more detailed architectural review before being scheduled for implementation. This sounded fine to Swen. All he wanted was to have some control over what was done and an understanding of when things were going to be ready to use.

I sketched the queuing idea in Figure 5.4 as a management approach:

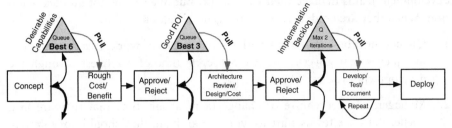

**Figure 5.4** *Pull system for managing a workflow*

With this system, Swen agreed to be limited to a maximum of six requests at a time. Karl committed to having a rough cost/benefit analysis (that would take about four hours) done within a week of each request. At that point Swen could either put it into the architectural review queue or reject it, but he agreed to have no more than three architectural requests in the queue at a time. If the queue was already full, a new request would either replace one of the existing requests in the queue or be rejected. Swen agreed that when the architectural queue was full, he would not submit any more requests that were less important than the three in the queue.

Karl agreed to complete an architectural review and more detailed cost estimate within two weeks. Then Swen could either accept or reject the result. Accepted requests went into the backlog, and every two weeks the team would pull an iteration's worth of work from the backlog. Swen agreed to limit the number of items in the backlog to no more than two iterations worth of work.

The important point is that Swen would "own" the queues. By keeping them short, he could tell at a glance approximately when any feature would be complete. Swen could reorganize the queues, add, or take away items at any time until the items were pulled by Karl's teams. Karl's organization would always be busy but never swamped, and they would always be working on exactly what Swen wanted.

Karl had a few other customers, but Swen accounted for 65 percent of his workload. Karl felt that he could integrate his other customers into this queuing system or else have separate teams work on their requests.

—Mary Poppendieck

Cascading queues (as shown in Figure 5.4) are possible, and are often used at organizational boundaries. Queues are a useful management tool, because they allow managers to change priorities and manage cycle time while letting the development teams manage their own work. But queues are not an ideal solution. When they are used, here are some general rules to follow:

1.  Queues must be kept short—perhaps two cycles of work. It is the length of the queues that governs the average cycle time of a request through the development process.

2.  Managers can reorganize or change items at any time that they are in a queue. But once teams start to work on an item, they should not interfere with day-to-day development.

3.  Teams pull work from a queue and work at a regular cadence until that work is done. It is this pull system that keeps teams busy at all times while limiting work to capacity.

4.  Queues should not be used to mislead people into thinking that their requests are going to be dealt with if the team does not have the capacity to respond.

### Summary

The measure of a mature organization is the speed at which it can reliably and repeatedly execute its core processes. The core process in software development is the end-to-end process of translating a customer need into deployed product. Thus, we measure our maturity by the speed with which we can *reliably and repeatedly* translate customers' needs into high quality, working software that is embedded in a product which solves the customers' whole problem.

# Try This

1.  How many defects are in your defect queue? How fast do they arrive? At what rate do they get resolved? At that rate, how many days, weeks, months, or years of work do you have in your defect queue? How many of the defects in your queue do you have a reasonable expectation to resolve? How much time do you spend on managing and reviewing the queue? Is it worth it?

2.  How many requests are on your list of things to do? At what rate do they arrive? How much time, on the average, has already been spent on each item? How much time do you spend on managing and reviewing the queue? How much work (in days, weeks, months, or years) do you have on

your list of things to do? Do you keep things in the list that you will never get around to? Why? What percent of the queue does this represent?

3. Does high utilization of people's available time cause logjams in your environment? Does your organization measure "resource" (i.e., people) utilization? If so, what kind of impact does this measurement have: Is it taken seriously? Does it drive behavior? Is that behavior beneficial?

4. What determines your batch size: Release schedule? Project size? Can you reduce time between releases or the size of projects? What is a reasonable target? What would it take to change to that target?

5. At a team meeting, review the list of ways to reduce cycle time:

   - Even Out the Arrival of Work

   - Minimize the Number of Things in Process

   - Minimize the Size of Things in Process

   - Establish a Regular Cadence

   - Limit Work to Capacity

   - Use Pull Scheduling

   Which one of these shows the most promise for your environment? Experiment by implementing the most promising approach and measure what happens to cycle time.

# Chapter 6

# People

## A System of Management

"Year after year, Toyota has been able to get more out of its people than its competitors have been able to get out of theirs,"[1] according to Gary Hamel. "It took Detroit more than 20 years to ferret out the radical management principle at the heart of Toyota's capacity for relentless improvement....Only after American carmakers had exhausted every other explanation for Toyota's success—an undervalued yen, a docile workforce, Japanese culture, superior automation—were they finally able to admit that Toyota's real advantage was its ability to harness the intellect of 'ordinary' employees."

Lean is a management system that creates engaged, thinking people at every level of the organization and most particularly at the front line. If you implement all of the lean principles save one—respect for people—you will reap only a shadow of the potential advantages that lean can bring. If you implement only one principle—respect for people—you will position the people in your organization to discover and implement the remaining lean principles.

## The Boeing 777

In 1988 Boeing made the rounds of its customers with plans for a new plane, a larger version of the 767 that would carry maybe 350 passengers. But somehow no one at Boeing had really understood what customers were looking for, and the proposed design got a collective yawn. So Boeing found itself designing a brand new airplane, listening carefully to customers this time. Two years later the Boeing 777 design competed with the McDonnell Douglas MD-11 and the Airbus A 330—both existing airplanes—for a large order from United Airlines. Boeing won the order, but with two conditions: First, the plane would be deliv-

---

1. "Management Innovation," by Gary Hamel, *Harvard Business Review*, February, 2006, p. 74.

ered certified for extended range operation within five years, and second, since the plane didn't exist yet, Boeing and United would work together to be sure that the airplane would truly meet United's needs.

This was a "bet the company" deal, an incredibly aggressive deadline with fierce penalties for not meeting it, coupled with a once-in-a-decade opportunity to define the next generation aircraft. Alan Mulally was charged with making it happen, and he responded by creating an entirely new management system for the Boeing 777 program. There were those who argued that this was not the time for a new management system—the old one had worked well for years. But root cause analysis of every problem that delayed the schedule of previous programs led to only one conclusion: Delays were caused because people were not working together, not looking for problems early enough, not paying attention when a problem arose, not communicating with each other promptly or effectively. So Mulally focused his energies on Working Together—an enormously successful example of organizational teamwork that has been largely credited with the extraordinary success of the Boeing 777 program. He created more than 200 design/build teams with members from design, manufacturing, suppliers, and customer airlines—everyone from pilots to baggage handlers. These teams captured the insight of those who would use the plane while it was being designed. For example, one team discovered that the fuel port on the wing was so high that no United fuel truck could reach it, something that would probably not have been caught until delivery under the former approach to development.[2]

Mulally urged everyone to "share early and share often," and he insisted on no secrets. Every problem was to be raised with and discussed by the team until a solution emerged. Suppliers worked on the basis of trust, and customers were given an unprecedented insight into the development process and status, as well as a large voice in trade-off decisions.

Mulally preached a "test early and fail fast" philosophy. Testing was moved as early in the development process as possible at all levels. For the first time the entire plane was designed using a 3-D modeling system. 3-D modeling provided a sort of unit test for each part, to be sure it fit and did not interfere with other parts. This resolved a problem that had plagued the early manufacturing stage of all previous models.

Testing was aggressive at every stage of integration. The new Pratt & Whitney engine was considered so well-tested that flight tests could be bypassed. But the collective wisdom of the engineers was biased toward testing it anyway, so

---

2. *Deadline! How Premier Organizations Win the Race Against Time*, by Dan Carrison, AMACOM (American Management Association), 2003, Chapter 5.

at considerable expense, one of the new engines was mounted to a 747 and tested in real flight. The engine backfired badly, and a critical part had to be redesigned. Mulally's reaction was: "Isn't that great! We found the problem early."

We know his reaction because Boeing allowed the Public Broadcasting System (PBS) to film the entire five-year development effort without exercising editorial control. The resulting five hour, publicly available documentary[3] brings home how Working Together solicited and quickly acted on the ideas of everyone—a wing sealer on the production line could get a suggestion implemented in an hour instead of weeks. It showed how a small company in Australia manufacturing the rudder was handed one impossible change after another by Boeing, but working on the basis of trust, they figured out how to deliver the rudder on time.

Boeing had to work creatively with the Federal Aviation Administration (FAA) to obtain long-range flight certification before delivery of the plane to United, because twin engine planes were supposed to be tried in actual use for a couple of years before being allowed to fly more than an hour from an airport. Boeing proposed a set of tests so rigorous that pilots and regulators alike were intrigued: Could a brand new plane really pass such a rigorous test regime? The "test early and fail fast" strategy worked. The new plane passed the extensive testing with ease, and was the first twin engine plane to receive "out-of-the-box" long-range certification.

The 777 was Boeing's first fly-by-wire aircraft—controlled by software and electrical actuators rather than hydraulics and cables. As part of the Working Together program Boeing insisted that everyone use the same software language: Ada. Although suppliers were initially resistant, they came to like the discipline that a strongly typed, object-based language imposed at compile time. The largest part of the software was the Airplane Information Management System developed by Honeywell's Air Transport Systems division. Honeywell used a loosely coupled architecture that allowed the seven main functions to be developed independently by teams of 60–100 engineers. In the end, all of the 777 software was delivered and working on time except the passenger phone system.

On June 7, 1995, three Boeing 777s took off on their first commercial flights, meeting the deadline established five years earlier. For more than a decade, Boeing has delivered 777 aircraft at the rapid pace of about 50 per year, and as of this writing it holds orders for another five years of deliveries.

---

3. *21st Century Jet: The Building of the 777*, Produced by Skyscraper Productions for KCTS/Seattle and Chanel 4 London, 1995.

## I Worked On the 777

I worked at Honeywell's Air Transport Systems division in Minneapolis at the time the 777 was being developed. We designed the triple redundant inertial navigation system—the laser gyroscopes that tell an aircraft exactly where it is even in the absence of GPS data. There was a lot of evidence of Boeing's Working Together program. This was before the Internet brought ubiquitous e-mail to the world, so we linked our internal e-mail systems together, which was novel at the time. We used FTP to exchange current versions of documents electronically, and we held status and feedback meetings every week via teleconference.

Those were challenging times for the aircraft industry, which experienced one of its cyclical downturns in the mid 1990s. There were industry-wide layoffs, so many people moved on to do different things. But every time I meet others who worked on the 777, their memory of the experience is uniformly positive.

—Tom Poppendieck

Boeing has moved on to the defining program of this decade, the 787 Dreamliner. This program brings another management innovation: an unprecedented degree of collaboration between Boeing and its global partners in the design and development of the aircraft. Boeing has created a worldwide innovation network and directs design challenges to the center of expertise around the world that is best equipped to handle the challenge. The 787 development is supported by far superior electronic collaboration tools than were available to the 777 teams, but it is Boeing's Working Together culture that makes the collaboration work.

## W. Edwards Deming

In July of 1950, a US statistician named W. Edwards Deming, who had been to Japan to help with the census a few years earlier, was invited to return and give a series of lectures to some of Japan's most influential industrial leaders. Deming was asked how to change the world's perception that Japan produced inferior products. He responded that production is a "system" that includes the supplier and the customer, and that business leaders should focus on continually improving the overall system. One way to do this is to use statistical process control to build quality into products instead of inspecting it in later. Recordings of Deming's lectures were translated into Japanese, and proceeds from their sale were used by JUSE, the Union of Japanese Scientists and Engineers, to fund the prestigious Deming award.

Deming traveled to Japan several times over the next 15 years, but back home in the United States, he was relatively unknown. Then in 1980 the NBC report "If Japan Can...Why Can't We?" featured Deming chiding US companies for the poor quality of their products. At 80 years old, Deming had finally been discovered by his own country. The TV show aired only once, but it shocked the country and put quality on corporate agendas. Deming was at the forefront of the quality movement in the United States until his death in 1993.

Deming espoused a System of Profound Knowledge that has four main points:

1. **Appreciation for a System.** Deming taught that the synergy between parts of any system is the key to the overall success of the system. Since he saw production as a system, he emphasized that it is important to manage the relationship between its parts—the relationship between departments in a company—the relationship between suppliers, producers, and customers. Above all, Deming believed that a systems view was fundamental; suboptimizing any part of the system was not in the best interest of the whole.

2. **Knowledge about Variation.** Deming was appalled at the way in which workers were blamed for problems that were inherent in the system in which they worked. His lectures focused on making sure managers understood that most system variation was what he called common cause variation, that is variation inherent in the system. He did exercises to show that trying to eliminate this variation from the system is not only futile, it just makes things worse. Deming emphasized that the bulk of the causes of low quality and low productivity were inherent in the system and thus, lie beyond the power of the individual worker. Deadlines and slogans do nothing to address systemic problems. What was needed instead, Deming insisted, was leadership in changing the way the system works.

3. **Theory of Knowledge.** A physicist himself, Deming espoused the scientific method for developing a data-based understanding of the system and making decisions. The steps of the scientific method—hypothesize, experiment, learn, incorporate learning—give us the well-known Deming Cycle [4]—plan, do, check, act (PDCA). A version of this cycle is found in virtually every quality and process improvement program. For more on this, see Chapter 7.

---

4. Deming called this the Shewhart Cycle, since it was originally taught by Walter Shewhart, who developed statistical process control in the Bell Laboratories in the United States during the 1930s.

4. **Psychology.** Deming admonished managers that numbers don't tell the whole story, and when it comes to people, the things that make a difference are skill, pride, expertise, confidence, and cooperation.

Deming summed up his multidimensional perspective on quality in 14 points for management (see sidebar).

## Deming's 14 Points[5]

1. Provide for the long-range needs of the company; don't focus on short-term profitability. The goal is to stay in business and provide jobs.

2. The world has changed, and managers need to adopt a new way of thinking. Delays, mistakes, defective workmanship, and poor service are no longer acceptable.

3. Quit depending on inspection to find defects, and start building quality into products while they are being built. Use statistical process control.

4. Don't choose suppliers on the basis of low bids alone. Minimize total cost by establishing long-term relationships with suppliers that are based on loyalty and trust.

5. Work continually to improve the system of production and service. Improvement is not a one-time effort; every activity in the system must be continually improved to reduce waste and improve quality.

6. Institute training. Managers should know how to do the job they supervise and be able to train workers. Managers also need training to understand the system of production.

7. Institute leadership. The job of managers is to help people do a better job and remove barriers in the system that keep them from doing their job with pride. The greatest waste in America is failure to use the abilities of people.

8. Drive out fear. People need to feel secure in order to do their job well. There should never be a conflict between doing what is best for the company and meeting the expectations of a person's immediate job.

9. Break down barriers between departments. Create cross-functional teams so everyone can understand each-other's perspective. Do not undermine team cooperation by rewarding individual performance.

---

5. True to his philosophy of continuous improvement, Deming continually modified the wording of his 14 points. This list is our summary of the 14 points and their discussion, found in Chapter 2 of *Out of the Crisis*, by W. Edwards Deming, MIT Press, 2000; originally published in 1982.

10. Stop using slogans, exhortations, and targets. It is the system, not the workers, that creates defects and lowers productivity. Exhortations don't change the system; that is management's responsibility.

11. Eliminate numerical quotas for workers and numerical goals for people in management. (We add: Eliminate arbitrary deadlines for development teams.) This is management by fear. Try leadership.

12. Eliminate barriers that rob the people of their right to pride of workmanship. Stop treating hourly workers like a commodity. Eliminate annual performance ratings for salaried workers.

13. Encourage education and self-improvement for everyone. An educated workforce and management is the key to the future.

14. Take action to accomplish the transformation. A top management team must lead the effort with action, not just support.

—W. Edwards Deming

Alan Mulally created a management system for the 777 straight out of Deming's playbook at a time when many companies throughout the US were discovering the power of Deming's ideas. The design/build teams, the weekly team meetings to expose, discuss, diagnose, and dispose of problems went to the heart of creating pride of workmanship in everyone working on the plane. Although the deadline loomed, it was never allowed to get in the way of doing the right thing.

Deming said that the real purpose of a company was not to make money, it was to create customers who were so pleased that they would continue to buy products. Mulally made sure that the 777 development team was not focusing on hitting deadlines at the lowest possible cost; instead it was to develop a plane that would be efficient to manufacture, cost-effective for airlines to operate, easy for pilots to fly, simple to maintain, and comfortable for the people who flew in it.

Deming emphasized that suppliers should be chosen based on their ability to work closely with the producer to minimize total system costs. Boeing not only followed that principle, it went one step further and maximized system value over a long timeframe. For example, Boeing felt that the parts for the airplane needed to come from around the world, if it expected to sell the plane around the world. Thus, for example, 20 percent of the 777 would be manufactured in Japan, one of the biggest buyers of Boeing's wide body jets.

The innovation in management thinking that Deming brought to the world is this: When things go wrong, the cause is almost always inherent in the system, and therefore it is a management problem. Managers who push harder on people to meet deadlines or reduce defects are ignoring the system problem and will usually make things worse. Instead, leaders must envision and institute fundamental changes that address the systemic causes of current problems.

## Why Good Programs Fail

We have seen many corporate initiatives over the years, from the quality programs spawned by Deming (and others) to the lean programs in the early 1990s to the Six Sigma programs that followed. We've noticed that lean is currently making a comeback. We've watched CMM and ISO 9000 as their focus changed from quality improvement to certification. These initiatives started out with the best of intentions, and they made a difference. But after a while their implementations tended to lose the original potency and become bureaucratic. Every one of these initiatives has generated large and sustainable improvements in some companies and mediocre to disappointing results in many others. So why is this?

Gary Hamel suggests that the largest improvements in companies come from a management innovation—a marked departure from traditional management principles, processes, practices, or organizational forms—that confers a competitive advantage on the innovative company.[6] When a management innovation creates a competitive advantage, it is a big one, and it is very difficult to copy, because management innovations are such a marked departure from accepted norms.

But that doesn't keep companies from trying to copy the best practices of a competitor and attempting to mimic their perception of the management innovation. Almost without exception, the fundamental principle of the innovation is overlooked by the mimicking company, because as Gary Hamel says, "Management orthodoxies are often so ingrained in executive thinking that they are nearly invisible and are so devoutly held that they are practically unassailable. The more unconventional the principle underlying a management innovation, the longer it will take competitors to respond. In some cases, the head scratching can go on for decades."

In other words, the central point of a management innovation is invisible to most management teams trying to copy the innovation. For example, many companies have tried to copy lean practices, but they often missed the central point. As Hamel noted, Toyota's real innovation is its ability to harness the

---

6. "Management Innovation," by Gary Hamel, *Harvard Business Review*, February, 2006, p. 74.

intellect of "ordinary" employees. Successful lean initiatives must be based first and foremost on a deep respect for every person in the company, especially those "ordinary" people who make the product or pound out the code.

## Do You Think We Want to Steal Your Hangers?[7]

When Deming was a patient at Sibley Hospital in the early 1990s he called the chief operating officer, Jerry Price, into his room and said, "You don't trust your patients, do you?" Price was puzzled.

"Look in the closet," Deming roared. He shouted a lot, particularly at top management. Price looked in the closet, and it was filled with the coat hangers used in expensive hotels, the hangers that have little balls that must be fitted into tiny holes.

"How would you like to be 92 years old and sick and you couldn't even hang up your clothes?" Deming demanded. "Do you think your patients want to steal your coat hangers?"

Deming sent the hospital a $25,000 check with instructions to buy new coat hangers for all the patients' rooms.

Price did so, had a number of them sanded down, and had Deming sign them. Today, the quality awards at Sibley are sturdy wooden hangers with hooks and Deming's signature mounted in a frame.

—Clare Crawford-Mason
Producer of the 1980 NBC report "If Japan Can...Why Can't We?"

Consider the kind of messages that your policies and practices telegraph to the "ordinary" people in your company and to your suppliers. Do you trust your employees, or do you have locked stock rooms? Do you say that quality is important but only look at deadlines? Do you ask people to work in teams but then rank them against each other or base bonuses on individual performance? Do you talk about trust with suppliers, but insist on fixed price contracts? If you do these things, you are missing the central point of lean thinking: respect for people.

---

7. Special to *The Washington Post*, by Clare Crawford-Mason Tuesday, April 23, 2002, p. HE01, used with permission.

# Teams

Our children were competitive swimmers when they were in high school. For almost a decade our son's name was on the record board at the high school swimming pool until someone finally swam the backstroke faster and replaced him. We liked swimming as a sport because our son and daughter, three years apart in age, were in the same swimming club. They practiced together, went to meets together, and developed a mutual language and mutual respect. The sport demanded discipline and helped them develop good habits. But swimming didn't really teach them a lot about teamwork.

The difference between individual sports and team sports is fairly clear. In individual sports, contestants win or lose based on their individual abilities. In team sports, the entire team wins or loses together based on the team members' ability to work together. When our son was in college he was the coxswain of a crew team. He sat in the back of a long narrow boat synchronizing the efforts of eight hefty rowers as they sped down the water. Rowing is clearly a team sport.

We might call diving and gymnastics team sports because individual scores are totaled to a team score. But that's not the same as basketball or soccer, where team members have to synchronize their efforts in order to perform. We should keep the same distinction in mind with work teams. People who work side by side are not necessarily a team, even when they sum up their individual efforts into a collective result. A work group becomes a team when the members hold themselves mutually accountable to produce a "collective work product."[8]

There is nothing wrong with individual sports, they're simply different than team sports. And there is nothing wrong with work groups, but they are different than teams. Putting a group of people together and calling them a team doesn't make them a team. The thing that turns a group into a team is the mutual commitment of the members to pool their various skills and work together for a common purpose.

## What Makes a Team?

What got our son up early every morning to coast his bike down the steep Ithaca hill to the Cornell University boat house? After all, the bike ride back up the hill was punishing. But the team had races to win, and to win races they had to

---

8. See *The Wisdom of Teams*, by Jon R. Katzenbach and Douglas K. Smith, Harvard Business School Press, 1992.

work hard every day to learn to synchronize their efforts so that they could row faster and smarter than the teams from other schools. If anyone didn't show up, or didn't put out his best effort, the team wouldn't make the progress it needed to make in order to win races.

Creating good software is a lot more like rowing than swimming. Software development involves constant problem solving; people make complex decisions many times a day, often with implications far beyond their own work. Pooling skill and knowledge from many different perspectives is critical to excellent results.

Teams need a challenge, a common goal, and a mutual commitment to work together to meet the goal. Team members depend upon each other, and help each other out. A wise organization will focus its attention, training, and resources on creating an environment where teams are challenged by their work and engaged with their teammates in doing the best job they can.

---

### A group or a team?

1.  *At the morning meeting everyone reports on what they have done in the last day. After each report the project manager says "Great, Joe, today I'd like you to...." Everyone leaves with their assignments for the day.*

    This is a group. By assigning work, the project manager has taken over the responsibility of making sure that everything gets done. Team members have not mutually committed to accomplishing the project goal.

2.  *At the morning meeting everyone reports on what they have done in the last day, what they expect to do today, and where they need help. Sanjiv reminds everyone that a tough feature is still waiting to be tackled by saying, "If someone doesn't get at that, I'm afraid it won't get done in time. I would do it," Sanjiv continues, "but I really have to solve this other problem first."*

    *In response, Mike says, "That's probably more important than what I'm working on, but it's not an area I'm good at."*

    *Sanjiv offers to take a couple of hours to get Mike started.*

    *Next, the ScrumMaster notes that the team is struggling with an interface to the firmware. She asks if it might help if she rounds up someone from the firmware team to meet with a couple of people that afternoon. Three developers jump on the opportunity.*

    This is a team. The meeting is focused on figuring out how to reach the goal they have jointly agreed to meet. The ScrumMaster focuses on helping where the team needs assistance.

**But it's not so easy....**

1.    *I tried the team approach, but I can't get the team to take the iteration goals seriously. They punch the clock and go home at the end of the day. At the end of an iteration, the work the team supposedly committed to is not done, and no one really cares.*

You get what you expect and what you inspect. Do the immediate supervisors of the team members consistently expect the team members to commit to team goals and deliver on those commitments? What is their reaction when commitments are not met? When evaluation time comes along, what will be rewarded—individual accomplishments or contributions to the team that help it meet its goals? When the expectation and measurement system of the organization promotes individualism over teamwork, it is almost impossible to sustain healthy teamwork over time.

2.    *We have a computer system that assigns projects to teams. You work with one team for a few months, then another and another. It's really hard to get people to commit to a common objective.*

Indeed, you aren't going to have teams in an environment that keeps reshuffling people; you have continually reforming groups. An occasional group may become a team, but after they get split up, they rarely bring the team spirit to the next group.

3.    *In my organization, we have a ranking system. Everyone needs to hand to their supervisor all the ammunition possible to get the highest rank. Helping other people out on the team doesn't show up on the ranking system, and worse, the other guy gets credit for my good ideas.*

As long as you have an individual ranking system or an individual bonus system, you may as well forget about teams. Do the best you can with work groups.

4.    *People would like to commit to team goals, but they are working on five teams at a time. They never know when an emergency is going to arise on another team, and after a while they just get burned out.*

We are sure that our son would never have been a top swimmer in high school or a top coxswain in college if he had tried to compete in more than one sport at a time. He had two priorities—top grades first, top athlete second. That's about the maximum number of commitments that anyone can honestly make at one time. People can be members of five groups at a time, but only one—or maybe two—teams.

## Expertise

A crew boat is narrow, goes fast, turns slowly, and tips easily. A crew team has to concentrate hard on working together just to stay dry. Racing in water is all about current, wind, drag, and strategy. Consistently synchronized power is essential in order to keep the boat motion smooth and conserve energy for the final push. To win races, the rowers must first of all be excellent athletes, and secondly, they have to focus on synchronizing their efforts with their teammates every time they work out. It takes many workouts for powerful athletes to develop into excellent rowers.

Toyota believes that consistent excellence in product development starts with "towering technical competence in all engineers."[9] And the company does not think that such competence is learned in college; it is developed over time—several years—with experience and mentoring. Toyota starts by sending new engineers to automobile plants to make cars. Then they work in dealerships for a few months, selling cars and talking to customers. After about a half a year, new engineers are assigned to a department to work under the guidance of a senior engineer. The first thing they do is a "freshman project"—an improvement project which provides a challenge and teaches the engineer Toyota's approach constant improvement. At the end of a year or so, new engineers start a rigorous, two year, on-the-job-training program in which they acquire a standard set of skills. Only then do they move up to entry level engineer and begin to be a serious team contributor. After this initial period, an engineer can expect to spend five or six years within the same specialty before being considered a first-rate engineer.

---

**The Bell Curve**

1.  *We have hundreds of developers. When you have that many people, their expertise falls along the bell curve—some are excellent, some are average, some are below average.*

    We believe that when an organization sets out to do so, it can consistently turn "ordinary people" into excellent contributors. The place to start is to make it the top priority of every manager to develop the capabilities of the people for whom they are responsible. At Toyota, "Developing people is fundamental to the manager's job. All managers view the performance of their teams as a direct reflection of their own ability. It is personal."[10]

---

9.  James Morgan and Jeffrey Liker, *The Toyota Product Development System: Integrating People, Process, and Technology*, Productivity Press, 2006. See Chapter 9.
10. James Morgan and Jeffrey Liker, *The Toyota Product Development System: Integrating People, Process, and Technology*, Productivity Press, 2006, p. 169.

Excellent software products start with highly competent technical experts in many areas—architecture, object-oriented technologies, coding strategies, data structures, test automation. This is not a function of the methodology used for development; behind every excellent product, no matter how it was developed, you will find excellent technical people. In lean development, we acknowledge this fact and focus organizational policies on hiring and developing such experts.

A development team should have among its members the expertise necessary to meet its goals. Team members should mutually commit to specific team goals, and reliably achieve those goals by working together, pooling their expertise, and helping each other out whenever necessary. It is easier to help each other out when there are multiskilled people on the team. As development progresses, there may be more need for testing and less for development, or more need for user interface coding rather than database work. Developers can help testers, user interaction designers can test user interactions, junior members can pair up with more experienced team members to help out and learn new skills. Every person on the team is first of all a member of the team, and second a specialist in some particular discipline. No one on the team gets credit for being done until all the work the team committed to is done, so everyone pitches in however they are able.

### Specialists

1.  *Our team always gets hung up because the technical writers are all working on several projects at a time. User documentation is a critical part of our product, but the technical writers just can't keep up with the team, what with all their other work.*

    Technical writers, as well as people with other critical specialties, need to be part of the team from the beginning. It's almost impossible for a person to really contribute to more than two teams at a time, and one team is much better. Yet there might not be enough work for technical writing to do at all stages of a development project.

    There are several remedies—the one you choose will depend on your situation. One approach might be to broaden the role of technical writers and get them involved in the design of the product. Perhaps they can help with user interaction designs or write user stories or use cases, since technical writers have to have a good understanding of the way users think. Technical writers might also help in testing, or they might write any necessary technical documentation as well as the user documentation.

A second approach could be to rethink the way in which technical writing is done. New methods such as the Darwin Information Typing Architecture (DITA), which is essentially a technique for creating documentation incrementally and making it more reusable, can allow technical writers to spread out their work more evenly over the development cycle.[11]

Or perhaps someone else might take a first crack at user documentation as an assistant to the technical writer. For example, people from the technical support team know exactly how users struggle with the system and its documentation, so they make great team members who have a good idea of what kind of documentation users need.

2. *We have silos in our company. For example, the graphics designers get much more esteem from designing a great screen than from getting it working with the rest of the system. The security people have their own silo, and they are paranoid about us writing any code at all.*

Silos are a pretty good indication that there are measurements and rewards at a functional level that encourage functional optimization at the expense of the overall system. This is most common in large organizations where it is difficult to see how to optimize the whole, so functional optimization is substituted instead. A possible remedy is use a value stream map to demonstrate how functional measurements are at odds with the overall good of the value stream. Substituting value stream cycle time for functional measurements can do a lot to promote cooperation between functions.

3. *We are having a problem bringing junior people up to speed. We have teams of senior people working on the most critical projects, while the junior people work in other areas.*

Teams should have a mix of skills. Teams with all-senior people lack anyone to do the "grunt" work, have no one to bring a fresh perspective, and the experienced people are not passing on their skills to the broader company. Teams with all-junior members have to reinvent too many wheels, have no sense of the patterns that work in the business, and generally lack a high-level view of the problem. Mix skill levels as well as skill sets.

---

11. The OASIS standards organization approved DITA in June of 2005. DITA is an XML-based standard and a set of design principles for creating "information-typed" modules at a topic level. DITA aims to deliver content from a single repository directly to the point-of-use.

## Leadership

During a race, a team of eight rowers needs a coxswain to focus on hydrodynamics, aerodynamics, and race strategy. The coxswain should be smart, confident, quick thinking, and weigh as little as possible. A coxswain is the "onboard" leader of a crew team, keeping the rowers focused on applying consistent, synchronized power so the boat glides smoothly through the water and air. During a race, the coxswain's job is to read the weather, the course, and the competition, to make quick decisions, to steer the boat, and to keep the rowers' effort paced so they have both a good position and enough reserve for the final sprint to beat the other boats across the line.

A large team without leadership is like a crew team without a coxswain. The team can perhaps go fast in the right direction, but it is unlikely to apply synchronized power and make the subtle course corrections that create a winning product. Toyota operates from the basic principle that teamwork is essential, but someone always needs to be responsible.[12] We concur. All too often we find that "Everybody's job is nobody's job." In Chapter 3 we discussed the importance of a champion who brings to a development team a deep understanding of the market need and the technology that can meet that need in a unique way. The question we address now is this: Does a development team also need a process leader? How many leaders does a team really need, and what are the appropriate roles?

Don't make the mistake of thinking that process leadership is a substitute for product and technical leadership. It is not. The role of champion remains essential; there should be one or two people who deeply understand the customer and deeply understand the technology. If there are two people, they should speak with one voice and have joint responsibility for the success of the product. When an organization puts a new process in place, a process leader may be a good idea. However, the process leadership role must synchronize well with the role of champion, either through close cooperation or by adding process leadership to the champion's role. If there are two people in the champion role already, three may be too many. If there is one champion, she or he may welcome the assistance of a process leader.

---

12. Jeffrey Liker and James Morgan, Ibid., p. 103.

**Leaders**

1. *We have ScrumMasters, but their job is to manage the process. They are not supposed to make product or technology decisions.*

   We question why a ScrumMaster should be limited to process leadership, since product and technical leadership are so critical to the success of any large development effort. If the ScrumMaster is not supposed to provide this leadership, then look for it elsewhere. Once a team has become a high performing agile team, the process leadership devolves to functional management and to those providing technical and product leadership.

2. *We have Scrum Product Owners, but they aren't very involved and don't really understand the technology.*

   The champion or product manager is a full team member, deeply involved in the day-to-day tradeoffs of the team, balancing his or her customer instincts with the technology tradeoffs. Without this interplay at a deep level, you will get a mediocre product. A team cannot abdicate customer understanding to someone who is not engaged with the team and mutually committed to achieving its purpose.

3. *So where does a project manager fit in?*

   If you examine the roles of highly successful project managers, you will find they provide the same product and technical leadership that are present in all highly successful products. Alan Mulally's leadership of the Boeing 777 has often been called project management at its best. He was chief architect of the aircraft, of the innovative design/build teams, and of the unrelenting emphasis on delighting customers.

   On the other hand, a project manager who mostly updates Gantt charts and tells people what to do probably adds little value to the team.

## Responsibility-Based Planning and Control

Crew teams have coaches. The coach is usually in a motor boat with a megaphone, organizing workouts and critiquing performance. But once the boat heads out to race, the crew team is on its own. All the coach can do is watch. Responsibility-based planning and control operates on the same principle: There is a time to stop telling well-trained experts what to do and expect them to figure it out for themselves.

The way this works at Toyota is remarkable. The product development process has specific synchronizing events such as vehicle sketches, clay models, design structure plans, prototype, and so on. The dates for each event are scheduled by the chief engineer. Every engineer and supplier knows that these dates will not—ever—be moved. They know exactly what is expected of them at each synchronizing event, and they will—always—be ready with their contribution by the date. There are no excuses. Engineers are expected to obtain for themselves everything necessary to be ready on time. Thus, information is "pulled" by engineers as they need it instead of broadcast to long distribution lists. At Toyota, the engineering tasks required for each synchronization event are well known and standardized. But they are not tracked. The schedule is managed through the fundamental imperative that schedules are never missed. The rest is the responsibility of the engineers.

This may seem like an impossible development approach, except that you can find examples of the same approach being successfully applied in every major city in the world. Any city with a daily newspaper has a group of skilled people who develop a new product every day. They never miss a deadline, even when the news is changing right up to the cutoff, even when computers go down, and with surprisingly few exceptions, even while coping with local disasters. So if you would like to see a development process that never misses a deadline, go benchmark your local newspaper.

An important consideration to bear in mind when schedules become a commitment is that *people must always have the time to do the job* that they have committed to complete, and at the same time, the details of the job will always change. As we discussed in Chapter 5, if you expect teams to meet aggressive deadlines, *you must limit work to capacity.*

There is more than one way to accomplish this. Toyota has a good feel for how much effort will be required in any development cycle and staggers model development cycles so that the demands on each function are more or less leveled. Further, Toyota makes no attempt to schedule at the detailed level but expects that each function or supplier will back up their team members with additional help whenever it is needed.

PatientKeeper estimates features and tasks at a fine-grain level and dynamically adjusts that estimate daily. The new estimates give PatientKeeper an immediate alert when work exceeds capacity, and the amount of work is quickly adjusted make sure that there is no more work scheduled into an iteration than can be completed by the deadline.

Maintenance organizations maintain slack by working on routine requests that can be set aside, which provides the capacity to jump on emergencies when they arise. However you do it, remember that it is impossible to implement responsibility-based planning and control unless you understand the capacity of each team and limit the work expected of a team to its capacity.

## Schedules

1. *Shouldn't we schedule tasks?*

   Most task schedules are deterministic—they don't have any flexibility for variation. If you use deterministic schedules with inherently variable things like task completion dates, the real task completion dates will *always* be at odds with the schedule. Trying to force out the variation from task completion dates is exactly the wrong approach, as Deming taught us, because it is inherent in the system.

   You have to change the system, and you have three options:

   a. You can add probabilities to the schedule with Monte Carlo simulations. However, this works best at a feature level.

   b. You can use a project buffer with the schedule as advised by Critical Chain scheduling. (See Chapter 10.)

   c. You can simplify your life by not scheduling tasks at all; use responsibility-based planning and control instead.

2. *Don't we need a work breakdown structure?*

   A system design is essential—the major subsystems and their interfaces must be laid out. But this is a feature breakdown structure, not a work breakdown structure. Instead of tasks, decide what specific, working capabilities should be demonstrated, and when. Assign these to teams, making sure that the teams have the skill and capacity to deliver, and let the teams manage their own work. Expect them to deliver on time.

3. *What about dependencies?*

   First of all, do not assume that all dependencies are real. Break them whenever possible. The job of managing dependencies should fall to the systems design, not the schedule.

   At a high level, dependencies are handled by developing major subsystems in a logical sequence. At a detailed level, dependencies between subsystems should be handled through board information sharing across teams along with regular synchronization events. Individuals and teams should be expected to make dependent tasks happen so they can meet their goals. Simple, effective communication supported by an insightful systems design and an options-based approach to development (see Set-Based Design in Chapter 7) are the best tools for dealing with dependencies.

## The Visual Workspace

Airports are amazing places, especially hub airports. You can land on one air-plane and leave on another a couple of hours later without talking to anyone, log-ging into a computer, or making a phone call. It's your job to get yourself from your arriving aircraft to your departing aircraft on time, without any help from people, technology, or communication devices. Instead of having someone or something tell you how to do your job, the airport makes it easy for you—and all of the other people milling about the airport—to figure it out for yourself.

First you look at your ticket to see what flight you are supposed to take. Your ticket tells you the details: the airline, the flight number, and the originally scheduled departure time of your next flight. (In manufacturing, we would call such a ticket a *kanban*, a card with the instructions for your next job.) Your job is to get on that flight before it leaves. Now your question becomes, where is that flight leaving from, and how do I get there on time? To answer this ques-tion you find a big display to help you out. You look at the display to find out what concourse and gate the flight will leave from and when it is currently scheduled to leave. In larger airports there will often be another display to tell you how many minutes it will take you to walk to that concourse or gate to help you decide if you need to run or flag down an electric cart. Next, you fol-low easily visible signs to your concourse and go down the concourse where gates are numbered in order until you find the gate your plane is supposed to be leaving from. Finally, you check the display at the gate to be sure that the plane leaving from this gate is really the one your ticket says you should be on.

Airports use tickets, displays, and visible signs quite effectively. But one thing that's missing in most airports is a *dashboard*, something that gives everyone a general idea of how the airport is operating. That's OK when things are going well, but it is missed when something goes wrong.

### An Alternate Route Home

One morning some years back, I arrived at the Santa Ana airport only to find that an airplane had skidded off the end of the runway a few minutes earlier. No one was hurt, no damage was done, really, but landings and takeoffs were temporarily suspended. Now my job switched from catching my plane to finding a way home before midnight. The first question to get answered was how likely is it that my plane will eventually take off? Unlike most airports, the Santa Ana airport has a *dashboard*, a central board that shows the schedule and gates for all landings and takeoffs. By watching this dashboard, I could soon tell that my aircraft was not going to be able to land and was being diverted to Los Angeles, a 45-minute drive away. So I immediately got my ticket reassigned to a Los Angeles flight, hopped on a bus provided by the airline, caught the Los Angeles flight, and actually arrived home a bit ahead of my original schedule. Unfortunately, many people did not see the big picture in time to react as quickly as I did, and quite a few spent the night in Santa Ana.

—Mary Poppendieck

## Self-Directing Work

When lots of things have to happen really fast, the execution strategy must switch from dispatching to enabling. A taxi, for example, is dispatched. I call from my home; the taxi picks me up and takes me to the airport. But there are only so many taxis and only so much space on the highway. Therefore many cities, including our home city of Minneapolis, provide rapid transit to the airport. Now someone in Minneapolis can walk out of their downtown hotel, hop on the Metro, and quickly get to the airport—along with a whole lot of other passengers. It's no longer necessary for people to get involved in dispatching a taxi, picking up travelers at their hotel, navigating the traffic, and delivering them—alone—to the airport.

Dispatching involves planning every step of someone else's job. Making work self-directing involves setting up an environment so people can figure out how to do their job without being told what to do. When a lot of things have to happen quickly, self-directing work is the only approach that works, and it works very well. In busy downtown areas, flagging down a taxi often works better than having one dispatched to your hotel. If managers really want things to happen quickly, they will focus their attention on organizing the work space so that work becomes self-directing.

When work is self-directing, everyone showing up for work in the morning can figure out exactly what to do without being told, and what they choose to do will be the most important thing for them to be working on. As people complete one job, it is immediately obvious what to do next. Throughout the day when people have questions, the workspace is organized so that people can look around and find the answers. Think of self-directing work as a package that you ship overnight. You attach instructions to the package, and from then on, every person and machine that handles your package can simply look at the instructions and know exactly what to do with the package.

If you are a manager who's been wondering what you are supposed to do once responsibility-based planning and control relieve you of a lot of your current dispatching work—here's part of your new job: Organize the work space so that work becomes self-directing. There are three key levels of information to focus on when organizing a self-directing workspace: kanban, andon, and dashboard.

### Kanban

*Kan* is the word for *card* in Japanese, and *ban* is the word for *signal*. So a *kanban* is a *signal card*. In the airport, your ticket is the signal card that tells you—personally—what flight you need to catch. Index cards make good signal cards. Each card contains a small amount of work, say a story to develop and some clarifying testable examples. Cards can be organized and reorganized easily, so that when someone needs to know what to do next, they select a card from the top of a stack and get to work on it. Cards can be attached to physical message boards—perfect for a local team—or they can be electronic—useful for dispersed teams. The number of cards can give a quick indication of the length of the queue. When the queue gets so long that the cards become unwieldy, perhaps the queue should be shortened.

The challenge with *Kanban* is not really figuring out how people might go about choosing what to do next. That's the easy part. The challenge is figuring out how to be sure that the content of the card and its location are correct, so that when the card is selected, it contains a sufficient description of a job that is the right size and is the right thing to do next. The card is not the specification of the job; it is a signal that the next job is to bring together the right people to create the detailed designs, verifications, and implementation of the story on the card.

Whatever mechanism is used to make work self-directing requires some thought and experimentation. Each job must be succinctly described, the set of jobs must be both complete and correctly sequenced, and the rules for posting and choosing jobs must assure that they will be done by people with the expertise to do them well.

---

**Organizing the Work**

*How does this work in practice? Have we gotten to tasks yet?*

Let's say that a company is spinning off a subsidiary in four months. As a first step, the looming deadline is broken into a set of relatively independent activities. One of these activities is to split all of the servers and data apart, so each new company has their own. A team of eight people is assembled representing every function that will be involved.

The first thing the team does is lay out on a wall, with Post-it Notes, all of the steps they can think of that have to get done to separate the servers and data. Their goal is to create a high-level picture of the work that needs to be done, not a detailed task breakdown. The best way to make sure that the overview touches on all of the affected functions is to have knowledgeable representatives involved. Managing this process means making sure the right functions are represented, the right people are there, they are mutually committed to meeting the deadline, and the process is organized so as to discover all the jobs that need to be done.

When everyone is confident that the notes on the wall adequately represent all of the general categories of what must be done, the team organizes them into a workable schedule—breaking whatever dependencies they can, and acknowledging the real dependencies.

This is just a high-level schedule—the next step is to agree on what must and will happen in the next month and break that down into more detail. (In the hectic environment of a spin-off, planning detailed tasks beyond a month is usually a waste of time.) Finally the team is getting to tasks. Development will have to write—and test—scripts to sort out data and applications; operations had better get the new hardware on order, but first someone has to do some experiments to nail down correct sizing; security is going to have to create different permissions for log-in, and they may as well implement that right away so they can test it… and so on.

Managing these tasks means making sure that each job has a testable outcome, that everyone agrees what will be done and tested by the end of the month, and that the team meets every day to review how everything is coming along and who needs help. At the end of the month everyone gets together, their commitments met, to review the big picture and modify it if necessary. Then the next set of tasks—and verification criteria—are addressed.

### Andon

An *andon* is a portable Japanese lantern made of paper stretched over a bamboo framework. Toyota used the word *andon* to name the cord that workers could pull to "stop-the-line," since pulling an *andon* cord usually cause lights to flash, calling attention to the problem area. The idea behind *andon* is to make problems visible so they can be addressed immediately.

Over time, *andon* has also come to be used for any kind of visual message board or other display device that can be easily changed. The message boards at train stations that display departure tracks are sometimes called *andon* boards. An *andon* board calls attention to any abnormality that requires attention, dynamically displays changing status, and shows locations of things that are frequently reconfigured (for example, which sever is currently the test server).

> **Visible Signals**
>
> A software development andon system might be two lava lamps, one red and one green, which are triggered by the results of the build and test system. If the build is successful and passes the tests, the green lava lamp bubbles cheerfully. If the red lamp begins to gurgle, developers know they have just a few minutes until it begins bubbling rapidly to either find the problem or back out the code they just checked in. Of course, an andon system might also be a simple e-mail, but where's the fun in that?

### Dashboard

People like to be on successful teams. It's interesting to succeed at local goals—for example, developing an electronic control system for the 777. But it's truly exciting to contribute to the overall success of a program—for example, watching the first 777 take off with the control system your team developed. Alan Mulally tried to bring the whole team working on the 777 together frequently to see how the aircraft was coming along. The biggest event happened two years before the first scheduled flight, when the first airplane rolled off the assembly line on its own wheels. He invited 10,000 or so workers and their families to a dramatic event to congratulate everyone on their progress and inspire their continued dedication to the cause.

It is important for teams to see the overall progress of their work in its context and in the context of the broader goals of the company. For this we use various kinds of dashboards. Every team room should have big, visible charts on the wall that show off to everyone how well the team is doing—or not—and make status visible to anyone who walks in the room. Things like burn-down charts, graphs of acceptance tests written and passed, and so on are very useful. Charts of the overall status of a multiteam effort should be available in the main "war room," as Boeing called it, for everyone to see. Dispersed teams should have visibility into status also, and here an electronic dashboard might be the perfect tool. Electronic dashboards are also useful for key metrics that are easier to generate electronically than manually.

We often ask our classes, "In your organization, how do people know their progress toward meeting the overall goal of their work?" (See exercise 4 at the end of this chapter.) We have been surprised by the number of times the answer is, "Actually, that information isn't readily available." Organizations that do not engage people in the ultimate goal of their work are squandering a great opportunity to inspire people and teams to enthusiastically contribute their best efforts to the cause.

## Incentives

In the book *The Living Company*,[13] Arie de Geus discusses why some companies have long life spans—a century or more—and others do not. "Companies die because their managers focus on the economic activity of producing goods and services, and they forget that their organizations' true nature is that of a community of humans."[14] de Geus says. "The amount that people care, trust, and engage themselves at work has not only a direct effect on the bottom line, but the most direct effect, of any factor, on your company's expected lifespan."[15]

There are two kinds of companies, according to de Geus, the economic company and the river company. The purpose of the economic company is to produce maximum results for minimum resources and produce wealth for a group of managers and investors. The purpose of a river company, on the other hand, is to keep on flowing, that is, to stay in business and provide jobs over the long term. For example, Sakichi Toyoda and Kiichiro Toyoda had as their primary purpose to provide jobs for Japanese workers by figuring out how to manufacture complex products that would otherwise have to be imported.

In the economic company, de Geus says, there is an implicit contract between the company and the individual: The individual will deliver a skill in exchange for remuneration. In a river company, the implicit contract is different: "The individual will deliver care and commitment in exchange for the fact that the company will *try to develop each individual's potential to the maximum*."[16] Commitment is a two way street: People are committed to a company if they feel that the company is committed to them.

### Performance Evaluations

Probably the most ignored piece of Deming's advice is this: Eliminate annual performance ratings for salaried workers; do not undermine team cooperation

---

13. *The Living Company*, by Arie de Geus, Harvard Business School Press, 1997.
14. Ibid., p. 3.
15. Ibid., p. 10.
16. Ibid., p. 118. Italics in original.

by rewarding individual performance. Deming was quite adamant about his belief that annual merit ratings create competition rather than cooperation and kill pride in workmanship. But the performance evaluation serves different purposes, depending on the implicit contract that the individual has with the company. In an economic company, where the employee contract is about exchanging remuneration for skill, the purpose of the performance evaluation is to determine the amount of remuneration an individual should receive. Indeed, this purpose will have a great tendency to foster competition rather than cooperation.

On the other hand, when a company is committed to developing each individual's potential to the maximum, a performance evaluation can be a time set aside to reflect on where that potential lies and what steps that the company and the individual can take to further develop the individual's potential. Thus, we do not have a rating system as much as we ponder honestly and openly whether the individual would be best aiming toward a technical ladder or a management ladder, what training and job assignments would be best for the coming year, what specific areas (public speaking, for example) need improvement to support further career growth.

Annual performance evaluations should never surprise employees with unexpected feedback. Performance feedback loops should be far shorter than an annual, or even a quarterly, evaluation cycle. If the annual performance evaluation is the only time employees finds out how they are doing, something is truly wrong with the evaluation system. Performance review criteria should put strong emphasis on teamwork, making contribution to team success as important—if not more important—than individual contributions. You get what you reward, so if you find effective ways to reward collaboration, you will get more of it.

One-directional evaluations give the appearance that only the evaluated person needs to improve, but Deming insists that most performance issues are a management problem. When an employee isn't performing, the first question a manager should ask is, "What am I doing wrong?" Managers should take personal responsibility for the performance of their organization and collaborate with their people to improve the performance of the *system*.

### Ranking

Consider a team trying to recover from a mistake that created a challenging problem. In a lean world, they work together, brainstorm ideas, try things out, and when they find a solution, they go out of their way not to allocate blame. After all, any of them could have made the same mistake. Instead they keep on working to find a way to mistake-proof the system so that the problem can never happen again.

Now consider the same team, only the members know that once a year their supervisors have to go into a secret session and rank the entire department so that raises and promotions can be handed out in order of value and contribution to the company. The team members must give their supervisors ammunition to show why they are better than their teammates, so as to get a higher rank and a better raise and better shot at a promotion. The incentive to allocate blame and take individual credit for finding a solution is high; collaboration is strongly discouraged by such a ranking system. If you have a ranking system in your company, a lean initiative will be hollow at best. The behaviors that ranking systems encourage are competition, hiding information so as to look good, and hiding problems so as not to look bad.

## Compensation[17]

Nothing is more likely to create contention and interfere with collaboration that the system used to determine compensation, no matter what system is in place. Although no compensation system will ever be perfect, some are better than others. We offer the following guidelines.

### Guideline No. 1: Make Sure the Promotion System Is Unassailable

In most organizations, significant salary gains come from promotions that move people to a higher salary grade, not from annual pay increases. Where promotions are not available, as is the case for many teachers, annual or "merit" pay increases have a tendency to become contentious, because these increases are the only way to make more money. When promotions are available, employees tend to deemphasize annual raises and focus on the promotion system. This system of promotions tends to encourage people to move into management as they run out of promotional opportunities in technical areas. Companies address this problem with "dual ladders" that offer management-level pay scales to technical gurus.

The foundation of any promotion system is a series of job grades, each with a salary range in line with industry standards and regional averages. People must be placed correctly in a grade so that their skills and responsibilities match the job requirements of their level. Initial placements and promotion decisions should be carefully made and reviewed by a management team.

Usually job grades are embedded in titles, and promotions make the new job grade public through a new title. A person's job grade is generally considered

---

17. Parts of this section are from an article originally published by Mary Poppendieck in *Better Software Magazine*, August 2004, under the title "Unjust Deserts."

public information. If employees are fairly placed in their job grades and promoted only when they are clearly performing at a new job grade, then salary differences based on job grade are generally perceived to be fair. Thus, a team can have both senior and junior people, generalists and highly skilled specialists, all making different amounts of money. As long as the system of determining job grades and promotions is transparent and perceived to be fair, this kind of differential pay is rarely a problem.

### Guideline No. 2: De-emphasize Annual Raises

When the primary tool for significant salary increases is promotion, then it's important to focus as much attention as possible on making sure the promotion system is fair. When it comes to the evaluation system that drives annual pay increases, it's best not to try too hard to sort people out. Use evaluations mainly to keep everyone at an appropriate level in their salary grade. Evaluations might flag those who are ready for promotion and those who need attention, but that should trigger a separate promotion or corrective action process. About four evaluation grades are sufficient, and a competent supervisor with good evaluation criteria and input from appropriate sources can make fair evaluations that accomplish these purposes.

Even when annual raises are loosely coupled to merit, evaluations will always be a big deal for employees, so attention should be paid to making them fair and balanced. Over the last decade, balanced scorecards have become popular for management evaluations—at least in theory. Balanced scorecards ensure that the multiple aspects of a manager's job all receive attention. A simple version of a balanced scorecard might also be used for evaluations that impact annual raises, to emphasize the fact that people must perform well on many dimensions to be effective. Input to the scorecard should come from all areas: teammates, customers, senior management, those receiving guidance from a leader. It is important that employees perceive that the input to a scorecard is valid and fairly covers the multiple aspects of their job. It is also important to keep things simple, because too much complexity will unduly inflate the attention paid to a pay system which works better when it is understated. Finally, scorecards should not be used to feed a ranking system.

### Guideline No. 3: Reward Based on Span of Influence, Not Span of Control

There is no greater de-motivator than a reward system which is perceived to be unfair. It doesn't matter if the system is fair or not, if there is a perception of unfairness, then those who think that they have been treated unfairly will rapidly lose their motivation. People perceive unfairness when they miss out on rewards they think they should have shared. Excellent products are developed through cooperative efforts of many people, so in a development environment, individuals rewards will inevitably leave the overlooked people feeling that they have been treated unfairly. Moreover, when individual rewards foster competition in an environment where cooperation is essential for success, even those who receive rewards are unlikely to appreciate them.

## We Don't Want Bonuses!

We visited a company where the senior management was planning to give incentive bonuses to developers who met individual deadlines and productivity targets. Since the management team was from marketing, they were most familiar with commission-based compensation and were trying to develop a technical version of the same thing.

The developers were appalled and told us so. "If someone comes to me now and asks a question, I'm glad to help out." One person said. "With the incentive pay system, I'd be nuts to spend my time helping out someone else. Not only would I get less money because I wasn't working on my stuff, they would get more because they would look good."

Fortunately, the development team manager was at the meeting and listened to these remarks. Later he intervened to have the proposed incentive bonus system reconsidered.

—Mary Poppendieck

Conventional wisdom says that people should be rewarded based on results that are under their control. However, when information sharing and cooperation are essential, rewards should be based on a person's span of influence rather than his or her span of control. For example, testers should not be rewarded based on the number of defects they find, but rather, developers and testers alike should be rewarded based on the team's ability to create defect-free code. Development teams should not be rewarded based on the technical success of their efforts; instead, the whole team should be rewarded based on the business success of its efforts.

### Guideline No. 4: Find Better Motivators Than Money

While monetary rewards can be a powerful driver of behavior, the motivation they provide is not sustainable. Once people have an adequate income, motivation comes from things such as achievement, growth, control over one's work, recognition, advancement, and a friendly working environment. No matter how good your evaluation and reward system may be, don't expect it to do much to drive stellar performance over the long term.

## The Contentious Bonus

A vice president of engineering told me about the time his company gave a team of 14 a $100,000 bonus. The team members were told to distribute the bonus however they wanted. This should have been a good thing, but it was impossible for the group to agree on how to allocate the money. In the end, the money was split evenly among the team members, but many were angry because they thought this was unfair.

—Mary Poppendieck

In the book *Hidden Value*,[18] Charles O'Reilly and Jeffrey Pfeffer present several case studies of companies that obtain superb performance from ordinary people. These companies have people-centered values that are aligned with actions at all levels. They invest in people, share information broadly, rely on teams, and emphasize leadership rather than management. Finally, they do not use money as a primary motivator; they emphasize the intrinsic rewards of fun, growth, teamwork, challenge, and accomplishment.

Treat monetary rewards like explosives, because they will have a powerful impact whether you intend it or not. So use them lightly and with caution. They can get you into trouble much faster than they can solve your problems. Once you go down the path of monetary rewards, you may never be able to go back, even when they cease to be effective, as they inevitably will. Make sure that people are fairly and adequately compensated, and then move on to more effective ways to improve performance.

---

18. O'Reilly, Charles A., III, and Jeffrey Pfeffer, *Hidden Value: How Great Companies Achieve Extraordinary Results with Ordinary People,* Harvard Business School Press, 2000.

# Try This

1. Review Deming's System of Profound Knowledge, which we paraphrase thus:

   a. It's the whole product, the whole team, the whole system that matters.

   b. When something goes wrong, in all probability it was caused by the system, which makes it a management problem.

   c. Use the scientific method to change and improve.

   d. With people, the things that matter are skill, pride, expertise, confidence, and cooperation.

   Imagine that Deming was scheduled to tour your organization next week. Prepare a presentation for him on how each of these points is addressed in your organization. What do you think his advice would be? Would you be prepared to act on it?

2. Review Deming's 14 points with your team. For each one, discuss: Is this point relevant today in our organization? Is it important? If we regard it as relevant and important, what does it suggest we should do differently? What would it take to make the change?

3. How are teams formed, chartered, and led in your organization? Are they actually work groups or true teams? How many teams are individuals typically on?

4. Fill out the Visual Workspace Assessment on the next page:

   a. In column 2, answer the question posed in column 1 as it relates to your organization.

   b. In column 3, rate how self-directing your organization is. Give your organization a score of 0–5, with 0 = people are told what to do and 5 = people figure out among themselves what to work on next.

| Question | Current Practice | Score |
|---|---|---|
| 1) How do people know what customers really want? | | |
| 2) How do people get technical questions answered? | | |
| 3) How do people know what features to work on next? | | |
| 4 How do people know what defects to work on next? | | |
| 5) How do people know if tests are passing? | | |
| 6) How do people know their progress toward meeting the overall goal of their work? | | |

5.  The next time your company does an employee survey, add these questions:

   a.  Do you feel that the compensation system is fair?

   b.  Do you feel that the promotion system is fair?

   c.  Rate how the compensation affects your dedication to your job (Scale of 1–5):

      1. It angers me and gets in the way of doing a good job.
      2. It sometimes annoys me and occasionally affects my performance.
      3. It doesn't make much difference.
      4. It occasionally motivates me to work harder.
      5. It motivates me to work hard every day.

# Chapter 7

# Knowledge

## Creating Knowledge

Centuries ago, the critical constraining resource was land. Those who controlled the land controlled everything. At some point, the constraint became skills, and guilds and merchants created more wealth than did landowners. Later, the industrial revolution moved the constraint to capital, and power became financially driven. Today, the constraint is knowledge: technical knowledge, management knowledge, process knowledge, and market knowledge. Much of this knowledge is being expressed as software.

Most of our current paradigms remain rooted in industrial/financial thinking and measurements. Those organizations that will dominate this century are those that shift to a focus on knowledge.

## Rally[1]

"We set out to create a tool for managing agile software development," said Ryan Martens, Chief Technical Officer of Rally Software Development.[2] "But much of our team's experience was driven by waterfall success, and we found ourselves doing waterfall in time-boxed increments." Ryan knew from first-hand experience that software companies could be quick and responsive at the beginning of their life, but after a while the code base always grew (that's the point, after all) and got increasingly difficult to change. He understood that agile development was supposed to be an antidote for these growing pains. What he hadn't quite gotten his arms around was that code is tolerant to change in the exact proportion that it is insulated from defects.

---

1. Full disclosure: The authors have served on a technical advisory board for Rally Software Development and have a minor financial interest in the company.
2. This section comes from an interview with Ryan Martens. Used with permission.

Anything that makes code difficult to change is technical debt. You can pay full price for code while you build it, or you can go into technical debt. Be warned, however, that technical debt extracts a very high interest rate, and the longer you are in debt the harder it will be to pay off. Ryan discovered that technical debt was Rally's biggest constraint: "We found that the only way to get ahead is to have a team, process, technical infrastructure, and guiding ideas that never let debt accumulate."

"During the first year we had a lot of technical debt." Ryan says. "We released software in eight or ten week cycles, and two weeks of the cycle was spent 'hardening' the software. [Hardening is another way of saying "test-and-fix."] We used JUnit for unit tests, of course, but a large part of our product is the user interface [UI]. We used HTTPUnit for testing the UI, but we found that it was not capable of testing page flows. Because of this, a lot of UI testing, along with all our acceptance testing, was manual. We had maybe 300 or 400 manual tests, and we could never run them all. Our technical debt increased every release. The testing load was the killer, and it just kept going up.

"Early in the second year, we set out to tackle the root cause of the debt: Our page flow platform did not let us get inside and test it with application-level unit tests. At the same time, we generated statistics which showed that our page flow structure was wasting users' time with too many clicks. So we decided to move our page flow platform to Spring and AJAX and unit test the page flows with Fitnesse.[3] If we could use this architecture going forward, it would at least stop the manual testing debt from accumulating.

"We tried the new architecture for some new and relatively experimental pages to learn how it really worked. The few customers who had asked for features changes in this part of the application were thrilled and tolerated the occasional problem as we learned. After two releases of isolated parts of the application, we were confident enough to gradually retrofit our old pages with the new architecture. As an industry, we have been trained to think of new releases as driven by big bang architectural changes. Learning to think in small incremental and iterative chunks is a critical guiding idea of agile. We learned that incremental architectural changes work very well; you don't need—or want the risk of—big-bang architecture.

---

3. Fitnesse is an Open Source framework that runs FIT within a wiki. FIT is an Open Source tool that creates annotated, human-readable specifications that are also acceptance tests. See www.fitnesse.org and *Fit for Developing Software: Framework for Integrated Tests*, by Rick Mugridge and Ward Cunningham, Prentice Hall, 2005.

"Spring proved to be easy to test. AJAX, however, needs direct execution through the browser. We brought in JIFFIE, which binds Java to Internet Explorer, so we could write unit tests in Java that test AJAX through the browser. Hardening went down from two weeks to one. But (there is always a but) we found that only a few test engineers had the background to write the new tests, and we were also accumulating automation debt. Automated testing became a bottleneck, so again our manual test coverage started going in the wrong direction.

"As we moved into year three, we moved responsibility for maintaining the UI test harness to our developers, who were already responsible for writing the JUnit tests and FIT fixtures. Testers remained responsible for creating Fitnesse tables and JIFFIE tests. This has become increasingly important because we have introduced multiple hosted configurations, so we have to test many different configurations of the application. The testing infrastructure has become more complex and thus it needs to be more robust; it can only really be maintained by the team that knows the architecture of the user interface—the developers. We are using Fitnesse to script all of our tests. We're putting a lot of effort in one button builds for the system testing harness that tests all our product configurations.

"We hired a contract firm to help us, finally, pay down our remaining manual test dept by automating all of our remaining manual tests. We have finally replaced all of our original UI architecture, 14 months after making the decision to switch to Spring. Now that we are realizing the full benefit of running without debt, we can release every month with no hardening, which enables us to move to monthly updates and use quarterly releases to focus on major functionality enhancements.

"We have invested a lot of effort in our testing framework because it is the key to growing the complexity of the application without growing the development team at the same pace. We have learned that acceptance-test-driven development is the way to go—it's the only way to keep the technology agile as the application gets large. The key is to understand what creates debt, to slow down—occasionally—to catch up, and to realize that you are in it for the long haul.

"We have figured this out through constant reflection and adaptation. After every iteration and every release, we discuss what worked and what didn't work, then make a list of what we will *commit* to change—commitment is essential. We tackle the list one at a time and experiment to see what works.

"One of the things we tried turned out to be amazingly successful. When we reduced hardening from two weeks to one, we decided to use the free week to allow everyone to take a break from the high pressure of iterations. So instead of using the week to develop more code, we turned it into what we call "hack-a-thon." During hack-a-thon, which occurs immediately after a release, developers are free to experiment with anything they want. However, if customers find defects in the release, the developers have to stop hack-a-thon and create a patch. You can imagine that developers are extra careful not to let anything creep into the release that might cut into their hack-a-thon time. The biggest payoff from hack-a-thon, however, is that our most creative and novel ideas are hatched during this time—it is a time for building vision, design sets/continuums, and architectural spikes. It is undoubtedly the most productive time of all."

Rally's focus on technical debt underscores how we have moved from the financial world, where debt is a financial term, to the knowledge world, where technical debt means that the expression of our knowledge is incomplete. Ryan's story also emphasizes the best way to create knowledge: Find the biggest problem that is getting in the way of your company's success, and focus everybody on figuring out how to solve that problem. Go at it one step at a time, check where that got you, and do it again and again and again. Make this the essence of everyone's job.

## What, Exactly, Is Your Problem?

In 1950, Toyota almost went bankrupt and had to lay off one-third of its workforce. The Toyota Production System grew out of Toyota's commitment not to ever have to experience that painful situation again. The Toyota Production System was and remains fundamentally dedicated to reducing costs. The way Toyota figures it, the market determines what it will buy and pretty much sets the price. Profit is what's leftover after you subtract your costs from the market price—so the lower the costs, the higher the profits, and thus the better chance of staying in business and protecting jobs.

Toyota didn't have a lot of money or tools when the Toyota Production System was developed. It had four simple goals:[4]

1.  Deliver the highest possible quality and service to the customer

2.  Develop each employee's potential based upon mutual respect and cooperation

---

4. Isao Kato, retired manager of training and development for Toyota in Japan, quoted by Art Smalley, "TPS vs. Lean Additional Perspectives," www.superfactory.com/articles/Smalley_TPS_vs_Lean_Additional_Perspectives.htm.

3. Reduce cost through elimination of waste in any given process

4. Build flexible production sites that can respond to changes in the market

The Toyota Production System is Toyota's approach to meeting those goals.

Rally perceived that its biggest threat to long-term profits was measured in units of time. The longer hardening took, the more debt it had. The more debt it had, the more linear the relationship between system size and development team size. And Rally knew that over time, a linear relationship of people to product size would be certain death. So the company attacked technical debt with the same vengeance that Toyota has always attacked cost.

Art Smalley, is one of the handful of Americans who learned the Toyota Production System in the 1980s while working for Toyota in Japan. He is troubled by the tepid track record of lean initiatives and reflects on the root cause of the failure of most lean initiatives to gain traction. A couple of candidates he puts forward are 1) lean implementations seem to be focused on tools and practices rather than solving basic problems, and 2) lean training seems to be focused on staff specialists rather than on improving the problem-solving skills of natural work teams.[5]

Smalley believes that the first step in any improvement effort should be to ask two basic questions:

1. How do you intend to make a profit and satisfy your customers?

2. What exactly is your main problem?

Lean initiatives must always start with a clear vision of how you make money and a sharp understanding of the most critical problem that is keeping you from doing so. The problem might be technical debt. It might be making sure each new video game is "fun." It might be system response time. It might be hardware and firmware integration. Whatever the problem is, becoming lean starts with a crisply defined, top-priority problem that is constraining business success.

Once you have a clearly defined problem, the next step is to use a disciplined problem-solving method, informed by basic principles, to solve the problem. Train everyone how to do this with every aspect of their job. Create an environment in which work teams at all levels of the company continue to use a disciplined approach to solving their biggest current problem over many years. This is hard work and requires long-term thinking. Nevertheless, it is the path that Toyota has blazed to sustained success.

---

5. See Art Smalley, "TPS vs. Lean and the Law of Unintended Consequences," www.superfactory.com/articles/smalley_tps_vs_lean.htm.

## A Scientific Way of Thinking

Tom has a Ph.D. in physics. Our son, Dustin, has a Ph.D. in environmental engineering. Both of them spent several years under the direction of a major professor, using the scientific method to create and publish knowledge. As any scientist knows, the scientific method works like this:

1.  Observe and describe a phenomenon or group of phenomena.

2.  Formulate a hypothesis to explain the phenomena.

3.  Use the hypothesis to predict something—the existence of other phenomena or the results of new observations.

4.  Perform experiments to see if the predictions hold up.

5.  If the experiments bear out the hypothesis it may be regarded as a theory or rule.

6.  If the experiments do not bear out the hypothesis, it must be rejected or modified.

The scientific method is the DNA of the Toyota Production System. Every Toyota worker is taught to use basic problem-solving techniques as *the* primary approach to doing their job. Toyota workers operate like a community of scientists, conducting ongoing experiments, constantly learning, and codifying new knowledge for the future in the same way that scientists have been doing for a long time.

Figure 7.1 depicts Toyota's problem-solving method on the left and shows how it is similar to the plan, do, check, act (PDCA) cycle that Deming taught in Japan in the 1950s. Toyota embraced the scientific way of thinking, adding it to Sakichi Toyoda's concept of stop-the-line and Kiichiro Toyoda's vision of Just-in-Time. The result is the Toyota Production System—disciplined problem solving at a detailed level on a consistent, companywide basis, focused on removing the current biggest constraint that is getting in the way of making a profit.

The important thing to remember is that this problem-solving method is never used in a vacuum. It is used, consistently and repeatedly, to attack the current biggest problem facing the work team. As in any disciplined scientific environment, the work team is expected to keep track of all of their observations, their hypothesis, their experiments, and their results. There is at least as much knowledge created by experiments that fail as is created by finding a solution to the problem.

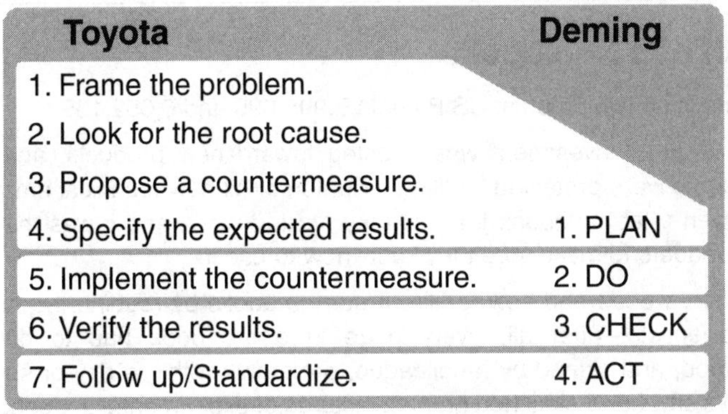

| Toyota | Deming |
|---|---|
| 1. Frame the problem. | |
| 2. Look for the root cause. | |
| 3. Propose a countermeasure. | |
| 4. Specify the expected results. | 1. PLAN |
| 5. Implement the countermeasure. | 2. DO |
| 6. Verify the results. | 3. CHECK |
| 7. Follow up/Standardize. | 4. ACT |

**Figure 7.1**   *The Toyota Production System problem-solving method and the PDCA cycle*

## Keeping Track of What You Know

"You know the biggest problem with iterative development?" a product manager asked us. "I like the ability to keep trying new things, but I really can't keep track of everything I've tried. I worry that I'm going to have to go back over the same territory and learn the same lessons all over again." If learning is not captured in a useful manner, then people will indeed forget what they've learned. Even when individual people remember what they've learned, the organization will not benefit from the learning unless it is captured in a useful manner.

Both Sakichi Toyoda and Kiichiro Toyoda were fundamentally inventors. They filed patents in countries around the world. Selling the patent rights to the automated loom provided seed money for Kiichiro to start an automotive company. Inventors who file patents have learned a lot about how to keep track of everything they learn, because the process of obtaining a patent depends heavily upon keeping detailed daily records of who knew what when, how they figured it out, and what the implications were at the time. Since inventors' notebooks are expected to be referenced regularly by inventor and colleague alike, they are concisely written and generously sprinkled with tables and graphs. Since they are legal records that may end up as evidence in a patent dispute, scientists make sure they are correct, complete, and contemporary.

## We All Had Notebooks

My name is on two patents: US Patents 5,995,690 and 6,052,135.

At 3M, a lot of investment was directed toward new products, and these investments were protected by filing for patents. All new technical employees were given a lab notebook the day they started work, and it was the job of their managers to make sure they knew how to use it.

In practice, we learned how to fill out our lab books by reading the notes of other scientists—after all, every page in a lab book had to be read, understood, and signed by a colleague, preferably within a day or so of the entry. We saw hand-sketched graphs, pictures of experimental set-ups, tables of data (often short computer printouts taped to the notebook pages), and brief summaries of conclusions.

We quickly understood that everything we did that generated knowledge was to be concisely recorded in our lab notebook. When it was full, we checked it into a library and got a new one. By that time the important information from the lab book had been extracted and used in further experiments, summarized in records of invention, or otherwise made available, so we usually didn't have to reference our lab books again—but if we did, we knew where to find them.

—Mary Poppendieck

In software development, the tests and code are often just the right combination of rigor and conciseness to document the knowledge embedded in the software. But experiments tried and options investigated on the way to making decisions about the product under development are easily forgotten, because they never make it into the software. Just writing something down does not necessarily turn it into knowledge, and information is just as easily lost in a sea of excess documentation as it is lost through lack of documentation.

*The Knowledge-Creating Company*[6] by Ikujiro Nonaka and Hirotaka Takeuchi is a book about the mechanisms and processes by which knowledge is created in a company. They note that Western companies think of knowledge as something that is written down. Japanese companies think of written knowledge as only the tip of the iceberg; most knowledge is contained in subjective insights, intuitions, hunches, and mental models. This knowledge, tacit knowl-

---

6. Ikujiro Nonaka and Hirotaka Takeuchi, *The Knowledge-Creating Company: How Japanese Companies Create the Dynamics of Innovation*, Oxford University Press, 1995.

edge, does not come from studying, it comes from experience. It cannot be easily processed by a computer or stored in a database. It is hard to formalize and transmit to others.

Some think that if we just "document" what we learn through iterative development—write down the decisions we made, why we made them, what we learned—we will create organizational learning. But most likely, the pile of documentation we create will gather dust or take up space on a disk, quite useless as a learning tool. We tend to write diaries, unconsciously associating the depth of ideas with the thickness of the binder.

But for those on the receiving end of documentation, the thickness of the binder is usually inversely proportional to its usefulness in transmitting knowledge. In order to create knowledge, we have to think not about the process of writing it down but about the people who will use what has been written. Technical writers do this for a living, so they might be asked play a key role in preserving team knowledge.

### The A3 report

Early in their careers, Toyota engineers learn the discipline of condensing complex thinking to a single A3 sheet of paper.[7] This forces people to filter and refine their thoughts so that anyone reading the A3 report will have all of their questions answered by reading a single sheet of paper. Different A3 reports have different purposes, but all of them capture critical knowledge in a way that is easy to store in a database, easy to post in a work area, easy to send to a manager, and is easy to incorporate into future experiments.

---

**A3 Documentation**

Place two A4 sheets side by side (or two 8.5"×11" sheet if you are in the US) and you have an A3 sheet (11"×17" for the US). One large sheet of paper should be all that is necessary to describe a customer job, capture knowledge about a devious system crash, or summarize all points necessary for a decision. Lengthy reports waste time and are ineffective, especially when complex ideas need to be communicated.

---

7. There are many examples of A3 reports in Morgan and Liker, *Toyota Product Development System*, pp. 269–276, and one example in Liker, *Toyota Way*, pp. 244–248.

**Guidelines:**

1. Use as few words as possible.

2. A picture is worth a thousand words. Use figures, graphs, tables.

3. Everything must fit on one side of an A3 sheet.

4. A3s are dynamic documents. Use and change based on feedback.

5. If it doesn't fit on an A3 sheet, condense it to an A4 sheet (8.5X11)!

6. The content and structure should support its purpose:

   - A problem-solving A3 might contain:

     a. Summary of the problem

     b. Root cause analysis

     c. Suggested countermeasure

     d. Planned experiments

     e. Measurements and feedback

   - A knowledge-sharing A3 might contain:

     a. Identification of specific database lockup problem

     b. Scatter plot showing instances of lockup plotted against suspected triggering mechanisms

     c. List of known lockup triggers

     d. Tradeoff curve of nested calls plotted against time-spent-in-nest, with a line showing where lockups occur and do not occur

     e. Discussion of additional suspected lockup triggers

   - An A3 describing a minimum useful feature set might contain:

     a. Description of customer job to be done with software

     b. Economic value to customers/development organization

     c. What customers will be able to do when the feature set is complete

     d. Diagram showing what is and is not included

     e. Diagram showing interactions with other systems

     f. Desired timeline

   - A customer goal A3 might contain

     a. A one page use case

     b. UI design for achieving the goal

### The Internet Age

Now that we are in the Internet age, we have some tremendously powerful ways to create and find knowledge. Powerful search engines change the way we think about indexing content. Blogs bring out the author in a large number of technical people. Wikipedia is a model for rapid and effectively collecting and arbitrating the content of very large of information libraries. At the same time, "knowledge management systems" didn't even show up in a recent survey of media used by knowledge workers.[8] Internet-age search and publishing tools do not excuse us from our obligation to concisely summarize our knowledge in a disciplined and useful way. But they will no doubt influence our approaches to keeping track of what we know.

## Just-in-Time Commitment

A friend of ours is a commercial pilot from Innsbruck. He recently augmented his pilot's license with an instrument rating at a school in the United States. He told us that the focus of his instrument flying class was on decision making, because research indicated that the cause of most single-pilot plane accidents is faulty pilot decisions. Here is what he learned:

> When you have a decision to make—say it's foggy and you have to decide whether or not to land—the first thing you should do is decide *when* the decision must be made. Then, you should wait until that time to make the decision, because that is when you will have the most knowledge about the situation. But you must never wait until *after* that time to decide, because then you might end up flying into something hard—there are rocks in the clouds over here.[9]

As we guide our product development process, we need to recognize that developing a product is all about learning, and the longer we defer decisions, the more we can learn. But we don't want to crash into a mountain, so the key is in timing. Lean development organizations make decisions Just-in-Time, and they start by deciding exactly what that means.

Software is a unique product because it is by its very nature meant to be changed, so typically we can defer decisions for a good long time. Unfortunately, this feature of software encourages some to procrastinate on the front end of development. If we aren't creating focused increments of technical

---

8. See Andrew McAffe, "Enterprise 2.0: The Dawn of Emergent Collaboration," *MIT Sloan Management Review*, Spring 2006.
9. Thanks to Werner Wild for this story. Used with permission.

progress, we are probably not making progress at all. If we are not doing experiments and getting feedback, we probably aren't learning much, and in the end, the work of any software development process is to create knowledge that gets embedded in the software.

## Set-Based Design

Two different approaches to learning have evolved in the software development world, both based on knowledge generation through iterative experiments. In the first case, the experiments are done by building a system which is change tolerant, so that as we learn we can easily fold the learnings into the system through what we call "refactoring." In the second case, the experiments are constructed as well-formed and thoroughly investigated options, so that at the last possible moment we can choose the option that gives the best overall solution to the puzzle.

The second approach is called set-based design, and it is the appropriate approach for making high-impact, irreversible decisions. There are a lot of these kinds of decisions in hardware development, so set-based design is particularly suited for hardware and, quite often, hardware-oriented aspects of embedded software. There are fewer high-impact irreversible decisions in software development, but they are certainly not absent. User interface approaches can be difficult to change once users get used to them. A hosted service is well advised to think through its security and performance strategies before the first release. Single-release products with seasonal release dates, such as games and tax preparation software, make good candidates for an options-based approach to development. Set-based design is the preferred approach for making key architectural decisions that, once made, will be very expensive to reverse.

How does set-based design work? Assume that some disaster befalls your company. You must make an immediate response and two things are clear: 1) There is a completely unmovable deadline, and 2) failure to meet it is not an option. What would you do? If you want to be absolutely certain of success, you commission three teams to develop the response: Team A is chartered to develop a very simple response that absolutely will be ready by the deadline. The response will be far from ideal, but at least it will be ready. Team B is chartered to develop a preferred solution that may be ready by the deadline if all goes well. Team C is chartered to develop the ideal solution, but the likelihood that it will make the deadline is slim.

Team A develops its suboptimal solution, but the team members hope that Team B makes the deadline because they know Team B's solution is better. Team B works very hard to make the deadline while simultaneously cheering on

Team A, because that's their backup, and hoping against hope that Team C comes through on time. Team C tries very hard to meet the deadline, but the team members are very glad that Teams A and B are backing them up.

When the deadline arrives, there *will* be a solution, and it will be the best one possible at the time. Moreover, even if the deadline is moved up, a functional solution can be still available while if the deadline moves back, the optimal solution might be ready. If the process is ongoing, the company can start out using solution A, then as soon as it is ready, switch to solution B, then eventually move on to solution C.

When it is absolutely essential to provide the best possible solution in the shortest possible time, set-based design makes a whole lot of sense. But when we apply set-based design to a development environment, it strikes many people as counterintuitive. The people who understand set-based development most readily live in environments that release products on a regular cadence with no tolerance for missing a deadline. Your daily newspaper is a good example; so are most magazines. Plays always open on opening night, news broadcasts happen on schedule every day, and seasonal clothing is always ready to ship when the season arrives.

Product development in these environments takes the form of readying various options and then assembling the best combination just before the deadline. When schedule *really* matters, it is not managed as an independent variable, it is a constant that everyone understands and honors.

So it should not be a surprise that Toyota has never missed a product delivery deadline. Nor should it be a surprise that Toyota uses set-based design. Set-based design is more than a method to meet schedules, it is a method to learn as much as possible in order to make the best decisions.

So how would this work in software? In Figure 7.2 we see a nine-month schedule with specific high-impact decisions scheduled at synchronization points. Each of these decisions is scheduled for the last possible moment; any later would be too late. For each of these decisions, multiple options are fully developed. When the synchronization point arrives, the system is assembled and tested with each option. The option that gives the best overall system solution is chosen. Note that the best option for each subsystem is not necessarily the choice. The option giving the best overall solution is chosen. This is the reason that each option set must be fully developed for testing at the synchronization point.

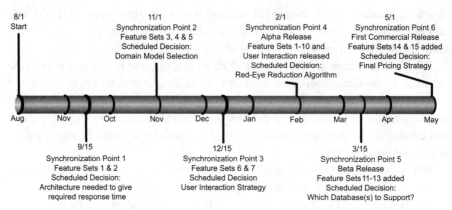

**Figure 7.2**  *Product release schedule with key decisions scheduled at synchronization points*

### Example 1: Medical Device Interface Design

One manager we spoke to uses a set-based approach to medical device interface design. His department is responsible for developing screen-based interfaces that technicians use to control medical devices. When a champion comes to him with a new product idea, he realizes that the champion has only a vague idea of what the interface really should do. So the manager assigns three or four teams to develop options during a six-week iteration. At the end of six weeks, the teams show their developments to the champion, who invariably likes some features from one option and other features from another option. The manager then assigns two teams to more fully develop two options over a second six-week iteration. At the end of that iteration, he finds that the champion can choose with certainty exactly which features he wants. "And at that point," the manager tells us, "the software is half done, and I know the champion will be completely happy with the product."

### Example 2: Red-Eye Reduction

After a talk, someone who managed software for printers proposed a dilemma to Mary. He said that he had 12 weeks to develop software for a new color printer, and the deadline simply could not be moved. The marketing people told him that they could sell a very large number of additional printers if they had an automatic red-eye reduction capability. At the time, red-eye reduction was a solved problem as long as an operator pointed a red eye out to the computer, but having a computer determine if there were red eyes in the picture and fix them automatically was not quite a solved problem.

The dilemma was this: There was a simple algorithm that the manager knew he could have ready on time, but he didn't think it was a very good algorithm. There was a far better algorithm, but he was not sure that it could be ready by the 12-week deadline. So what should he do—take a risk on the better algorithm, or take the safe route and do the simple one?

"Quite obviously you should do both." Mary said.

"But how am I going to get the resources?" he asked.

"You said you could sell a very large number of additional printers if you can provide red-eye reduction," Mary answered, "And you're asking me how you can get the resources?"

"You have a point," he said, "But how am I going to explain to my management that I'm doing two things when one will have to be thrown away?"

"You tell them," Mary said. "Don't worry, I guarantee you that we will have red-eye reduction ready on time. And better than that, we will have a spectacular algorithm that might make the first release, but if it doesn't it will be ready for the next one."

### Example 3: Pluggable Interfaces

Some decisions simply are not clear until the end of development. Maybe external interfaces are not clear, or in the case of embedded software, the hardware is not built yet. Often the exact role of various users has not been determined by the business, or technologies such as middleware or persistence layer have not been chosen. Some decisions might never be made. For example, a person might type on a keyboard for input in the initial release, but voice recognition will be substituted for some users later on. One solution in these cases is to create pluggable interfaces selected by build-time switches. Mock objects are useful as placeholders for decisions that are being deferred or for options that will be selected later.

Embedded software should be developed to run in two environments: a development environment with a simulator and the real environment. Usually the logging and actions upon errors will be different in each environment and will be selected by a flag. Pluggable interfaces to databases, middleware, and user interfaces are common, but building multiple cases of user roles is less common. In one class a developer described her strategy to determine file size: "It was unclear if the file had to be large or small, so I built both cases so I could decide at the last minute which one to use," she said.

"Surely you didn't waste time building two when you knew you would have to throw one away?" someone asked.

"Surely I did," she replied. "It didn't take much extra effort, and when the time came to deploy the software, it was ready to go."

### Why Isn't This Waste?

What we think of as "waste" is almost entirely dependent on how we frame the problem we are trying to solve. Remember the emergency response Teams A, B, and C. We have been asked: "Why not put people from Team A onto Team B and increase the chances of getting the better solution earlier?" Recall, however, that this was an emergency and *failure was not an option*. If we had said *this was a matter of life and death and failure would mean someone dies*, would Team A still seem like a waste?

In the examples above, missing market timing would have created far more waste—including time on the part of all of the rest of the team members—than the relatively small incremental effort of creating technical options. Developing technical options to be sure we make optimal decisions results in higher product quality—reducing support and warranty costs many times over the life of a product. If set-based design seems like waste, our frame of reference is probably limited to the immediate development issues rather than the big picture.

## Refactoring

As we noted in Chapter 2, the point of most software development is to create a change-tolerant code base which allows us to adapt to the world as it changes. As we will see in Chapter 8, we do this by using an iterative process, along with the disciplines that support change tolerance: automated testing, small batches, rapid feedback, and so on. There are two dangers with this strategy. First, we may make some key irreversible decision incorrectly if we make them too early. As we have seen, this danger should be identified and dealt with using set-based design.

The second danger of incremental development is that as we make changes, we add complexity, and the code base rapidly becomes unmanageable. This is not a small danger; it is highly probable unless we aggressively mitigate the risk. Refactoring is the fundamental mechanism for mitigating the risk and minimizing the cost of complexity in a code base. Refactoring enables developers to wait to add features until they are needed and then add them just as easily as if they had put them in earlier.

The rationale behind refactoring is this:

1.  Adding features before we are sure they are needed increases complexity, making it the worst form of waste in software development. Therefore, most features should be added incrementally.

2.  When adding features and changes to an existing code base it is essential not to add complexity.

3. Refactoring reduces the complexity of a code base simplifying its design. This allows new features to be accommodated with minimum complexity.

## Leave Room for What Needs to Happen

The YAGNI[10] style says, "Don't support what you don't need yet."

Gordon Bell said, "The cheapest, fastest, and most reliable components of a computer system are those that aren't there."[11]

It's an attitude that says that if you don't overbuild, you leave room for what needs to happen. The design decisions are all on a provisional basis. Then when you know more, you can plug in a better decision.

For example, today I use a simple list. When I run a performance test, I find out that searching is a bottleneck, so I use a fancier structure that still "looks" the same from the outside but performs better.

Development that's sensitive to what varies can "make room for variation"; the experiment style doesn't always have to happen first.

—Bill Wake[12]

Probably the biggest mistake we can make is to regard refactoring as a failure to "Do It Right the First Time." In fact, refactoring is the fundamental enabler of limiting code complexity, increasing the change tolerance, value, and longevity of the code. Refactoring is like exercise; it is necessary to sustain healthy code. Even the most time-pressed people in the world, executives and presidents, build in time to exercise to maintain their capacity to effectively respond to their next challenge. Similarly, even the most time-pressed developers in the world build in time for refactoring to maintain the capacity of the code base to accommodate change.

Refactoring requires an aggressive approach to automated testing, similar to the one used at Rally, which we described at the beginning of this chapter. As changes are being made to reduce the complexity of the code base, developers must have the tools in place to be certain that they do not introduce any unin-

---

10. YAGNI means "You Aren't Going to Need It." It's another way of saying: No Extra Features, or Write Less Code.
11. Quoted in *More Programming Pearls* by Jon Bentley, Addison-Wesley, 1988, p. 62.
12. We'd like to thank Bill Wake for this insight. Used with permission.

tended consequences. They need a test harness that catches any defects inadvertently introduced into the code base as its design is being simplified. They also need to use continuous integration and stop-the-line the minute a defect is detected.

The time and effort invested in automated testing and continuous improvement of the code base and associated tests is time spent eliminating waste and reducing complexity. The lean strategies of eliminating waste and reducing complexity are the best known way to add new capability at the lowest possible cost. Refactoring is like advertising: it doesn't cost, it pays.

### Legacy Systems

There are two kinds of software—change tolerant software and legacy software. Some software systems are relatively easy to adapt to business and technology changes, and some software systems are difficult to change. These difficult-to-change systems have been labeled "legacy" systems in the software development world. Change tolerant software is characterized by limited dependencies and a comprehensive test harness that flags unintended consequences of change. So we can define legacy systems as systems that are not protected with a suite of tests. A corollary to this is that you are building legacy code every time you build software without associated tests.

Legacy systems are everywhere, and thus a large portion of software development is aimed at legacy code. Brian Marick identifies three approaches to dealing with legacy systems:[13]

1. Rewrite and throw away

2. Refactor into submission

3. Strangle

Rewriting legacy software is an attractive approach for managers who dream of walking into their office one day and finding that all of their problems have disappeared as if by magic, and the computer now does all of the things that they could never do with the former system. The problem is, this approach has a dismal track record. Attempting to copy obscure logic and convert a massive database—which is probably corrupted—is very risky. Furthermore, as we have seen, perhaps two thirds of the features and functions in the legacy system are not used and not needed. Yet too many legacy conversions attempt to import the very complexity that caused the legacy system to resist change in the first place.

---

13. Brian Marick, "Exploration through Example," www.testing.com/cgi%2Dbin/blog/2005/05/11.

Refactoring legacy software is often a better approach. As we noted above, refactoring requires a test harness, but legacy code by definition does not have one. So the first step is to break dependencies and then place tests around independent sections of code to be able to refactor them. It is impractical, for the most part, to add unit tests to legacy code, so the idea here is to create acceptance tests (also called story tests) that describe by example the business behavior expected of the code. For help here we refer you to *Working Effective with Legacy Code*,[14] which is pretty much the bible on refactoring legacy code.

The third approach to dealing with legacy code is to strangle it. Martin Fowler[15] uses the metaphor of a strangler vine that grows up around a fig tree, taking on its shape and eventually strangling the tree. Ultimately the tree withers away, and only the vine is left. To strangle legacy code, you add strangler code—with automated tests—every time you have to touch a part of the legacy code. You intercept whatever activity you need to change and send it to a new piece of code that replaces the old code. While you are at it you may have to capture some assets and put them into a new database. Gradually you build the new code and database until you find that the parts of the old system that are actually used have all been replaced. At the beginning of this chapter, we saw how Rally used the strangler approach to replace its UI platform over fourteen months.

### Example

At Agile 2005, Gerard Meszaros and Ralph Bohnet[16] of ClearStream Consulting in Calgary reported on their successful port of a complex billing system of about 140,000 lines of Smalltalk code, with about 1,000 classes and over a dozen algorithms for charge calculations. Their approach was to create a set of regression tests for the existing system and then port the code until the new system produced the same results as the existing system. The regression tests took the form of tables in Excel spreadsheets. These tables were run against the legacy system and the results it produced were considered the "correct" answer. Then the developers went to the part of the legacy system that produced the results and ported the code to Java. (It was pretty good code, since it was Smalltalk). As the team developed the new system, they used Fitnesse to run the tables against the developing code every day, until the results produced by the legacy system were duplicated. At that point the feature was considered com-

---

14. Michael Feathers, *Working Effectively with Legacy Code*, Prentice Hall, 2005.
15. Martin Fowler, "StranglerApplication," www.martinfowler.com/bliki/StranglerApplication.html.
16. Gerard Meszaros and Ralph Bohnet, "Test-Driven Porting," Agile 2005 Experience Report. Additional information via e-mail correspondence. Used with permission.

plete. Meszaros and Bohnet report that they ported the system on schedule in six months, with only 20 open defects throughout a month-long user acceptance test. Most importantly, Ralph reports that perhaps 55 percent of the legacy code was left behind because they found that it was not being used.

## Problem Solving

We often have our hotel bill paid by companies we visit. The interesting part comes when we arrive at the hotel desk and they ask for a credit card. "This will be billed to company XZY, won't it?" Mary will say. Half the time the answer is, "Oh yes, your credit card is just for incidentals." And the other half of the time the answer is, "No, I don't see any information about XYZ paying for your room." Then comes the familiar hassle of getting the hotel to direct bill company XYZ before we check out. The most frustrating part about this hassle comes when the person at the hotel desk says, "Oh, yes, we have this problem all the time." And Mary inevitably responds, "If you have this problem all the time—why don't you *do* something about it?"

The mark of an excellent organization is not that they are without problems; it is that they are without systemic problems. In an excellent organization, everyone, at all levels, has a regular, reliable channel to address problems that they encounter in their everyday work. More than once we have been wrongly billed by a top-rated hotel, which signals to us that the hotel, despite its high rating, lacks a systematic improvement process.

It does no good to have a software development process if it is not accompanied by a way for those who struggle with its idiosyncrasies to fix them. Every team should have a regular time to systematically find and fix the things that make their lives difficult. Rally, for example, takes time out at the end of each iteration to discuss problems and commit to specific changes, and then it follows up on these commitments one by one.

The first rule of process improvement is not to try to do everything at once. When process improvement efforts are sporadic, people have a tendency to want to solve every problem at once. This is reminiscent of big projects and long release cycles, which have a similar tendency to create large batches of work. The idea is to establish a cadence of continuous improvement.

Frequent, regular meetings allow a team to find its biggest annoyance, get rid of it, and then move on to the next one. Usually the biggest annoyance can be described in sweeping terms, for example, "Our life would be so much easier if we had enough time to do all the stuff that everyone wants us to do." But such a broad statement doesn't provide much traction for actionable problem resolution.

## A Disciplined Approach

A disciplined approach to problem solving moves a team from wishful thinking to new knowledge, specific countermeasures, and permanent results. The scientific method discussed earlier in this chapter provides a good outline of how to proceed:

1. Define the problem.

2. Analyze the situation.

3. Create a hypothesis.

4. Perform experiments.

5. Verify results.

6. Follow-up/standardize.

### 1. Define the Problem

It's nice for a team to say "we want to be more responsive to customers," but how, exactly, does a team go about doing this? Let's follow a team through the problem-solving process. This team's biggest problem was a long list of complaints from customers who said their requests were being ignored, so the team decided to take a closer look at the problem.

### 2. Analyze the Situation

First the team looked at the features that had been deployed in the last four releases and plotted the feature cycle time on a Pareto chart. The data (Figure 7.3) looked fairly good—more than three-quarters of the features were deployed within six weeks of receiving the request.

However, the team members knew that there were a lot of items in their request queue that they were ignoring, especially since new features kept on being added all the time. So they plotted a Pareto chart of the age of the features that were currently in the queue (Figure 7.4).

The data showed that more than 60 percent of the requests in the queue were more than eight weeks old. Yet in the previous graph they saw that only nine requests they actually delivered were more than eight weeks old. They seemed to be working only on the most recent requests, not the older ones.

## Cycle Time of Deployed Features

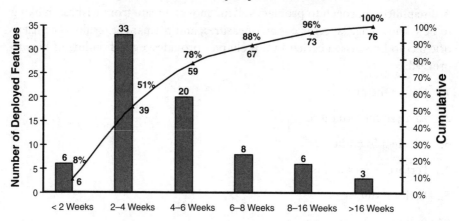

**Figure 7.3**   *Pareto chart: cycle time of deployed features*

## Request Age

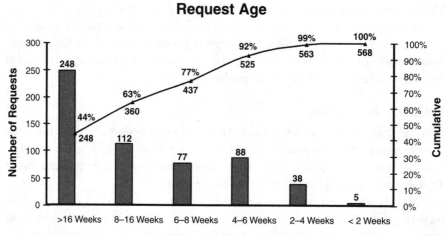

**Figure 7.4**   *Pareto chart: age of active customer requests*

The data also showed that the team had closed a total of 76 requests in the last four releases, or an average of 19 per release. The releases were two weeks apart, so their current rate was about ten requests a week. Since there were 568 requests in the queue, at the rate they were going it would take them more than a year (55–60 weeks) to work off the current queue, even without new requests.

The team next plotted the request input rate by priority category (Figure 7.5).

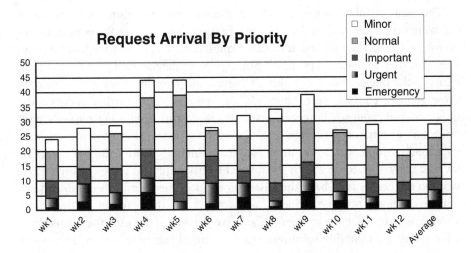

**Figure 7.5** *Request arrival rate*

### 3. Create a Hypothesis

A critical part of the scientific method, and one which is often overlooked by teams racing to solve problems, is to form a hypothesis that can be tested. The team members noted that the average input rate of the three highest priority request categories (emergency, urgent, and important) was ten per week, which was approximately the same as their current output rate. So their hypothesis was that if they could reduce the queue to 40–50 requests, stop accepting "normal" and "minor" requests, and increase their request completion rate slightly, they could complete new requests in four weeks 90 percent of the time.

### 4. Perform Experiments

The team members decided to see if they could reduce the backlog by sending an e-mail to everyone who had requests older than eight weeks. The e-mail said they were trying to reevaluate the request backlog and would like confirmation that the person would like their request to stay in the queue. If they didn't get confirmation in a week, they would assume that the request could be canceled. Table 7.1 shows the response to the e-mail:

**Table 7.1** *Response to Request for Confirmation of Need for Request*

| Age Category | Total | Withdraw | | Confirm | | No Response | |
|---|---|---|---|---|---|---|---|
| 8–16 weeks | 112 | 1 | 1% | 26 | 23% | 85 | 76% |
| >16 weeks | 248 | 20 | 8% | 3 | 1% | 225 | 91% |

The team members noted that 99 percent of requests more than 16 weeks old were no longer desired, 77 percent of requests more than 8 weeks old were no longer valid. They looked at the 29 requests that were confirmed and discovered that they all had "important" priority. Next they looked at the remaining items in the queue and sent a similar e-mail, but this time they sent it to only those whose requests were "normal" or "minor." This further reduced the queue to 100 requests; however, customers were still submitting requests with "normal" or "minor" priorities, and the team felt that if they removed this designation, customers would simply assign a higher priority. So they experimented with ways to deal with the lower priority requests. The experiment that worked the best was to have the customer support member of the team call initiators of lower priority requests and work with them to see if there was another way to solve the problem. Sixty-five percent of the time there was a relatively quick alternative solution. Ten percent of the time the requestor was convinced that the request was not justified based on the effort involved. Thus three quarters of the lower priority requests were withdrawn through this personal contact.

### 5. Verify Results

The team was able to increase its average completion rate to 25 requests per release (every two weeks). Over the next several weeks the queue was gradually reduced to about 50 requests through a combination of canceling older requests and completing higher priority requests slightly faster than they came in. The team measured its ability to provide reliable turnaround. The data showed that the queue length was the determining factor in request response time, so team members were confident that with the queue at 50 requests, they could promise a four-week turnaround on requests 90 percent of the time.

### 6. Follow Up/Standardize

The team members announced to their customers that they would complete most requests within four weeks, but they found that this encouraged more customers to submit requests, so they had a second team member assist with the customer service calls aimed at limiting the rate of request arrival and finding alternative solutions for low-priority requests. In addition, they were able to increase their average completion rate to 28 requests per release, due in part to the shortened turnaround time. Within a month the queue stabilized at four weeks of work. The team prepared a report on their experiences and presented it to other teams at an internal company seminar.

## Kaizen Events

We have just followed a work team through a typical problem-solving process, something that should be embedded in the everyday activity of existing work teams. Sometimes it is a good idea for teams to take a step back from everyday activities and focus solely on improving a key aspect of their process. This is particularly useful if the change will affect multiple areas of the company, and thus members from several different functions or different teams need to get involved.

Consider an organization that has determined that its key problem is deployment, so it decides that the most important thing it needs to do right now is automate deployment of software to customers. This will take a lot more than writing scripts. It will involve changing jobs and processes, interactions with other departments, customer expectations of what they will receive on deployment, and so on. This is a good opportunity to hold a Kaizen event.

The word Kaizen means "change for the better" in Japanese. Kaizen events are a well-known lean tool that brings together representatives from different functional areas to work intensely for a few days or a week to solve a well-defined, critical problem. During the event, all of the processes necessary to solve the problem are actually changed by the Kaizen team. After the event, the Kaizen team disbands and members go back to their ordinary jobs, with the improved process in place.

### Large Group Improvement Events

Sometimes a change is too momentous for a small team to be formed and chartered to implement it in a few days. For example, a value stream map may have shown that the biggest opportunity lies in moving testing much further forward in the process, which might mean a complete rethinking of many jobs and some organizational structures. This is a much bigger problem, so big in fact that it will probably languish unless it is addressed head on. For such a problem, a large group event may be the answer.

Large group improvement events are often modeled on the GE Workout,[17] arguably a key force behind GE's remarkable success in the 1990s. Implemented by Jack Welch long before—and, at first, instead of—Six Sigma, the GE Workout was designed to cut through bureaucracy and solve organizational problems that no one seemed to have the time to address in the newly downsized company. Similar techniques have been widely used in other organizations

---

17. See *The GE Workout*, by Dave Ulrich, Steve Kerr, and Ron Ashkenas, McGraw-Hill, 2002.

to enable ordinary employees to initiate and carry out both small and large cross-functional changes.

In a large group improvement event, a large, cross-functional and multilevel group of people is assembled and challenged to come up with solutions to a specific and critical organizational problem. These solutions should be based on lean principles and should be practical enough to be implemented in the near future—in, perhaps, 90 days. This kind of event is usually a facilitated meeting that lasts about three days. After a clear charter by a sponsoring executive, small groups brainstorm ideas for solving the problems, come up with recommendations, meet with each other to consolidate ideas, and gather supporting information for the recommendations. By the end of the event, those attending have put together a set of recommendations with supporting material. Each recommendation is championed by someone who will inherit the responsibility to implement the recommendation immediately, should it be approved. Toward the end of the meeting the sponsor returns, the recommendations are presented and discussed, and the sponsor (hopefully) approves or rejects each one. The champions of approved recommendations are chartered to implement them and can expect to receive both the time and support to do so.

That's the theory. And quite often it works in practice. But quite often large group improvement events fail for a variety of reasons:

1.  A lack of focus on core business processes leads to:

    • Random improvements

    • Local rather than global optimization

    This can also be a problem with small group Kaizen events; improvements should address the most critical outstanding business problem.

2.  Many ideas are approved, few are implemented, because:

    • No one "owns" responsibility for implementing each idea.

    • There is no charter to make changes across boundaries.

    • No time is allocated for people to make the changes.

    • There is no follow-up by the sponsor.

    Lack of follow-up is particularly a problem with large group events, and leads to broad discouragement. It is better not to hold such an event than to let it fail. Failure to follow-up shows a lack of respect for the people who were involved.

Kaizen events and large group events are good places for people to learn problem-solving skills, attack cross-functional problems, and make dramatic changes in a short time. But generally, improvement should fall to the natural work teams, which should constantly and in a disciplined manner identify and remove the largest current constraint that keeps their process from making the maximum possible contribution to the improvement of overall business results.

## Try This

1. At your next team meeting, discuss this: What, exactly, is our biggest problem? And what, exactly, are we going to do about it?

2. Talk about set-based design at a team meeting. Find out if anyone has any examples of when they used such an approach while developing software. (In a group of eight, there will usually be someone who has. If not, try for an experience of set-based design outside of software.) Have the person describe the experience, the rationale, and whether or not it was a good idea.

3. What is your team's practice regarding refactoring? Before you add any new features, do you first change the design to simplify it, without making any feature changes, and test the new design to be sure nothing has changed? Do you refactor to simplify immediately after getting a new feature working?

4. Take one document that your team is expected to produce and at a team meeting work to figure out how it can be fit into the A3 report format. Does the new format adequately summarize all of the information in the old document? The next time the document is distributed, attach the A3 version on the front. After doing this a few times—if it is practical—try distributing just the A3 report and not the longer document. What happens?

5. If something small goes wrong on a regular basis, do the people annoyed by the problem have a way to fix it? Does your team have a regular meeting for discussing these annoying problems, reflecting on how things are done and what could be done better? How often is it held? Does the team work together using a disciplined problem-solving approach to do something about the issues that arise? Does it work on one problem at a time?

# Chapter 8

# Quality

## Feedback

Customers who wanted new information systems used to be told that it would take a lot of time to develop high-quality software. But for some customers, this was simply not acceptable. Getting the software they needed—quickly—was essential for survival, yet they could not tolerate poor quality. When faced with no alternative but to break the compromise between quality and speed, a few companies have discovered that there *is* a way to develop superb software very fast—and in the process, they have created an enduring competitive advantage.

When it becomes a survival issue and old habits are not adequate to the task, better ways of developing new products have been invented out of necessity. In every case, these more robust development processes have two things in common:[1]

1. Excellent, rapid feedback

2. Superb, detailed discipline

## The Polaris Program[2]

On October 4, 1957, a crisis hit the US Defense Department. The Soviet Union successfully launched Sputnik I, the first artificial satellite to orbit the world. The surprised American public reasoned that since the Soviets had already fired short-range missiles from surfaced submarines, and now that they had the technology to make long-range missiles, adding the two together would result in the capability to launch a nuclear weapon that could penetrate the country's

1. See Kim B. Clark and Takahiro Fujimoto, *Product Development Performance*, Harvard Business School Press, 1991.
2. The Aegis Program and the Atlas Program have similar histories; however, the Polaris Program has superior independent and unbiased documentation.

defenses. The crisis intensified a month later, when Sputnik II was launched. This was a much bigger satellite; it even carried a dog named Laika.

The US Navy had just started the Polaris program, a program to develop submarines that could launch missiles while submerged. The first Polaris submarine was scheduled to be operational in 1965. Obviously, taking nine years to launch the submarine was no longer acceptable. Two weeks after Sputnik I circled the world, the deadline was changed to 1959. Two-and-a-half years later, on June 9, 1959, the first Polaris missile was launched from a submarine. By the end of 1960 two Polaris submarines were patrolling at sea.[3]

How could such a technically complex objective that was supposed to take nine years be accomplished in such a short time? To begin with, the minute the deadline changed, Technical Director Vice Admiral Levering Smith focused his team on one simple objective: Deploy a force of submarines in the *shortest possible time*. This meant no wasted time, no extra features, and no delays—in short: *Make every minute count.*

Within weeks, Vice Admiral Smith had commandeered the two submarines currently under construction as attack submarines, and had them stretched out 130 feet (about 40 meters) to provide a place for missiles.[4] Since 16 missiles would fit in the newly stretched submarines, 16 missiles is the standard number of missiles in a submarine to this day. Admiral Smith needed the submarines right away because he had modified the development objective from creating the ultimate system in nine years to creating a progression of systems: A1, A2, and A3.[5] The A1 version would contain technology that could be deployed in about three years. The A2 version would be developed in parallel, but proceed more slowly to allow it to use more desirable technologies. The A3 version would incorporate everything learned in the development of the earlier versions.

Within each version, Admiral Smith orchestrated rapid, sharply focused increments of technical progress. He carefully controlled the systems design and tightly managed the interfaces between components, personally signing the coordination drawings. But rather than manage the details of the subsystems, he had several competing subsystems developed in virtually all areas of technical uncertainty. This allowed him to choose the best option once the technology

---

3. "The Polaris: A Revolutionary Missile System and Concept," by Norman Polmar, Naval Historical Colloquium on Contemporary History Project, at www.history.navy.mil/colloquia/cch9d.html, January 17, 2006.

4. Ibid.

5. See Harvey Sapolsky, *The Polaris System Development: Bureaucratic and Programmatic Success in Government*, Harvard University Press, 1972.

had been developed. Finally, Admiral Smith demanded the highest reliability, so from the beginning Polaris submarines were tested thoroughly and had built-in redundancy.

As historian Harvey Sapolsky notes:[6]

> The Polaris program is considered an outstanding success. The missile was deployed several years ahead of the original FBM [Fleet Ballistic Missile] schedule. There has been no hint of a cost overrun. As frequent tests indicate, the missile works. The submarine building was completed rapidly. Not surprisingly, the Special Projects Office is widely regarded as one of the most effective agencies within government.

The Polaris project gave us PERT (Program Evaluation and Review Technique), an innovative new scheduling system developed for the managing the Polaris program. PERT has been widely regarded as the reason for Polaris's remarkable success, but Harvey Sapolsky calls this a myth.[7] Sapolsky makes the case that the PERT system, at least in the early stages of the Polaris project, was mostly a façade to assure continued funding of the program. In those early years, PERT was unreliable as a scheduling system, because the technical objectives changed so fast and frequently that the PERT charts could not be kept up to date. Later on, the Polaris program was a victim of its own publicity; eventually its managers were required to use the PERT system that they had largely ignored and would have preferred to abandon.

Sapolsky attributes the success of the Polaris program not to PERT, but to the technical leadership of Admiral Smith and his laser-like focus on synchronized increments of technical progress, the option-based approach to developing components, the emphasis on reliability, and a deep sense of mission among all participants.[8]

## Release Planning

When political events suddenly collapsed the Polaris program timeframe, the first thing Admiral Smith did was switch from a nine-year plan for the perfect system to an incremental plan for a minimalist system that would grow increasingly better. He planned to demonstrate the most risky capability (submarine-launched missile) one-quarter of the way into the program. Then he would develop the simplest system that could possibly work and deploy it as soon as possible (A1). At the same time, he would develop a better version and deploy it

---

6. Ibid., p. 11.
7. Ibid., Chapter 4.
8. Ibid., Chapter 5.

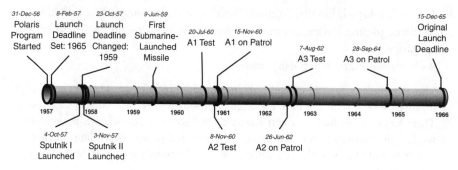

**Figure 8.1**   *The Polaris timeline*

as a rapid follower (A2). Once the first version was deployed and the second version was well underway, he would start developing the "ultimate" version (A3). This approach resulted in significantly more capability, faster delivery, and lower cost than the original plan (see Figure 8.1).

If this approach is good for technically complex hardware, it's even better for software. Let's take a software development program through the same process.[9] The program starts with the identification of a market need (or business need), product concept, target cost, and launch timing. This establishes the general constraints of the program. People experienced with the customer domain and the available technology make a quick "rough order of magnitude" determination of what capabilities the organization can reasonably expect to develop within the constraints.

Instead of spending the initial investment time developing a detailed long-range plan, we take a short time to create an incremental release plan. We plan near-term development to check out the most critical features and establish the underlying architecture. We plan an early launch of a minimum useful set of capabilities to start generating revenue (or payback). We stage additional releases to add more capabilities on a periodic basis.

Figure 8.2 shows a nine-month release plan divided into six releases of feature sets. Each release is further divided into three two-week iterations to develop the feature sets.

The goal of the first release is to develop the feature set that will establish feasibility and preliminary architecture, so it should create a thin slice through

---

9. For a thorough background on planning, see Mike Cohn's *Agile Estimating and Planning*, Addison-Wesley, 2005.

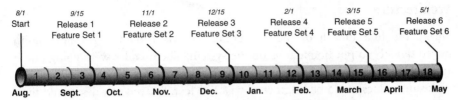

**Figure 8.2**  *Release plan for a nine-month effort with 18 two-week iterations and six releases*

all layers of the application, showing how everything fits together. After that, feature sets should be chosen based on the following considerations:[10]

1.  Feature sets with high value before lower value

2.  Feature sets with high risk and high value before lower risk

3.  Feature sets that will create significant new knowledge before those already well understood

4.  Feature sets with a lower cost to develop or support before higher cost

A release plan gives you a basis for testing technical and market assumptions before investing a large amount of money in detailed plans. You can get an early reading of the plan's feasibility by starting implementation and tracking progress. By the first release you will have real data to forecast the effort needed to implement the entire project far more accurately than if you had spent the same six weeks generating detailed requirements and plans.

If you implement a release plan and find that you are behind at the first release, you should assume that the plan is too aggressive. The preferred approach at this point is to simplify the business process or product under development, simplify the technical approach to implementing the features, or remove features entirely. It is generally best to maintain a fixed "timebox" of iterations and releases and limit features to those that can be fully implemented within the timebox.

There are certainly environments—games for example—where incremental releases to the public are not feasible. But in most of these environments incremental development is still a very good idea. You just "release" the product internally to an environment which is as close to the production environment as possible. Getting a product "ready to release" every three months gives everyone a concrete handle on actual progress. This is a particularly good way to manage risk in custom software development.

---

10. Ibid., pp. 80–87.

## Architecture

During the first month of the accelerated Polaris program, Admiral Smith moved quickly to put boundaries on the system. The missiles were going into a submarine, two submarines were about to be built, and the practical amount these submarines could be lengthened was 130 feet. Sixteen missiles would fit in this space, and without further ado the highest level architectural constraints were established. After that it did not take very long to create the high-level systems design (architecture). It was pretty much dictated by the limited space of submarines and the existing missile technology. The underlying principle of the system design was to tightly define and control interfaces while making sure that subsystems were complete feature sets that could be developed and tested independently by different contractors with a minimum of communication. This was necessary because Admiral Smith's small staff could not possibly get involved in the details of each subsystem, and in any case, giving contractor teams the freedom to be creative was necessary because the system required a host of innovations if it was going to work.

The starting point of large a complex system should be a divisible systems architecture that allows creative teams to work concurrently and independently on subsystems that deliver critical feature sets. A subsystem is a set of user-valued capabilities. It is not a layer—the idea is *not* to have separate teams develop the database layer, the user interface layer, and so on. A subsystem should be sized so that it can be developed by a team or closely associated group of teams.

As it becomes apparent that change tolerance is a key value in most software systems, architectures that support incremental development—such as service-oriented architectures and component-based architectures—are rapidly replacing monolithic architectures. Even with these architectures there are still some constraints, particularly those that deal with nonfunctional requirements (security, performance, extensibility, etc.), that are best considered before feature sets development begins. However, the objective of a good software architecture is to keep such irreversible decisions to a minimum and provide a framework that supports iterative development.

Architecture itself can, and usually should, be developed incrementally. In *Software by Numbers*, Mark Denne and Jane Cleland-Huang make the case that software architecture is composed of elements, and these elements should be developed as they become required by the feature sets currently under development. In successful products whose lifetimes span many years, a major architectural improvement can be expected every three years or so, as new applications are discovered and capabilities are required that were never envisioned in the original architecture. It is time to abandon the myth that architecture is something that must be complete before any development takes place.

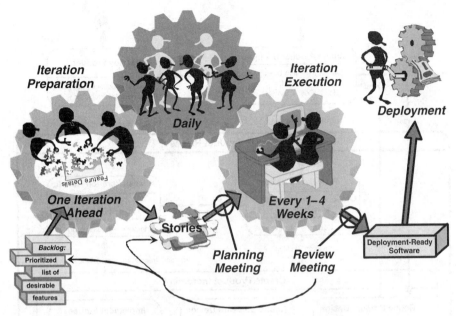

**Figure 8.3** *Iterative development overview*[11]

## Iterations

Iterative development is a style of development that creates synchronized increments of technical progress at a steady cadence. Figure 8.3 depicts a typical iterative software development process.

Starting at the lower left of Figure 8.3, we find a backlog, a prioritized list of desirable features described at a high level. Shortly before it is time to implement a feature it is analyzed by team members who understand the customer domain and the technology. They break it into "stories,"[12] units of development that can be estimated reliably and completed within a few days. At a planning meeting, the team determines how many stories it can implement in the next iteration—based on its track record (velocity)—and commits to completing these stories. During the iteration the whole team meets briefly every day to talk about how iteration planning is going, keep on track toward meeting its implementation commitment, and to help each other out. At the end of

---

11. Screen Beans art is used with permission of A Bit Better Corporation. Screen Beans is a registered trademark of A Bit Better Corporation.
12. For the details of using user stories, see Mike Cohn's *User Stories Applied*, Addison-Wesley, 2004.

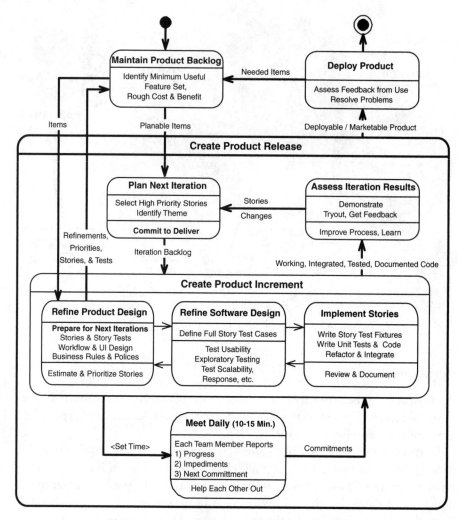

**Figure 8.4** *An example of iterative development*

the iteration, the stories must be *done*—integrated, tested, documented, and ready to use. A review meeting is held to demonstrate progress and obtain feedback, which may be captured as story or a change to the backlog. After a few iterations, a useful feature set is completed and ready to deploy.

We'll now take a more detailed walk through a typical implementation of iterative software development (see Figure 8.4).

*Preparation*

Figure 8.4 begins with a backlog that is initially assembled at the beginning of the development effort. The backlog is a list of desirable features, constraints, needed tools, and so on. It is better used as a succinct product roadmap rather than a long queue of things to do. The backlog is dynamic—that is, it can be added to or subtracted from at will based on the team's learning. Each backlog item has a rough estimate, and the total of all estimates gives a ballpark estimate of the time to complete the effort. Someone (the champion, or in Scrum, the Product Owner) is responsible for keeping the priorities of the backlog current with business needs.

Backlog items start out as large-grain bullet points, since the lean approach is to delay detailed analysis until the last responsible moment. As items near the top of the priority list they need to be broken into smaller, more manageable pieces. A backlog item is not ready to be developed until its design is packaged as one or more stories. The people who will implement each story must understand the story clearly enough to reliably estimate its implementation effort—reliable delivery requires reliable estimates.[13] Each story should have some clear value from the perspective of the business, but the criteria for sizing a story is its implementation effort—a good story is typically one-half to four days of work. The people designing the product must decide if the value of the story is worth its implementation cost.

Backlog items are usually features expressed in terms of business goals; high-level goals can be more like epics than stories. Team members who have a good understanding of the customers' job (Product Owners, analysts, etc.) lead the effort to break the epics into stories as they near the top of the priority list. Standard analysis techniques such as essential use cases combined with conceptual domain models, business rules and policies, and paper user interface (UI) prototypes are effective for thinking through this aspect of designing the product. If a use case is small enough, it may map to a story. Or it may take several stories over more than one iteration to realize the main scenario of a complicated use case with its associated interfaces, rules, and persistence.

The objective of iteration preparation is to design the portion of the "whole" product that will be developed next. Decisions need to be made about business rules, policies, workflow, functionality, and interface design. This design activity creates "just enough" carefully thought out stories "just-in-time" for the next iteration. A good story is a well-defined unit of implementer work, small enough so that it can be reliably estimated and completed within the next itera-

---

13. For details on estimating stories, see Mike Cohn's *Agile Estimating and Planning*, Addison-Wesley, 2005.

tion. The objective is *not* to create extensive analysis documents for the entire product. Instead, the objective is to provide enough sample tests to make the business intent clear to the implementer.

### Planning

At the beginning of an iteration there is a planning meeting. The whole team, in collaboration with the champion or Product Owner, estimates how long the top priority stories will take to develop, test, document, and deploy (or have ready for deployment). Team members pick the first story and commit to complete it. They pick a second story and decide whether they can commit to deliver this one as well. This process continues until the team members are no longer confident that they will be able to deliver the next story.[14] Team members commit to an iteration goal, which describes the theme of the feature set they agreed to implement during the iteration. No one tells the team how much work it should take on, but after a few iterations, each team establishes its velocity, which gives everyone a good idea of how much the team can complete in an iteration.

Team members should regard the commitment as a pledge that they will work together as a team to accomplish the goal. Occasionally, a team may over-commit, or unexpected technical difficulties may arise. When this happens, the team should adapt to the situation in an appropriate manner, but they should also look for the root cause of the overcommitment and take countermeasures so that it does not happen again.

### Implementation

During the iteration, the whole team works together to meet the iteration goal. Everyone attends a 10–15 minute daily meeting to discuss what each member accomplished since the last meeting, what they plan to do by the next meeting, what problems they are having, and where they need help. The team interaction at this meeting provides sufficient information for individual members to know what to do next to meet the team goal without being told.

The preferred approach is story-test driven development (also called acceptance-test driven development). Working one story at a time, team members focused on designing the functional details, workflow, and user interface work with the developers to express precisely what the product needs to do in terms of test cases. This discussion leads to a definition of the relevant variables and the applicable policies and business rules from the domain. Using this shared language, they define specific behaviors in terms of inputs or sequences of steps and expected results.[15] While some team members flesh out a sufficient number

---

14. Ibid.
15. See Eric Evans, *Domain Driven Design*, Addison-Wesley, 2003.

of test instances, the developers create fixtures to interface the test cases to the application and they create the code to satisfy these test cases. When the developers need clarifications or additional detail, team members who understand the customer needs are available to discuss the issue and help define additional example tests to record the agreements reached. The full set of example tests becomes, in effect, a very detailed, self-verifying product design specification.

## How FIT Works

In the book *Fit for Developing Software*,[16] Rick Mugridge and Ward Cunningham present the Open Source tool FIT as a tool to help teams communicate with each other by creating concrete examples of what the code should do. The examples are in table format. When text is added between the tables, the result is a readable specification. Developers write "fixtures," which connect the application code to the tables. The FIT framework executes the application to verify that each behavior specified in the tables is correctly implemented. Once a fixture is written, analysts and testers can write as many test cases as they want to assure the application is doing what is expected as its functionality grows. When FIT runs, it produces reports that are the input tables marked with green for tests that passed and red for tests that failed. This output can be kept on file for regulatory purposes or simply measured to determine how close to "done" the code is.

—Tom Poppendieck

To implement behavior specified by a story test, developers use unit-test driven development. They start by selecting a simple behavior for the code that will contribute to the story-test objective. To implement that behavior the developers select suitably named objects, methods, and method parameters. Whenever possible they choose names consistent with the names used in the story-test. They document their design decision by writing a unit test, which fails until new code returns the intended behavior. They then write simple code to make this test pass without breaking any previous tests. The final step in the cycle is to assess the resulting code base and improve its design by refactoring it to remove any duplication, to make it simple and easy to understand, and to ensure that the intent of the code is clear. They repeat this cycle, adding each

---

16. Rick Mugridge and Ward Cunningham, *Fit for Developing Software: Framework for Integrated Tests*, Prentice Hall, 2005.

additional behavior until the selected story test passes. When the full set of story tests pass, it is time to go on to the next story.

A story is not done until the team updates associated sections of any user, customer, or regulatory compliance documentation as far as practical. There should be *no partial credit* for stories. Stories don't count until their fully working code is integrated, tested, documented, and ready to deploy. At the end of each iteration, the goal is to have complete, "releasable" features. Some teams go further than this and release software into production at the end of each iteration.

*Assessment*

At the end of an iteration, a review meeting is held for the team to show all concerned how much value they have created. (Applause is appropriate.) If the review turns up anything that needs to be changed, small issues become new stories while larger issues go into the backlog where they will be prioritized with other items. And without further ado, the planning meeting for the next iteration commences.

Notice that we have described three nested learning cycles, once for the entire iteration, once for each story, and once for each small piece for the code. (see Figure 8.5). The growing suites of story tests and unit tests express the current knowledge of how the product and the software need to work to do the customers' job. As the team learns, the test suites will need to be adapted to

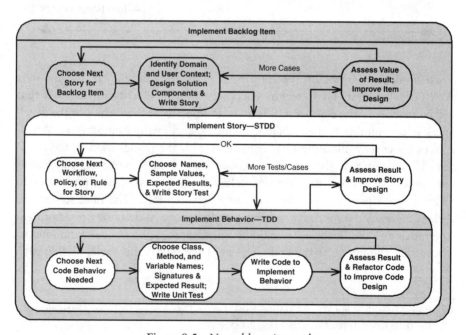

**Figure 8.5** *Nested learning cycles*

express the newly created knowledge. The magic is that the tests make the cost of change very low because if anyone unintentionally breaks a design decision made earlier, a test will fail immediately, which alerts the team to stop the line until they fix the code and/or update the tests, which express the design.

### Variation: User Interface

In practice most organizations modify the iterative process to suit their circumstances. One special context that may require modification is user interface development. In Chapter 3 we introduced Alias (now part of Autodesk), a 3-D graphics company whose products center on user interactions. Since excellent user interaction design is a key competitive advantage of the company, most development teams are assigned two dedicated interaction designers. During every iteration, these interaction designers have several jobs:

- Gather customer data for future iterations

- Test the user interaction developed in the previous iteration

- Answer questions that arise as coding proceeds in the current iteration

- Design in detail the user interface to be coded in the next iteration

Figure 8.6 shows how development proceeds. Before a user interaction design is coded, customer data is gathered, various options are tested through

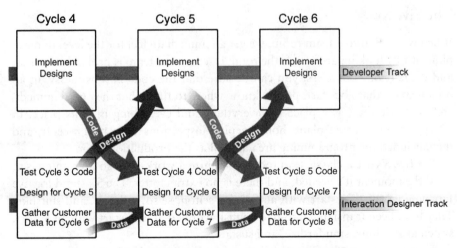

**Figure 8.6** *Iterative user interaction design*[17]

---

17. From Lynn Miller, director of user interface development, Autodesk, Toronto, used with permission. Originally published in "Case Study of Customer Input for a Successful Product," Experience Report, Agile 2005.

prototypes, and a detailed design ready for coding is finalized. Usability testing of the production code occurs one iteration after coding.

# Discipline

We were teaching a class at a company whose development processes were relatively chaotic. The class went well until we got to the part on quality, and then a bit of discouragement set in. "You mean we have to do all that stuff? We thought lean meant going fast, but that quality stuff looks like a *lot* of work!" Indeed.

Shortly after that class, we gave a seminar to aerospace developers. When we got to the part on quality we heard: "Oh, we've been doing *that* for years." And indeed they had. The people in this group probably knew as much about automated testing as anyone we have met.

You can't go fast without building quality into the product, and that takes a lot of discipline. We find that such discipline is second nature to people working on life-critical systems, companies with Six Sigma programs, and organizations with high CMM assessments. But to a small and rapidly growing company that hasn't thought much about quality, becoming lean means becoming very disciplined about the way software is developed.

## The Five S's

When we walk into a team room, we get an immediate feel for the level of discipline just by looking around. If the room is messy, the team is probably careless, and if the team is careless, you can be sure that the code base is messy. In an organization that goes fast, people know where to find what they need immediately because there is a place for everything and everything is in its place. In Mary's manufacturing plant, housekeeping inspections were held weekly, and they included the programming area as well as the production floor.

The five S's are a classic lean tool to organize a workspace so everything is at hand the moment it's needed, and there is no extra clutter. The S's stand for five Japanese words that start with an S: seiri, seiton, seiso, seiketsu, and shitsuke. They have been translated into five English words that also start with an S: sort, systematize, shine, standardize, and sustain.

We recently remodeled our kitchen, and as we moved into the new space we found ourselves using the five S's to reconfigure our workspace.

1. **Sort (Seiri):** First we sorted through all our kitchen tools and set aside anything we had not used in the last year. Only the things we actually used went back into the kitchen.

2. **Systematize (Seiton):** The big project was to find a place for everything that would make it easy to find and close at hand. We moved shelves and invested in drawer organizers and wall hooks. We rearranged things several times before we found the right place for each tool and appliance.

3. **Shine (Seiso):** With everything finally put away, we cleaned up the kitchen and were ready to start cooking.

4. **Standardize (Seiketsu):** Then we agreed on two (new!) policies: We would fill and run the dishwasher every night, and we would put everything away first thing every morning.

5. **Sustain (Shitsuke):** Now we just have to keep up the discipline.

The software development workspace is not just the physical workroom, but also the desktop on a computer screen, the layout of the team server, and the code base everyone is working on. So after you apply the five S's to the team room, think about applying it to the logical workspace behind the screen. And since software is a reflection the organization that developed it, take a good look at the code base as well.

1. **Sort (Seiri):** Sort through the stuff on the team workstations and servers, and find the old versions of software and old files and reports that will never be used any more. Back them up if you must, then delete them.

2. **Systematize (Seiton):** Desktop layouts and file structures are important. They should be crafted so that things are logically organized and easy to find. Any workspace that is used by more than one person should conform to a common team layout so people can find what they need every place they log in.

3. **Shine (Seiso):** Whew, that was a lot of work. Time to throw out the pop cans and coffee cups, clean the fingerprints off the monitor screens, and pick up all that paper. Clean up the whiteboards after taking pictures of the important designs that are sketched there.

4. **Standardize (Seiketsu):** Put some automation and standards in place to make sure that every workstation always has the latest version of the tools, backups occur regularly, and miscellaneous junk doesn't accumulate.

5. **Sustain (Shitsuke):** Now you just have to keep up the discipline.

## The 5 S's for Java

1. **Sort (Seiri):** Reduce the size of the code base. Throw away all unneeded items immediately. Remove:

   - Dead code
   - Unused imports
   - Unused variables
   - Unused methods
   - Unused classes
   - Refactor redundant code

2. **Systematize (Seiton):** Organize the projects and packages. Have a place for everything and everything in its place.

   - Resolve package dependency cycles
   - Minimize dependencies

3. **Shine (Seiso):** Clean up. Problems are more visible when everything is neat and clean.

   - Resolve unit test failures and errors ( passed == 100%)
   - Improve unit test coverage ( > 80%)
   - Improve unit test performance
   - Check AllTests performance
   - Resolve checkstyle warnings
   - Resolve PMD warnings
   - Resolve javadoc warnings
   - Resolve TODO's

4. **Standardize (Seiketsu):** Once you get to a clean state, keep it that way. Reduce complexity over time to improve ease of maintenance.

5. **Sustain (Shitsuke):** Use and follow standard procedures.

This is the way we do things.

—Kent Schnaith[18]

---

18. From private e-mail communication. Used with permission.

**Figure 8.7**  *Standards?*

## Standards

As we travel around the world, we have come to appreciate the importance of standards. We really appreciate the train system and metro transportation we find in almost every European city, but we are especially appreciative in the United Kingdom, because we try very hard not to drive a car there. We couldn't avoid driving in New Zealand recently, but even after two weeks we had to be vigilant at every turn or we would find ourselves on the wrong side of the road. Every electrical gadget we own can operate on any voltage, and we carry a bag full of plug converters (see Figure 8.7). We have learned to think of temperatures in Celsius and distances in kilometers, but we have not gotten used to electrical switches where up is off.

Standards make it possible to operate reflexively and move information without conversion waste. A standardized infrastructure with a common architecture reduces complexity and thus lowers cost. Any organization that wants to move fast will have standards in place. Here are some of the standards that a software development organization should consider:

1. Naming conventions

2. Coding standards

3. User interaction conventions

4. File structures

5. Configuration management practices

6. Tools

7. Error log standards

8. Security standards

Of course, standards are useless on paper; they have to be used consistently to be valuable. In a lean environment, standards are viewed as the current best way to do a job, so they are always followed. The assumption, however, is that there is *always* a better way to do things, so everyone is actively encouraged to challenge every standard. Any time a better way can be found and proven to be more effective, it becomes the new standard. The discipline of following—and constantly changing—standards should be part of the fabric of an organization.

## Appreciating Standards

I know of a case where there were two programs, both with the name "SYNC." They were stored in the same location on two different systems. On System 1, SYNC saved local files by merging them into the master file, while on System 2 SYNC reset the local files by replacing them with the master file. An operator who frequently worked on System 1 happened to be working on System 2. She found SYNC in the same location she always found SYNC, so she assumed that it <u>was</u> SYNC. She ran SYNC to merge a large number of recent transactions into the master file. To her horror, the master file was copied over her local flies, completely wiping out everything she was trying to save. It was a very expensive "mistake," and the root cause was probably the absence of naming standards.

—Mary Poppendieck

### Code Reviews

"Are code reviews waste?" people often ask in our classes. Good question. We think that using code reviews to enforce standards or even to find defects is a waste. Code analyzers and IDE checks are the proper tools to enforce most standards, while automated testing practices are the proper way to avoid most defects. Code reviews should be focused on a different class of problems. For example, the code of inexperienced developers might be reviewed for simplicity, change tolerance, absence of repetition, and other good object-oriented practices. Code reviews can also be a good tool for raising awareness of issues such as complexity. One organization we know of computes the McCabe Cyclomatic Complexity Index[19] for newly committed code, and when it reaches a threshold of 10, a code review is triggered.

---

19. The McCabe Cyclomatic Complexity Index is a measure of the number of execution paths through a program. See "A Complexity Measure," by Thomas J. McCabe, *IEEE Transactions on Software Engineering*, Vol. Se-2, No.4, December 1976.

## Formal Code Review

In our organization, a group of Cobol developers was transitioning to Java. They had training in Java syntax, but object-oriented thinking is counterintuitive to people who have done procedural programming for years. We used code reviews to help show the developers how to use standard patterns while writing and refactoring object-oriented code. When a developer finished a section of code and requested a review, it was held as soon as possible and was open to anyone who wanted to attend. The developer showed the code to two technical leaders, who then discussed how it might be improved. The two experts did not always agree, and the ensuing discussion gave the developers thinking tools rather than answers. The atmosphere of the reviews was so open and educational that they became very popular. Soon more and more developers were sitting in on the reviews, because they learned so much. The collective capability of the new Java developers increased dramatically through this process.

—Jill Aden[20]

Some policies that require code reviews prior to check-in create a large accumulation of partially done work waiting for review, but in a lean environment this is an unacceptable situation that should be avoided aggressively. One way to provide code review with no delays is to use some form of pairing while the code is being written.

### Pairing

Pairing (also called pair programming) is the practice of having two people work side-by-side on the same task. This provides continuous code review in a flow rather than a batch. The judicious use of pairing can be very valuable. Developing code in pairs can enhance learning, teamwork, and problem-solving skills. Moreover, pairing often increases productivity because both the quality and the robustness of the code are enhanced when viewed through two sets of eyes. In addition, pairs tend to deflect interruptions and keep each other on task. Anyone who has ever programmed will tell you that developing software is a continuous exercise in solving problems, and pair problem solving is a pattern we find in many occupations. Pairing makes it easier to add new people to a team, because there is a built-in mentoring program.

---

20. From a presentation at the Twin Cities OTUG meeting, on June 17, 2003, and later conversations. Used with permission.

Pairing is not for everyone nor for all situations. But pairing often creates synergy: Two people will frequently deliver more integrated, tested, defect-free code by working together than they could produce working separately. And pairing is one of the best ways to achieve the benefits of reviews without building up inventories of partially done work.

## Open Source Reviews

In Open Source communities, "committers" review all code before it is committed to the code base. Committers are trusted developers who have demonstrated their competence and commitment to the project. Typically there is one committer for about every ten contributors, and code is always submitted in small batches. This allows submissions to be reviewed and committed very quickly. After submission, the code is subject to the review of the entire community, where scrutiny is immediate and advice is freely given. It's been said that if you really want to learn how to code, try your hand at Open Source, and you will get plenty of feedback on how to improve.

—Mary Poppendieck

## Mistake-Proofing

When you connect a projector to a laptop with a video cable, it's difficult to plug it in wrong, because it is mistake-proof. One side is wider than the other and has more pins. After a quick look, most people will get it right. A USB cable, on the other hand, is not so simple. How many times do you try it one way, push a bit, realize that it's backward, turn it over, and try again? Although it is virtually impossible to plug a USB cable in wrong, it is not always obvious which way it should be oriented. This cable is not quite mistake-proof enough for our tastes.

The worst offender, however, is no longer with us. The IDE cable appeared in 1984 on the IBM AT, where it was used to connect the hard drive to the system board. For many years, the cable had 40 holes that plugged into 40 pins on the disk drive. There was a red stripe down the side to let you know which side was for pin 1, but it was often difficult to tell where pin 1 was on the drive, or the stripe was hard to see, or you just weren't paying attention. As a result, quite often the cable got attached upside down or misaligned, missing a couple of pins on one end or the other. Many a dead hard drive or fried controller can

**Figure 8.8**  *A keyed IDE connector*

be attributed to the fact that this cable was not mistake-proof. Various indents and tabs were added to the drive and connector, but these were not consistently located and most were not effective. It took years for the industry to remove pin 20 from each disk drive, fill in pin 20 on the connector, and finally make it impossible to make a mistake with an IDE cable (see Figure 8.8).

When we ask in a class if anyone has ever assembled a PC with an un-keyed IDE cable, we usually get a few groans, as people who've been around a while raise their hands. Then we ask anyone who had ever made a mistake with an IDE cable to lower their hands. Invariably, all hands go down. We have also had our share of IDE cable misalignments, and we know two things: Everyone who ever plugged in unkeyed IDE cables considered themselves to be an expert, and everyone knew enough to be very careful. Yet almost every one of us has, at one time or another, made a mistake plugging in that cable.

Mistakes are not the fault of the person making them, they are the fault of the system that fails to mistake-proof the places where mistakes can occur. With software, anything that can go wrong *will* eventually go wrong—just ask the people in operations if you don't believe us. So don't waste time counting the number of times individuals are "responsible" for defects and pressuring them to be more careful. Every time a defect is detected, *stop*, find the root cause, and devise a way to prevent a similar defect from occurring in the future. Perhaps a new unit test might be the proper countermeasure, but a development team should think broadly about effective ways to mistake-proof code. Get testing and operations involved in identifying potential failure points and add mistake-proofing before defects occur.

### Automation

One of most rewarding ways to mistake-proof development is to automate routine tasks.[21] Even small teams should automate everything they can, and even occasional tasks should be candidates for automation. Automation not only

---

21. For the ideas on what and how to automate, see *Pragmatic Project Automation: How to Build, Deploy and Monitor Java Applications,* by Mike Clark, Pragmatic Press, 2004. See also *Pragmatic Project Automation for .NET* by Ted Neward and Mike Clark, Pragmatic Press, forthcoming.

avoids the eventual mistakes that people will always make, it shows respect for their intelligence. Repetitive tasks are not only error prone; they send the message that it's OK to treat people like robots. People should not be doing things by rote; they should thinking about better ways of doing their job and solving problems.

---

**Examples of Automation**

1. **One Click Build:** Automating the build is the first step. After the build, fire off a set of automated tests to see if anything broke. Many teams use Ant.

2. **Scheduled Builds:** Once the build can be done in one step, it's easy to schedule it. A build can be triggered by a clock or a code check in. Quite often, teams use Cruise Control.

3. **Build Result Notification:** No sense doing a build if no one knows the results. It's easy to set up an e-mail notification if the build fails. It's fun to turn on a red semaphore or light up a red lava lamp to alert everyone to a failed build.

4. **One-Step Release:** A release probably means creating a release branch and packaging the code into a file or set of files that can be downloaded or distributed on a CD. This really should be an automated process. There is no room for error.

5. **Bullet-Proof Installation:** When the distribution files arrive at customer sites, the installation process should be automated, even if you send people on-site to help. The distribution media might include a few diagnostics tools to help when (not if) an installation fails.

---

## Test-Driven Development

As we mentioned in Chapter 2, Shigeo Shingo taught that there are two kinds of tests: tests that find defects after they occur and tests to prevent defects.[22] He regarded the first kind of tests as pure waste. The goal of lean software development is to prevent defects from getting into the code base in the first place, and the tool to do this is test-driven development.

"We can't let testers write tests before developers write code," one testing manger told us. "If we did that, the developers would simply write the code to pass the tests!" Indeed, that's the point. Some people feel that a tester's job is to

---

22. See Shigeo Shingo, *Study of 'Toyota' Production System*, Productivity Press, 1981, Chapter 2.3.

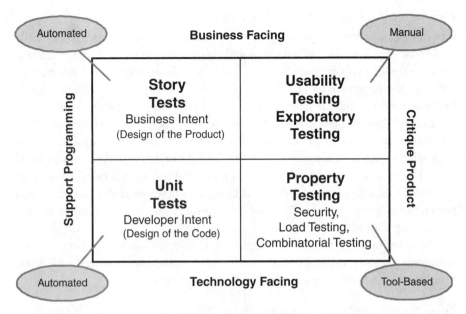

**Figure 8.9** *Types of testing*[23]

interpret the specification and translate it into tests. Instead, why not get testers involved with writing the specifications in the form of executable tests to begin with? This has the advantage of mistake-proofing the translation process, and if it's done with the right tools, it can also provide automatic traceability from specification to code. The more regulated your industry is, the more attractive executable specifications can be.

If the job of testing is to prevent defects rather than to find them, then we should consider what this means for the various kinds of tests that we typically employ. Brian Marick proposes that we look at testing from the four perspectives we see in Figure 8.9. This figure shows that testing has two purposes: We want to support programmers as they do their job, and we also need to critique the overall product that the software supports. We can do this from a technical perspective or from a business perspective. This gives us four general test categories, which we will describe briefly.

---

23. From Brian Marick, "Agile Testing Directions," available at www.testing.com/cgi-bin/blog/2003/08/21-agile-testing-project-1. Used with permission.

### Unit Tests (Also Called Programmer Tests)

Unit tests are written by developers to test that their design intent is actually carried out by the code. When developers write these tests first, they find that the code design evolves from the tests, and in fact the unit test suite becomes the software design specification. Writing tests first usually gives a simpler design because writing code that is testable leads to loose coupling of the code. Because of this virtuous circle, once developers start using test-first development, they are reluctant to develop software any other way.

A selection of unit tests are assembled into a test harness that runs at build time. The build test suite must be fast. A build and test should take less than 10 minutes, or else developers will avoid using it. Therefore the code tested with the build test suite is frequently separated from the database with mock objects to speed up execution.

The reason unit tests are sometimes called programmer tests is because programmers use unit test tools to test more than small elements of code. Unit test tools are used to test at any level: unit, feature, or system.

### Story Tests (Also Called Acceptance Tests)

Story tests identify the business intent of the system. They are the tests that determine whether the software will correctly support customers in getting their job done. When story tests are written before the code, they help everyone think through what the customers' job really involves and how it will be supported by software. The team works through examples of what the system should do, and the story tests become a specification-by-example. If we are going to write a specification ahead of time, it may as well be executable to save the waste of writing tests later and then tracing code to specifications.

Automated story tests are not usually run through the user interface; they should generally be run underneath the user interface. In order for this to work, user interfaces should be a very thin presentation layer; all logic and policies should be at lower, separately testable layers. Usually the remaining user interaction layer can be thoroughly tested separately from the business logic.[24]

Story tests should be automated and run as often as practical. Generally they are not part of the build test suite because they usually require a server or database. However, a selection of story tests should be run every day, a more complete set should run every week, and every one should pass by the end of an iteration.

---

24. Visually oriented interaction layers such as those found in graphical programs, games, and similar software are more likely to require manual inspection than transaction-oriented interfaces.

### Usability and Exploratory Testing

Usability and exploratory tests are, by definition, manual tests. When a system passes its automated tests, we know that it does what it is supposed to do, but we do not know how it will be perceived by users or what else it might do that we haven't thought to test for. During usability tests, actual users try out the system. During exploratory tests, skilled testing specialists find out what the system does at the boundaries or with unexpected inputs. When exploratory tests uncover an area of the code that is not robust, a test should be written to show developers what needs to be done, and the test should be added to the test harness.

### Property Testing

Property testing includes the so-called nonfunctional requirements such as response time, scaling, robustness, and so on. Specialized tools exist to test systems under load, to check for security problems, and so on. There are also tools that generate combinatorial tests that test every possible configuration the system might encounter. If these tools are appropriate for your environment, invest in them and develop the skills to use them well. Start using them early in the development process. Apply them in an environment that is as close as you can get to actual operational conditions.

## Configuration Management

Configuration management is a central discipline in any software development environment, and agile practices create significant demands on a configuration management system. Consider that:

1. Any area of code can be worked on by several people at a time.

2. Releases are small and frequent.

3. As one set of features is released to production, new features are being developed.

4. The entire code base constantly undergoes refactoring (continuous improvement).

   The configuration management system is the librarian that checks out code lines to people who will change them, then files the new versions correctly when they are checked back in. It can be used to manage repositories of not only code, but also documentation and test results, a particularly useful feature in a regulated environment. Every development organization should have a configuration management system that supports the scenarios used in the organization, and it should establish policies governing how the system is used.

Here are some typical scenarios handled by configuration management systems:[25]

1. Developers check out files into their private workspace. They make changes, then just before checking the code back in, they merge the changes with the current code base on their machine and do a private build and test. If everything works, they check their new code into the configuration management system, which triggers a public build and test.

2. At the time of a release, a branch is created that includes all the code to be included in the release. Developers continue adding new features to the main code line. Any changes that are made in the release during testing or maintenance are merged back into the main code line as soon as possible. (When code is released as part of the iteration, or a branch is deployed without modification, this scenario is unnecessary.)

## Continuous Integration

Whenever code is checked out to a private workspace or branched into a separate code line, incompatibilities will arise across the two code lines. The longer parallel code lines exist, the more incompatibilities there will be. The more frequently they are integrated, the easier it will be to spot incipient problems and determine their cause. This is so fundamental that you would expect continuous integration to be standard practice everywhere. But it's not so simple. First of all, it is counterintuitive for developers to check in their code frequently; their instincts are to make sure that an entire task is complete before making it public. Secondly, lengthy set-up times exacerbate the problem. Private builds take time. Checking in code takes time. Public builds and tests can take a lot of time. Stopping to fix problems discovered in the builds and tests can really slow things down. So there is strong incentive to accumulate large batches of code before integrating it into the code base.

Stretching out the time between integration is false economy. The lean approach is to attack the set-up time and drive it down to the point where continuous integration is fast and painless. This is a difficult discipline, partly because developing a rapid build and test capability requires time, skill, and ongoing attention, and partly because stopping to fix problems can be distracting. But a great epiphany occurs once a software development team finds ways

---

25. For many additional scenarios and considerations on how to use configuration management systems, see Brad Appleton's articles at: www.cmwiki.com/AgileSC-MArticles.

to do rapid builds and continuous integration and everyone faithfully stops to fix problems as soon as they are detected. We have been told many times that this is a very difficult discipline to put in place, but once it is working, no one would ever think of going back to the old way of doing things. Invariably teams experience an accelerating ability to get work done, which makes believers out of the skeptics.

## Nested Synchronization

As we mentioned earlier in this chapter, large systems should have a divisible architecture that allows teams to work concurrently and independently on subsystems. But that is not the whole story. What happens when the independent teams try to merge these subsystems? In theory, the interfaces have been well defined and are stable, and there are no surprises when the subsystems are eventually integrated. In practice, it hardly ever works that way. In fact, the failure of subsystem integration at the end of development programs has been one of the biggest causes of escalating schedules, escalating costs, and failed programs.

If you think of software as a tree and the subsystems as branches, you might get a picture of where the problem might be. Generally you would not grow branches separately from each other and then try to graft them onto the trunk of a tree. Similarly, we should not be developing subsystems separately from each other and then try to graft them onto a system. We should grow subsystems from a live trunk—if the trunk doesn't exist, we should build it first. The subsystems will then be organically integrated with the system, and we don't have to worry about trying to graft everything together at the end.

The rule we stated for parallel code lines also holds for larger subsystems: The longer parallel development efforts exist, the more incompatibilities there will be. The more frequently they are integrated, the easier it will be to spot incipient problems and determine their cause. Instead of defining interfaces and expecting them to work, we should actually *build* the interfaces first, get them working, and then build the subsystems, synchronizing them with each other as frequently as practical.

How does this work in practice? It starts with continuous integration. Several times a day developers check in code, which triggers an automatic build and test to verify that everything is still synchronized at the micro level. An acceptance test harness is run overnight. Various configurations and platforms may be tested over the weekend. Every iteration the entire code base is synchronized and brought to a "releasable" state. It may also be synchronized with other subsystems or perhaps with hardware. Every release the code is deployed to synchronize with customers.

With large systems and geographically dispersed teams, nested synchronization is even more critical, because it provides a basis for continual communication and regularly aggregates the collective knowledge of the teams in one place. Teams working on closely related subsystems should synchronize their work by working off of a common code base. Major subsystems should be brought together at the end of every iteration. On large projects, the entire system should be synchronized as frequently as practical. Using Polaris as an example, full-system synchronization points occurred when the first missile was launched, when the A1 was tested, when it deployed, and so on. These full-system synchronization points were never more than 18 months apart, and you can be sure that there were many more subsystem synchronization points. Although 18 months may seem like a long time, full-system synchronization occurred six times more frequently than called for in the original Polaris schedule.

Full-system synchronization means bringing the system into a "ready to release" state, as far as that is practical. If there are any live field tests that can be run, synchronization points are the time to run them. All participating teams and key customers should be involved in analysis and critical decision making at each synchronization point. Major synchronization points are not a one-day event. They are several days set aside to thoroughly analyze the system's readiness, absorb what has been learned, focus on key decisions that must be made at that point, make any necessary course corrections, plan the next stage in some detail, and celebrate the current success.

## Try This

1. We have used the terms "release plan," "backlog," and "product road map" more or less interchangeably. Do these terms mean the same thing in your environment? If not, how and why are they different? How long is each one, in terms of weeks of work?

2. How long is an iteration in your environment? Why do you use that cadence? Does the work of clearly defining the details of the customer problem happen inside of or prior to the iteration?

3. Discuss in a team meeting: What is the difference between story-test driven development and unit-test driven development? What are the advantages and disadvantages of each? Which do you use? Which *should* you use?

4.  On a scale of 0–5 (with 0 = low and 5 = high) rate your organization on:

    a.  Standardized architecture

    b.  Standardized tools

    c.  Coding conventions

    d.  Configuration management

    e.  Automated unit tests

    f.  Automated acceptance tests

    g.  One-click build and test

    h.  Continuous integration

    i.  Automated release

    j.  Automated installation

    Total your score.

5.  At your next team meeting, ask the team to take a look at your team room. Rate its general appearance on a scale of 0–5 (high). Now rate the general neatness and simplicity of your code base on the same scale. Are the results similar? If you have a score of 3 or lower, propose to the team that you do a 5S exercise, first on the room and then on the code base.

6.  Who is responsible for setting standards? Who should be? How closely are standards followed? How easily are they changed? Is there a connection between the last two answers in your organization?

# Chapter 9

# Partners

## Synergy

"A world class 'varsity eight' (plus coxswain) can cover 2,000 meters over the water in about 5.5 minutes. However, a single sculler can at best row the same distance in about 7 minutes. The difference is synergy, and if rowing faster were a matter of survival, the cooperators would be the fittest."[1]

Partnerships are not about cost reduction, they are not about risk reduction, nor are they about adding capacity. The fundamental reason for partnerships is *synergy*, people—and companies—can achieve better results through cooperation than they can individually.

## Emergency!

**Tuesday, December 2, 2003.** A serious security breach was discovered in a Gentoo Linux server in an Italian University. The system administrator traced problem as best he could, then through a chain of contacts, got in touch with a developer in Australia who had once led the development of that area of code. The developer dropped everything and worked through the Italian night with the system administrator to pinpoint the exact location of the breach. Then he rounded up a friend, and they worked through the Australian night writing a patch. They sent the patch to a small group of Gentoo Linux user-developers. who had been alerted to stand by for testing. Less that 30 hours after the attack was discovered, an announcement of the breach and the tested patch were distributed to Linux users worldwide.

---

1. "The Synergism Hypothesis: On the Concept of Synergy and Its Role in the Evolution of Complex Systems," by Peter A. Corning, Ph.D., *Journal of Social and Evolutionary Systems*, 21(2), 1998.

This story was told by Philip Evans and Bob Wolf in the *Harvard Business Review* article "Collaboration Rules."[2] They summarized, "No one authorized or directed this effort. No one—amateur or professional—was paid for participating or would have been sanctioned for not doing so. No one's job hinged on stopping the attack. No one clammed up for fear of legal liability. Indeed, the larger user community was kept informed of all developments. Yet despite the need for the highest security, a group of some 20 people, scarcely any of whom had ever met, employed by a dozen different companies, living in as may time zones and straying far from their job descriptions, accomplished in about 29 hours what might have taken colleagues in adjacent cubicles weeks or months."[3]

**Saturday, February 1, 1997.**[4] An early morning fire leveled Aisin plant number one, the one that made all of the P-Valves that go into Toyota automobiles. A P-Valve is a cigarette-box-sized part that controls pressure to rear brake lines, and Toyota had maybe two or three days of inventory on hand. P-Valves are high-precision parts made by specialized tools, but theoretically they could be made with general purpose machine tools. Aisin immediately put out a call asking every company with machine tools for help. Sixty-two companies responded, and within hours, blueprints for the valve were picked up and tooling systems were improvised. The volunteers coordinated among themselves as they figured out how to produce the high-precision valves, and Denso stepped in to coordinate the messy logistics. Even as Toyota shut down all of its plants on Tuesday, a small supplier, Kyoritsu Sangyo, proudly delivered the first 1,000 production quality valves. By Thursday, 36 suppliers, aided by 150 subcontractors, were producing small batches of P-Valves, and Toyota began reopening its plants. One week after the fire, Toyota was back at full production of over 16,000 cars a day, each one containing two hand-machined P-Valves. It took Aisin six weeks to rebuild its line, and eventually it paid all of the interim suppliers for their time. Toyota also gave each first-tier supplier a bonus to show its appreciation, which they promptly passed down to second- and third-tier suppliers.

"The parallels between these stories are striking,"[5] according to Evans and Wolf. "In both of them, individuals found one another and stepped into roles without a plan or an established command-and-control structure. An extended

---

2. This section is a summary of two stories told in "Collaboration Rules," Philip Evans and Bob Wolf, *Harvard Business Review*, July–August, 2005.

3. Ibid., p. 99.

4. Ibid. See also "The Toyota Group and the Aisin Fire," by Toshihiro Nishiguchi and Alexandre Beaudet, *Sloan Management Review*, Fall, 1998.

5. Ibid., p. 100. Italics in original.

human network organized itself in hours and 'swarmed' against a threat. People, teams, and companies worked together without legal contracts or negotiated payment. And despite the lack of any authoritarian stick or financial carrot, those people worked *like hell* to solve the problem."

The people and companies that responded to these two emergencies were used to working together. They had already established an understanding of how to communicate with each other to get things done. They had learned to do this with no visible leader, each person or organization taking on whatever needed doing if they had the skills to contribute. Fueled by trust and paid with applause, each community was governed not by contracts or hierarchies, but by rules about how people and teams work together and how they communicate.

## Open Source

We know that excellent software can be developed and maintained by volunteers working around the world with a few simple communication tools and some basic rules. In fact, many of the people developing Open Source software have day jobs as software developers. Some might even get paid by their employers to contribute to an Open Source effort. More often than not, Open Source contributions come from developers who modify an existing program to solve a problem of their own and then share the results. But none of this explains the underlying success of the Open Source model.

Most Open Source projects have a leader, at least in the beginning. All Open Source projects have "committers," a trusted inner circle of people who have the authority to commit new code to the code base. Originally, the project originator is the committer, but as the project grows, more developers earn the right to join the inner circle of committers. The committers enforce any standards that may have been established and act as a first-line reviewer. It is an honor for new members to have their code committed, although contributing code that hasn't been thoroughly tested is embarrassing. The active community for any project provides merciless reviews of code once they see it, enforcing standards through aggressive peer pressure. This is definitely a challenging team sport with great psychological rewards for making an outstanding contribution.

Many people have obsessions that thoroughly absorb their attention outside of work. With Open Source that obsession just happens to be writing code. There is something about software that can be terribly engaging. We might ask ourselves what we can do to make software development similarly engaging in our organization.

Going back to Deming's 14 points, point 12 is probably the most important: Eliminate barriers that rob people of their right to pride in workmanship. Artificial deadlines, managers with no idea about what good code really is, sloppy code bases and coding practices, no way to see if new code works, no idea what the users really want, individual rewards for team contributions—all of these rob every member of the development team of pride in workmanship. Pride builds commitment, and without mutual commitment a group really isn't a team.

What if a software development leader had a job description similar to a project leader in Open Source? To get volunteers to work on Open Source, a new project leader needs an attractive idea and a good approach. To keep volunteers committed, the leader—and later the committer community—must recognize, appreciate, and applaud good work. Good work means solving the problem (the developers are also the customers in most cases so they really understand the problem) with concise, readable code, committed into the system in very small pieces. Open Source developers will not waste their time working on software that is messy or broken—or if they do, they start by fixing it. And nobody, really, tells Open Source developers what to do. They are perfectly capable of figuring that out for themselves.

For a disciplined, competent development team, there is no currency that can beat respect, trust, and applause.

## Global Networks

The Boeing 787 Dreamliner is being designed and developed by a global network because Boeing believes that the synergy of many cultures with varying areas of expertise will result in a superior aircraft. Procter & Gamble decided that it needed new ideas faster than it could generate them, so now it searches for innovative ideas throughout a global network and brings them inside to develop into products.[6] Tapping into worldwide innovation talent is not the only reason for global networks. Both companies realize that they must sell their products worldwide, so global networks are necessary to help them understand and meet the needs of global markets.

---

6. "Connect and Develop: Inside Procter & Gamble's New Model for Innovation," by Larry Huston and Nabil Sakkab, *Harvard Business Review*, March 2006, pp. 58–66.

In software development we have our own well-respected global network: Open Source communities. From Open Source we learn that people don't need to be in the same time zone to work closely together on software. The question is, what *do* people need to collaborate closely on software development, especially if they are not in the same location?

Let's reexamine the two stories at the beginning of this section. The first thing Aisin did was put out a call for help, and 62 companies responded. Everyone was engaged in getting Toyota's production back on track; it was a matter of both pride and mutual economic necessity. With commitment established, the focus switched to communication. During the crisis after the fire, Aisin could give blueprints to everyone, but it couldn't help the suppliers figure out how to machine the P-Valve. Aisin made automated equipment; it had little experience in using machine tools. Suppliers figured out how to machine the part by organizing daily meetings among themselves so machinists could talk to other machinists about what they were learning.

Fixing the security breach in Linux started with the commitment of a former project leader in Australia to fix a flaw in code he had worked on. Many people had come to depend on it, so as matter of pride, he jumped in to help. He spent hours in one-on-one communication with the system administrator in Italy before they pinpointed the exact spot in the code that was at fault. Then he paired with a friend who lived nearby to develop the patch, because tough problem solving is better done by bouncing ideas off of someone else—especially when it takes all night.

We are often asked how to improve the communication channels of global teams, but all too often we find that the root of the problem is not communication, it is the absence of a committed team. Global networks and distributed work groups do not become teams just because someone calls them teams. Providing channels for rich communication is very important when team members are located in different time zones, but it is hardly sufficient to change a work group into a team.

The challenge of creating synergy among people who are geographically disbursed is very similar to the challenge of creating synergy among people who are co-located: Above all, team members must be mutually committed to achieving a common purpose. With global teams the challenge of mutual commitment simply has an added dimension: Effective communication among team members is more difficult.

**From Global Work Groups to Global Teams**

Here are some techniques that we have found helpful in creating commitment and facilitating communication among work groups that are widely separated by geography:

1.  **Frequent Integration:** Very often, a work group is made up of several small teams, each in a separate location. If team responsibilities reflect the system's functional architecture, then the teams can usually work on separable modules relatively independently. This can be a very effective structure, but the teams *must* use nested synchronization, integrating their efforts frequently. Regular, frequent integration has many benefits, from establishing mutual commitment to creating a common repository of knowledge. The faster knowledge is communicated through the code base, the easier the code is to understand, the better the programmer tests communicate what each local team intends, the better their combined results will be.

2.  **Exchange People:** All too often we find that a team in one country has all of the necessary technical capabilities to develop a system, but their "requirements" come in large batches of written documents developed many time zones away. Predictably, when the application is finished several weeks or months after the arrival of the requirements, it isn't what the customers really wanted. Large separations between customers or analysts and the implementation team—with over-the-wall communication—seldom works very well. The best way to deal with this situation is to locate a couple of people from one team on the other team for extended periods of time, preferably on a rotating basis. Either a couple of team members that understand customers should be located with the development team, or alternatively, a couple of people who are part of the development team should be located with those who understand the customers. Rotating people through these positions is even more effective.

3.  **Exchange Tests:** We are familiar with one case in which moving requirements between teams was handled by sending executable tests, rather than requirements, to the remote team. The people who understood the customers developed detailed tests that the code had to pass. They sent the remote team tests. If the code passed the tests then it was considered to be working. Nevertheless, they found that unless the iterations were closed out and tested at the customer site once a week, the distance was too great and the remote team would drift away from delivering what the customer really wanted.

4. **Proxy:** We have seen very successful dispersed teams that communicate through a single person. Someone from a remote site becomes a member of a core team and serves as a proxy for the remainder of the remote team. Every day this person assumes responsibility for a large amount of well-defined work and sends it to the remote team, calling them each day to describe what needs to be done, answer questions, and retrieve completed work. Thus, the remote team maintains rich communication with one person on the core team, and the core team considers the remote team an extension of this proxy, who can take on work for several people.

5. **Traveling Team Leader:** In one case we know of, each co-located subteam had an Oobeya, or "war room," with the big visible charts showing project status and issues. The status charts were maintained identically in each of four rooms around the world. The program leader traveled from one room to another, holding regular status meetings at each location. The other locations called in to the meetings, which renewed the mutual commitment of all teams to their common objective.

6. **No Second-Class Citizens:** When part of a team must work using a second language while other team members use their first language, or when one group is a subcontractor while the other is part of the contracting company, or when one group clearly has higher pay or status than the other, people can easily get the perception that one group is "better" than the other. Such perceptions will quickly destroy the respect, trust, and commitment that are essential for true teamwork.

## The Light Fiber Team

Nishijima-san decided that our plastic light conductor would make a great product for Sumitomo-3M. We toured the United States together for three weeks to look at possible applications, and Nishijima-san returned to Japan to form a team. At any given time over the next two-and-a-half years, he sent at least two engineers from his team to join my team in the United States. The engineers rotated so that everyone spent several months on the US team, contributing to our work and learning about the optics and the technology. Every night the Japanese engineers called in to a team meeting in Japan to keep everyone informed. Then at our meetings they brought us up to date on the progress in Japan.

We tried video conference calls, but they didn't work very well. Fortunately, they didn't need to, because whoever was in the United States from Japan was a full team member, and every night they drew their colleagues into our team. When we traveled to Japan we knew everyone on the team and felt like we were a part of their team. We jointly chose the brand name to work well in any language. If I were to do it again, I'd do it the same way, except that I would send two engineers to Japan in exchange for the engineers Nishijima-san sent us.

Probably the biggest concern was joint intellectual property, even though 3M and Sumitomo-3M were very closely associated and had intellectual property agreements. However, with the Sumitomo-3M engineers on our team full-time, we couldn't do much to sort out who came up with what ideas. So the vice president sponsoring the program told us to ignore the issue, and he asked the lawyers sort it out. I am convinced that this decision was critical in helping our teams feel like equals. Over time, we had several joint inventions. In fact, I was named on one of the joint patents.

—Mary Poppendieck

## Outsourcing

Global teams may exist entirely within a single company, or they may cross company boundaries. Actually, the same is true of local teams: Members may come from within a single company or from different companies. Outsourcing involves having some of your company's work done by another company—that may be a company down the street or half a world away. Outsourcing adds a different dimension than distance. It raises the question of allegiance. When workers make trade-off decisions, how do they weigh the interests of their own company, the other company, and the joint venture? And how do they balance that with the continued existence of their own jobs?

The best outsourcing arrangements make the answer to these questions very clear: The best interests of the individual companies and their respective employees will be best served by furthering the best interests of the joint venture. Without such clarity, we subject workers to veiled conflicts of interest. How can such conflicts of interest be avoided? The answer depends on what kind of work is being outsourced. Let's take a look at three possibilities: infrastructure, transactions, and development.

### Infrastructure

When we started our business in 1999, we knew we needed a Web site and e-mail capability, but we had no interest in setting up a server. So we found a company (which happens to be in Canada) that would host our Web site and provide e-mail for a modest monthly sum. Over the years the company has improved its offerings and lowered its prices to the point where we sometimes wonder why any small business would host its own Web site and e-mail server. We don't worry about downtime, security, or even growth. The service is very easy to use, and in the few instances where we've needed technical support, the response was more than satisfactory.

We have outsourced infrastructure—which is probably the easiest thing to outsource. The expected features of the infrastructure are well defined in the marketplace, provided by many vendors, and competitively priced. While we are technically competent to provide our own infrastructure, we get a lot better return on our time if we spend it elsewhere. It makes a lot of sense to outsource infrastructure when the market can provide it more competently and cost-effectively than you can. Most people are comfortable with outsourcing infrastructure.

### Transactions

Another thing that can be outsourced is transactions. For example, a company that has to transcribe a lot of paper documents to an electronic format can scan the documents and then ship them anywhere in the world for transcription. Because transcription is labor intensive, sending the documents to a country with low labor rates can be very cost-effective.

But there is a caution here: What if the real competitive advantage in the industry will go to the company that figures how to capture the data electronically and dispense with the paper documents? Companies that outsource the transcription to lower their costs will lose the incentive to ask themselves why the documents need to be transcribed in the first place. Before outsourcing transactions, simplify the value stream first and try to eliminate the need for the transactions.

Most of the conflict of interest in outsourced transactions lies in a piece-work approach to compensation. When an outsourcer is paid on a per-transaction basis, their incentive is to reduce the amount of time per transaction. But if the real value lies in reducing the *number* of transactions, piece-work compensation systems create a conflict between allegiance to one's employer and allegiance to the company that generates the transactions.

For example, in Chapter 2 we told the story of how BMI, a UK airline, outsourced its call center to Fujitsu. Typically call center outsourcers are paid based on the number of calls (transactions) that they handle, but Fujitsu was able to show BMI that it could reduce the number of calls it handled *and* decrease BMI's operating expenses at the same time. Thus, Fujitsu was able to convince BMI to shift the incentive so that payment was on based on *potential* callers, so they could make money by helping BMI save money—a win-win partnership. This approach to compensation makes it crystal clear that looking out for the good of the joint venture is in everyone's best interest.

### Development

Just as outsourcing infrastructure makes a lot of sense, outsourcing software development for common industry processes—purchasing for example—could also make a lot of sense. You can expect to get the industry average with this kind of outsourcing, however, because your outsourcing provider is usually working with other companies in your industry. If your practices are below par, then outsourcing is a quick way to bring them up to the industry average. Outsourcing this kind of development is basically the same as outsourcing infrastructure—and it rarely raises issues of allegiance.

Some companies outsource a portion of development—for example, manual testing through a user interface is often outsourced because it is so labor intensive. The real advantage, however, goes to the company that realizes that testing does not need to be done manually through the user interface. This company will automate testing beneath the user interface and then integrate that testing as far back in the development process as possible. In fact, it will try to write the tests first and then write the code to pass the tests. This company will have a significant competitive advantage in its entire software development process over the company that outsources the manual testing.

Outsourcing the development of key components of your product or the software that supports key differentiators in your process requires careful consideration. Some companies keep this kind of development entirely internal, providing a key lever to create competitive advantage. Other companies have learned to outsource these critical areas of development effectively. For example, in the United States, more than 70 percent of the parts in a Toyota car are both developed and manufactured by suppliers.[7] The global innovation networks of Boeing and Procter & Gamble mentioned earlier in this chapter give them access to the most technically advanced thinking in the world, no matter where it exists. Thus, advanced development that used to be done internally is now carried out in partnership with other companies.

Companies that gain a significant advantage from outsourcing critical development areas operate from a few basic principles:

1. The reason for outsourcing critical capabilities is motivated by the need for access to a broader set of technical capabilities than the company possesses or to broaden its market understanding and reach, or both.

2. Outsourcing of critical capabilities is always set up to be a win-win partnership. The partnership is not just *expected* to create synergy it is *managed* to

---

7. See Jeffrey H. Dyer, *Collaborative Advantage: Winning Through Extended Enterprise Supplier Networks*, Oxford University Press, 2000, p. 33.

create synergy. The compensation system, interaction rules, and management expectations give clear signals to the workers that loyalty to the joint venture is equivalent to loyalty to their individual companies, and a successful joint venture will serve their best interests

3. Companies exhibit a deep respect for their partners, and this respect is embedded in the processes and procedures they use to frame the details of the partnership.

Supplier management—done well—can bring the same dramatic advantages to the development world that supply chain management brought to the manufacturing world. It all starts with a recognition that outsourcing is not about cost reduction, it is not about risk reduction, it's not even about adding capacity. It's about creating a synergy. It's about coming to the realization that by rowing together, the companies can get to the finish line faster than even the strongest of them could manage alone.

## Contracts

What is the purpose of contracts? There are two schools of thought on this question:

1. The purpose of contracts is to protect each party from opportunistic behavior on the part of the other party.

2. The purpose of contracts is to set up appropriate incentives for companies to work together in a synergistic manner.

Depending on which approach you take, contracts can make lean software development impractical in a contracting environment, or it can set up a framework for all parties to work together to achieve the best results possible.

### The T5 Agreement

BAA manages most of the major airports in the United Kingdom, and it was a public entity until the 1987. It started building Terminal 5 at Heathrow airport in 2002 and is scheduled to open the terminal on March 30, 2008. The project is huge—it will cost of 4.2 billion. From the beginning, BAA realized that it simply could not afford the kind of cost overruns and extended deadlines that are so typical of projects of this size. Any significant delay in the project, for any reason, no matter who was at fault, would be a death knell for BAA.

So BAA studied what went wrong on airport projects with large delays and overruns, as well as other public projects that went badly astray. It came to the conclusion that the contracting process was the cause of the problems. In a stroke of management innovation, BAA realized that the essential problem was that contracts try to dispose of risk by selling it to contractors. The contractors charge more for assuming the risk, but in the end, if there are problems, it would be BAA that suffered, not the contractors. So BAA decided to assume and manage the project risk itself, because it could not afford to leave performance up to contracts and the courts.

BAA devised what it calls the T5 Agreement—a legally binding document that replaces conventional contracts and changes the rules of the construction game. BAA agrees to assume all risk—and in return the contractors agree to work in integrated teams, mitigate risks, and work to achieve the best possible results. The project is broken into about 150 subprojects, each of which has a team of contractors, an agreed target cost, and a pool of risk/incentive money. Contractors are paid for their time and materials. If something has to be redone, there are no arguments, they still get paid. If the subproject exceeds its target cost, the money comes out of the risk/incentive pool for that subproject. At the end of the subproject, the team that worked on it splits two thirds of any money remaining in the risk/incentive pool.

The T5 Agreement addresses both risk and incentives in a completely unorthodox way that BAA is convinced is saving it a significant amount of money while keeping its risks low. The agreement raises the threshold for conflict and lowers the cost of collaboration, putting all of the incentives in place for independent contractors to collaborate with each other. Between BAA supervision, peer pressure, and pride in workmanship, the teams have not only gotten things done on time, but they have caught up on several weeks of slippage due to bad weather. To date the project is "spot on schedule," and there is every expectation that Terminal 5 will be pretty close to ready for its planned opening on March 30, 2008.

## The PS 2000 Contract

The PS 2000 contract was developed by Norwegian Computer Society in alliance with the Norwegian University of Science and Technology (NTNU) and leading industry and public organizations in Norway. Developed specifically for use in large public IT projects, the PS 2000 contract came from the observation that it is often difficult to draw up a detailed specification of an IT system during the procurement and tendering process. It is based on the following premises:

1. Best practices show that a flexible iterative development model is more suited to the uncertainties and risks of many large-scale IT projects.

2. This requires mechanisms for establishing a common understanding between the contracting party and the customer.

3. The party developing the system is the most qualified to find the best way to meet the objectives and needs of the customer.[8]

The unique thing about the PS 2000 contract is that it is a contract about how the customer and the contractor will work together, not a specification of what will be delivered. The body of the contract establishes decision-making boards, names mediators in case of disagreement, and specifies the general rights and obligations of each party. The project objectives and target cost are called out in annexes. The contract specifies the method by which the system will be iteratively explored, and as more details are agreed upon, the objectives are replaced by the agreed-upon details in an iterative manner. The target cost annex specifies the method by which both parties will share in any savings or overrun and provides an upper limit and lower limit for the overall cost.

## Relational Contracts

Both the T5 Agreement and the PS 2000 contract are *relational contracts*[9]—that is, they describe the relationships of the parties rather than the expected results of the relationship. Relational agreements are focused on aligning the incentives of the parties with the good of the joint venture. The underlying assumption is that people will naturally look out for the interests of their own company, so a relational agreement is specifically constructed to make it clear to people doing the work that the best interests of their individual companies are best served when they focus on the best interests of the joint venture.

---

8. From http://dataforeningen.no/?module=Articles;action=ArticleFolder.publicOpen-Folder;ID=1044, February 2006. See this Web site for more information.

9. The Lean Construction Institute has more on relational contracts at www.leanconstruction.org.

## A Joint Venture

Our two companies had very novel, complementary technologies and we figured that by combining them we could come up with a truly innovative product. But separately, the technologies were the basis for a very large portion of the business of each company. There was no way we could risk working together until we signed a joint venture agreement, which protected the intellectual property of each company.

It was challenging to work out the details. My colleague at the other company and I knew exactly how we wanted to work together, but we needed a way to define how joint inventions would be defined, how they would be handled, how the prior intellectual property of each company would be protected, what would happen if either side opted out of the joint venture, and so on. We spent very little time and effort worrying about how the research would proceed—we set up a governing board to oversee that—or how the costs would be split—that would be easy. We spent just a bit more time ironing out the profit-sharing details of the agreement.

The really difficult part was creating an agreement that would allow scientists and engineers from both companies to sit in a room and jointly brainstorm ideas about how their technologies could work together to make a superior product. This was a true challenge because what was at stake was the most precious asset of each company: its intellectual property.

The agreement took a couple of months to work out, and in the end, it was all about how we would work together. With the document signed and tucked out of the way on a shelf, we could finally get on with the business of working together.

—Mary Poppendieck

Peter Drucker estimated that collaborative relationships can save a joint venture 25 percent to 30 percent of the cost of doing business.[10] We certainly see this in the case of BAA: Raising the threshold for conflict and lowering the threshold for risk among its many subcontractors significantly reduced both risk and cost for BAA. Throughout this book we have seen that a lean approach to software development can create significant improvements in the quality of the software, the speed of delivery, and the long-term maintainability of the system. We have seen that these benefits come from the synergy of people who

---

10. Peter Drucker, *Management Challenges for the 21st Century*, Harper Business, 2001, p. 33.

combine their skill and experience to create knowledge more effectively together than they can separately.

Most software development contracts are predicated on a different set of assumptions. They include a product specification as part of the language of the contract and assume that the specification substantially represents the desired result. If that assumption is in error, most contracts offer ineffective remedies. A relational contract starts with the assumption that the product cannot be effectively specified in the contract, so the language focuses on how the parties will work together to determine *what* to deliver.

Relational contracts generally designate a target cost and a target schedule. Both parties agree to work together, using the mechanisms in the contract, to deliver the best possible value within the cost and schedule targets. The contract sets up incentives for both parties to work collaboratively for the good of the joint venture and reduces incentives for parties to advance their separate interests.

The use of relational contracts in software development is a new and emerging area. We believe that those who learn how to forge synergistic relationships across company boundaries will see at least the 25 percent to 30 percent cost reduction predicted by Drucker, and quite possibly they will do significantly better.

## Try This

1.  At the next team meeting, find out if anyone has ever contributed to an Open Source project. If so, ask each one to answer these questions: Why did you spend your free time coding? How long did you do it? How much time did you spend?

    If appropriate, ask these questions as well: What kept you doing it for such a long time? Why did you stop? What did you like best about working on Open Source? What was the thing that annoyed you the most?

2.  Identify a "global team" in your world, and brainstorm with others involved with the team the answers to the following questions:

    a.  Is this a single team or an association of teams in different locations?

    b.  Are members of the team committed to a common goal? What is it? Would everyone on the team agree that this is a goal they are personally committed to achieve?

    c. How do people in different locations know if they have done a good job? Where does applause come from?

If you did not involve people at all locations in this exercise, then have people in a different location repeat the exercise and compare answers.

3. What is the primary purpose of outsourcing in your company? What kinds of activities does the company keep inside rather than outsource? Are the incentives of outsourcing agreements aligned with the best interests of your company and your customers? Can you imagine ways in which your outsourcing arrangements might create questions of allegiance in the minds of workers in your company? In the other company?

4. For contracting companies: What kinds of contracts do you routinely use? What do you see as the key benefit of that kind of contract? What is the key risk? If you were in the shoes of your contractors, what would you see as the benefits and risks of that kind of contract?

5. For contractors: What kinds of contracts do you routinely engage in? Are some types better for you than others? Consider your favorite contracting format and reconsider it from the point of view of the contracting companies. What do you see as the benefits and risks for them?

# Chapter 10

# Journey

## Where Do You Want to Go?

"What do I do next?" we often hear. "My company is in a world of hurt, and it *really* needs to get better. Lean principles make a lot of sense. But what do I do with principles? How do I implement them—right now—in my company?"

This reminds us of Alice as she wandered through Wonderland:[1]

'Would you tell me, please, which way I ought to go from here?'
'That depends a good deal on where you want to get to,' said the Cat.
'I don't much care where—' said Alice.
'Then it doesn't matter which way you go,' said the Cat.
—so long as I get somewhere' Alice added as an explanation.
'Oh, you're sure to do that,' said the Cat, 'if you only walk long enough.'

In Chapter 7 we recommend that you start a lean initiative by answering two questions:

1.  How do you create value for customers and make a profit?

2.  What, exactly, is your main problem right now?

To this we add two more questions:

3.  What threatens your continued existence in the future?

4.  What do you *really* believe about people?

---

1.  *Alice's Adventures in Wonderland* by Reverend Charles Lutwidge Dodgson under the pseudonym Lewis Carroll, originally published in 1865.

## A Computer on Wheels

During the late 1970s and early 1980s, Toyota was doing very well. But in 1985, the value of the yen started its steep fall against other currencies, prompting Japanese automakers to move manufacturing abroad to satisfy foreign markets. As a result, Japan found itself with more automotive manufacturing capacity than the domestic market could hope to absorb, which drove prices down and created a severe downward pressure on profits. As the low-cost producers, Honda and Toyota were able to sustain a high level of R&D, but the other Japanese automakers cut back on development, which led to a downward spiral in sales. Eventually the main Japanese automakers, except Honda and Toyota, were purchased by global groupings such as GM, Ford, Daimler-Chrysler, and Renault. Suddenly Honda and Toyota were competing with these global groupings on their home turf.[2]

At the same time, the Toyota Production System became well known and widely copied. As other automakers became more efficient, Toyota's lead as the world's most efficient auto producer narrowed. Technical advances in vehicle features were rapidly copied—for example, as the market moved to minivans and SUV's, most auto companies rapidly followed. Furthermore, with the rest of the world comparatively saturated with automobiles, it was clear that the future growth market would move to Asia.

In this atmosphere, Toyota developed a long-range strategy for creating a sustainable competitive advantage. That strategy, best expressed as *Smart Design, Smart Production, Smart Car*, centered on using information technology to make profit-generating innovations difficult to copy. During the 1990s, Toyota became a very competent information systems company.

Under the *Smart Production* banner, Toyota replaced the traditional single assembly line with a half dozen short lines separated by buffer stock and synchronized by software, giving it a boost in productivity that is difficult to copy. *Smart Design* included digitizing A3 production standards and developing a way to simulate manufacturing processes on CAD systems during the design process, greatly speeding up time to market for new cars. The *Smart Car* initiative prompted major investments in developing internal electronic manufacturing and embedded software capability, enabling Toyota to launch the Prius in

---

2. Information for this section came from *Automobiles: Toyota Motor Corporation: Gaining and Sustaining Long-term Advantage Through Information Technology,* case prepared for the Columbia Project: Use of Software to Achieve Competitive Advantage, by William V. Rapp Co-Principal Investigator The College of International Relations Ritsumeikan University Kyoto, Japan, April 2000.

Japan in 1999. With drive-by-wire throttle, brake, and shift controls, the surprisingly popular hybrid is truly a computer on wheels.

Toyota's success with information technology comes as something of a surprise, since the company has a reputation for its minimalist approach to IT. While competitors built highly automated plants to reduce the labor content in vehicles, Toyota experimented with automation and didn't find that it would pay off when the total cost was considered. While competitors invested heavily in computerized scheduling systems and cross-docking automation, Toyota felt that people should be at the center of the manufacturing process and that simple manual systems would work better. Toyota management has traditionally resisted using information systems to manage material flow and production scheduling.[3] We find it remarkable that a company that has been so cautious about using information systems would become such a leader in leveraging these systems in its production processes, in its development approach, and in its products.

## A Long-Term Perspective

Some companies survive for hundreds of years—but not very many. In *The Living Company*, Arie de Geus points out that the average life expectancy of a multinational corporation—Fortune 500 or equivalent—is between 40 and 50 years.[4] People live for an average of 75 years, so they can expect to outlast perhaps three quarters of the companies that existed when they were born. The average life expectancy of well-established companies is an order of magnitude less than the longest-lived companies. No living species has such a wide discrepancy between its average life expectancy and maximum life span.

Institutions such as churches, armies, and universities live for centuries. Why do large companies die or get acquired so young? More importantly, how can good companies survive more than a couple of generations of management? Just to make it into the list of companies de Geus studied, a company had to be very successful. Not only had the company made it past the startup phase and the growing pains of an expanding company, it had become a large multinational corporation. And then the world changed, and many of these very successful corporations failed to adapt to the new reality.

---

3. See *The Toyota Way Fieldbook* by Jeffrey Liker and David Meier, McGraw Hill, 2006, pp. 208–212.

4. Arie de Geus, *The Living Company: Habits for Survival in a Turbulent Business Environment*, Harvard Business School Press, 1997, 2002, p. 1.

Organizations that have become successful tend to establish their habits in the days when they are growing rapidly and there is plenty of market demand. But eventually all growth engines run out of fuel, and past success no longer points the way to future growth. At this point, the organizations that have developed the capability to learn and adapt are the ones that survive. De Geus believes it is the ability of managers to envision the future that enables them to adapt to that future before it is too late; but unfortunately, managers often develop "future-blindness," preferring to stay on the course that has led to success in the past.

This view of future-blindness is seconded by Clayton Christensen[5] who shows that companies that move up-market to maintain margins, leaving the less profitable down-market to their competitors, are frequently overtaken by disruptive technologies. These companies serve their current customers so well that they have little incentive to imagine a future filled with risk and low margins. We see disruptive technologies in the computer industry all the time, as smaller, faster, less power-consuming hardware replaces bigger, more profitable equipment. In software, we see inexpensive software packages replacing offerings with large per-seat fees and self-service software replacing consultant-intensive businesses. In an industry that moves as fast as ours, envisioning and being prepared to adapt to the future is a survival issue.

Toyota has a tremendous ability to learn and think in an evolutionary manner. Sakichi Toyoda counseled his son Kiichiro and nephew Eiji, "Stay ahead of the times." In 1934 the Toyoda company added car manufacturing to loom manufacturing, even though it would take two decades for the automobiles to start paying their way. In 1958, with sales of cars at barely more than 2,000 per month, Toyota built a new factory with a capacity of 10,000 cars per month to the astonishment of both its dealers and competitors.[6] But the factory positioned the company to lead the market as the Japanese economy expanded in the 1960s. In 1984 Toyota opened the New United Motor Manufacturing Incorporated (NUMMI) plant in Fremont California, positioning it to manufacture in the United States a year *before* the precipitous drop of the yen against the dollar. Toyota's *Smart* strategy was initiated with the purchase of an electronics plant in 1989, well *before* overcapacity began to plague the Japanese market. In 1995 Toyota purchased a controlling interest in Daihatsu to

---

5. See Clayton Christensen, *The Innovator's Dilemma*, Harvard Business School Press, 1997; Harper Business, 2000, and Clayton Christensen and Michael Raynor, *The Innovator's Solution*, Harvard Business School Press, 2003.

6. Eiji Toyoda, *Toyota: Fifty Years in Motion*, Kodansha, 1987. First published in Japanese in 1985.

strengthen its position in the Asian market. Today Toyota is focusing on environmentally sensitive cars and intelligent traffic systems as key avenues for future growth.[7]

An organization that expects to survive over the long term must consistently develop an insightful view of the future and base decisions on this long-range vision.

## Centered on People

Scientists will tell you that the first step in effective problem solving is to place the problem within a conceptual framework that reflects a sound understanding of how things actually work. For example, Frederick Winslow Taylor based his work on an incorrect understanding of the nature of workers—he started with the premise that front-line workers are inherently lazy and basically interchangeable. Management practices based on this attitude toward people are incapable of leveraging the intelligence of "ordinary" workers. When an organization with a culture based in mass production thinking attempts a lean initiative, the results will probably be mediocre.

There are two conceptual frameworks concerning the use of technology in the workplace. The first framework suggests that we should automate existing jobs to reduce the need for people or the skill level needed to perform the job. The second framework encourages us to use technology to enhance the capability of workers.[8] As we have seen, Toyota operates in the second framework. But what's wrong with the first? Automating routine tasks sounds like a good idea. In fact, as we noted in Chapter 8, automating repetitive tasks in the build and deployment process eliminates variation and gives us reliably consistent results.

However, removing people from a process—or expecting people to perform a process by rote—means that the process no longer has the capacity to change, to adapt, or to discover. For example, drug companies have spent billions automating the routine side of drug research. They have replaced lab technicians with robots, making it possible to test far more drug compounds than they could possibly have done before. This was supposed to lead to a lot more

---

7. See *Automobiles: Toyota Motor Corporation: Gaining and Sustaining Long-Term Advantage Through Information Technology,* case prepared for the Columbia Project: Use of Software to Achieve Competitive Advantage, by William V. Rapp Co-Principal Investigator The College of International Relations Ritsumeikan University Kyoto, Japan, April 2000.

8. Ibid., and see also Larry W. Hunter and John J. Lafkas, "Opening the Box: Information Technology, Work Practices, and Wages," Working Paper 98-02-C, Wharton, Financial Institutions Center, June 1999.

blockbuster drugs—but results have been disappointing. The reason, many speculate, is that by "deskilling" the job of drug experimentation and removing the human element, companies made implicit assumptions about what spaces should be explored and lost the human capacity to notice unexpected results and try out new experimental spaces.[9]

The difference between testing automation in drug industries and testing automation in software development is this: The drug testing automation "deskilled" testers (replaced them with robots), while effective automation of software testing "upskills" testers. That is, it automates the routine, repetitive testing in order to free testers up to focus on mistake-proofing the development process, making sure users find the software easy to use, doing exploratory testing, and property testing. In a nutshell, deskilling workers creates interchangeable people while upskilling workers creates thinking people.

The question to resolve before you embark on a lean initiative is this: What do you *really* believe about people? Consider your attitude toward process. Do you think that a well-documented process that everyone follows without question is the path to excellence? Or do you think that the reason to standardize a process is so that people doing the work have something solid to question and change? Lean principles are solidly based on the second viewpoint.

Consider your attitude toward schedules. Does it make you nervous when someone suggests that the development team should decide what can be done within a timeframe and tell managers, rather than the other way around? Or your attitude toward work assignments. Does it seem unnatural for people to figure out for themselves what to do next rather than being told?

In order for lean to work, your conceptual framework about people has to contain the fundamental belief that the people doing the work know how to do it best. You have to be nervous about automation that would eliminate people from the process or reduce the skill levels needed to do a job. You have to think it strange that many levels of authorization—or even one level of authorization—are required for decisions made on the front line. You have to really believe there is no better way to tackle problems than to give the people doing the work the training, the tools, the charter, and the support to solve their own problems and improve their own processes.

---

9. From "Supporting Cheap and Rapid Iteration (with a Human Touch)" by Robert D. Austin, Cutter Consortium Business-IT Strategies Advisory Service, April 19, 2006.

# What Have We Learned?

Before we set out to change something, it is always a good idea to survey useful ideas that already exist to see what we can learn from them. Here we will look at two initiatives: Six Sigma and Theory of Constraints.

## Six Sigma

One of the initial problems with Six Sigma initiatives, one that has long since been resolved, was an attempt to apply practices that were appropriate in manufacturing to development processes. As it became apparent that in development variation is a good thing and failed experiments generate as much learning as successful ones, companies have recognized that Design for Six Sigma (DFSS) is the right variation of Six Sigma for software development. With its strong focus on discovering the voice of the customer and clear emphasis on data-driven problem solving, DFSS has a lot of good tools to offer a development team.

### Process Leaders—Natural Work Team Leaders

Where Six Sigma programs differ from the Toyota Production System is in the role of change agents. Six Sigma programs often recommend that about 1 percent of the workforce be trained as Black Belts, process leaders who are not supposed to have line responsibility. But it is relatively silent on the training that first-line supervisors should receive. Instead of focusing on process leaders or change agents, Toyota focuses its training efforts mainly on the natural work team leaders, believing that these people should both lead and be responsible for the results of their work teams.[10] We believe that a lean initiative should closely track the Toyota approach and focus on training natural team leaders in preference to process leaders.

### Tools—Results

We know of a case in which a plant showed dramatic improvement on all bottom line results measured by the company, but when the plant was assessed by the corporate process experts, it received a very low score—because it had achieved the outstanding results without showing evidence of using the corporately sanctioned process improvement tools that the experts thought were

---

10. *TPS vs. Lean and the Law of Unintended Consequences*, by Art Smalley, www.superfactory.com/articles/smalley_tps_vs_lean.htm.

essential. This is clearly an improvement initiative gone astray. Every tool—including value stream mapping—has been developed to address specific kinds of problems. If the problem at hand is not best addressed with a tool, then it should not be used. The work team and work team leader should be trained in experiential problem solving and trusted to use the appropriate tool to solve their most important current problem.

## Theory of Constraints

Eliyahu Goldratt, who coined the term Theory of Constraints, starts his audio book *Beyond the Goal*[11] with the proposition that technology can bring benefit if and only if it diminishes a limitation (removes a constraint). If you accept this proposition, then you face the obvious fact that people were functioning quite well before the technology appeared, because there were rules or accommodations in place to deal with the limitation. For example, the Boeing 777 was developed before there was broadband or the World Wide Web. Phones and faxes were heavily used, but who uses faxes any more? Boeing created FTP sites and supported some of the earliest intercompany e-mail.

Just introducing a new technology will not necessarily remove the limitation it was designed to remove, because the accommodations made to deal with the limitation are so woven into the fabric of the company that they are not even recognized. For example, when e-mail became widely available from Internet service providers, large companies took years to open their e-mail systems to the outside world. We were sending e-mail to our college-age children from home long before we could communicate with vendors through our work e-mail systems.

The problem in removing limitations is that we not only have to overcome the constraint, we also have to recognize the accommodation that we were making to live with the constraint—always a difficult task—then we have to remove the accommodation and finally, replace it with new rules.

To successfully adopt a new technology, Goldratt says that we must answer four questions:[12]

1. What is the power of the new technology?

2. What limitation does the new technology diminish?

---

11. *Beyond the Goal*, by Eliyahu Goldratt, Your Coach in a Box Series, Gildan Autio, 2005.
12. Ibid.

3. What rules helped us to accommodate the limitation?

4. What rules should we use once the limitation is replaced?

Consider Enterprise Resource Planning (ERP), once a new technology that gives managers access to a vast amount of information to help make better decisions. Before ERP, decisions were made based on rules that created local optimization, because there was no data to make system-wide decisions. For example, manufacturing mangers tried to optimize efficiency of machines, and sales managers used product costing formulas to decide how to price products. Making decisions based on local optimization was an appropriate approach when it was the only alternative. These decision rules created much better results than random decisions. However, once ERP provides the data to make better system-wide decisions, local optimization rules must be abandoned or else the potential of ERP will go unrealized. Many of the failures of ERP can be attributed to a failure to remove the accommodations and revise the rules from pre-ERP days.[13]

## Changing the Rules

Every state in the United States and every province in Canada has a system for registering liens against property. When property is offered as collateral, a lending institution can check the system to see if the property is free of liens and then register the new lien. Almost all aspects of these systems are governed by state or province laws.

In the late 1990s I worked with a company that was automating property lien registration systems in several US states. The idea was to supply states with an imaging system to scan in the legally required paperwork and thus automate the workflow of data entry and collecting fees.

I was on a team that had two subject matter experts from British Columbia. "We considered an imaging system," the experts said, "but we decided it would be better to do away with paper and go to a Web-based data entry system. Since the law required a paper system, we drafted model legislation that would allow us to get rid of the paper and lobbied the lawmakers to get the new laws adopted. It took well over a year, but the laws passed, and after that, moving to a Web-based system was relatively fast and easy. Now all of the provinces in Canada are adopting the same legislation."

---

13. Ibid.

To my dismay, no one in the US considered adopting a similar paperless system. The laws requiring paper were so woven into the fabric of government work that it didn't seem to cross anyone's mind that paper was an accommodation that could easily be removed, even when prodded by the people who had changed the laws in Canada. The resulting imaging systems were very expensive to implement and continued to require manual data entry from images of paper forms.

—Mary Poppendieck

### Critical Chain

Critical Chain is Goldratt's term for the application of the Theory of Constraints to projects. Goldratt believes that the key constraint of projects—he considers product development to be a project—is created when estimates are regarded as commitments. People working on a project are asked to estimate the amount of effort that each activity will take, but they have to guess, because projects are unique endeavors, so by definition, they are filled with unknowns. Since the estimate will be regarded as a commitment, the estimator accommodates by including a large amount of "safety" time in case things go wrong. However, even if things go well, the estimated time will be used up anyway, since estimators don't want to look like they over-estimated.[14]

Goldratt recommends that estimates be acknowledged as just that—estimates—and the safety margin attached to individual estimates should be removed from the activities and accumulated in a project buffer. With this approach, individual activities will be completed much faster, and the project buffer can be spread across all activities to absorb variation. In the book *Agile Estimating and Planning*,[15] Mike Cohn explains in detail how to do this for software.

Note that project buffers will not speed up overall project execution until accommodations to past practices that are embodied in the expectation and reward mechanisms are changed. In order for Critical Chain to work, everyone—from senior management to those doing the estimates—must abandon the expectation that activities should be delivered within the estimated timeframe. In fact, if half of the activities don't take longer than their estimated time, the system will not achieve the desired improvement.

---

14. Ibid.
15. Mike Cohn, *Agile Estimating and Planning*, Prentice Hall, 2006, Chapter 17.

WHAT HAVE WE LEARNED?

An additional problem with using Critical Chain for software development lies in the assumption that all of the activities needed to complete development should be known in advance and that dependencies among them are understood. As we have seen, these assumptions are inappropriate for most software development. First of all we need to abandon the idea that all requirements should be known at the beginning of a development effort. Secondly, we should focus our creative efforts on breaking dependencies.

At a high level, the Critical Chain project buffer may make sense, but at a detailed level, it is an accommodation to the past. If we break dependencies and have a dedicated team develop in small, deployable increments, we no longer have the problems that Critical Chain was designed to solve. A master in the Theory of Constraints would recognize this as a natural result of the application of the Theory of Constraints, scrutinize the accommodation embedded in the Critical Chain approach, and develop the new rules to use now that the constraint has been removed.

### Accommodations

Hidden in our practices, processes, and rules are a large number of accommodations put there to deal with real or imagined constraints. These accommodations are so ingrained in the fabric of our lives that we usually do not realize that they are there. Many of the practices we have in place were put there to deal with specific problems that are no longer relevant or were never relevant to our particular situation. For example, the early definition of cost, schedule, and scope is largely an accommodation to a funding mechanism which commits all money at the beginning of a project. When projects are funded incrementally, as most new product development is funded, there is no reason to fix these parameters at the beginning of the development cycle.

The development environment of 30 years ago, 20 years ago, even 10 years ago is entirely different than it is today, and the accommodations we made to deal with limited memory, processor power, communication capability, and software options are no longer appropriate. Object-oriented development, automated unit and acceptance testing, service-oriented architectures, topic-oriented documentation, and innumerable tools for small-batch development have recently appeared and are being constantly improved. The Web has spawned innovations ranging from Open Source development to powerful search capability to Voice-over-IP. In an environment that is changing so rapidly, we would do well to be alert for the accommodations that we continue to make for constraints that are no longer present.

## Hypothesis

Once you have decided where you want to go and considered what you already know about change initiatives, the next step is to develop a hypothesis about how to embark on a lean journey. Our hypothesis is this:

The most effective way to get started with lean development is:

- Train team leaders and supervisors (in preference to change agents).

- Emphasize on-the-job thinking (rather than documentation).

- Measure a few key indicators (as opposed to many data points).

## Training

At the start of the 20th century, while Sakichi Toyoda was making looms in Japan, Henry Ford was starting up his automobile company, and Frederick Taylor was publishing his ideas on Scientific Management, a scientist named Charles Allen was developing an industrial education program in New Bedford, Massachusetts. He took a novel approach—he felt that most learning happens on the job, so he taught people how to learn through hands-on experience.

By 1917, Massachusetts had developed a model for American vocational education that was subsequently copied throughout the country, and Charles Allen was its director. There was a war going on, and the US Shipping Board decided to build a thousand new ships. Faced with an urgent need for a tenfold increase in the number of skilled ship builders, the Shipping Board tapped Charles Allen to oversee their training. During the next two years, 88,000 workers went through the training programs Allen developed, which were regarded as a great success. He summarized his experience and philosophy in the book *The Instructor, the Man and the Job*.[16]

Charles Allen felt that most training happened on the job, so he focused on teaching supervisors how to train workers. His first assumption was that supervisors were highly skilled at the work they supervised. Allen's training programs taught supervisors how to transfer this knowledge to new workers using four steps: preparation, presentation, application, and testing. At the same time that the automobile industry was teaching industrial engineers to find the "one best way" and tell workers what to do, Allen was teaching shipbuilding supervisors

---

16. Charles Allen, *The Instructor, the Man and the Job: A Handbook for Instructors of Industrial and Vocational Subjects*, J. B. Lippincott Co., Philadelphia, 1919.

to cooperate with workers to solve problems. His philosophy was, "If the learner hasn't learned, the teacher hasn't taught."

Fast forward 20 years to 1940. The US War Production Board faced a similar problem: A rapid escalation in the production of aircraft and munitions created a huge demand for skilled workers, which was exacerbated by the departure of most of the available young men to fight the war. Drawing upon Allen's success, the War Production Board developed Training Within Industry (TWI), a program focused on training supervisors how to train workers. The basic modules of this training program were:[17]

- **Job Instruction (JI):** This training program was based on the assumption that experienced workers might be very good at what they do, but they may have little experience teaching others how to do the same thing. Using Allen's four steps, supervisors are taught to 1) prepare the worker, 2) present the operation, 3) have the worker try the operation, 4) follow-up by checking frequently, encouraging questions, and gradually tapering off coaching as the worker becomes proficient.

- **Job Methods (JM):** This training program was based on the assumption that workers have many good ideas about how to improve things, but they may not be encouraged to act on these ideas. Supervisors were taught to help workers: 1) break down the job, 2) question every detail, 3) develop a new method along with colleagues, 4) sell the new method broadly, get approval and apply it.

- **Job Relations (JR):** This training program taught supervisors to treat people as individuals and helped them resolve "people" problems effectively and fairly. Supervisors were taught to: 1) get the whole story; 2) weigh the issues, don't jump to conclusions; 3) take action, don't pass the buck; 4) follow-up and check results.

Following Allen's lead, TWI training assumes that first line supervisors know how to do the job of the people reporting to them, and therefore can act as a teachers. It is interesting to note that Deming's sixth and seventh points address the same issues as the TWI training program:

6. Institute training. Managers should know how to do the job they supervise and be able to train workers.

---

17. See Jim Huntzinger, "The Roots of Lean," www.lean.org/Community/Resources/ ThinkersCorner.cfm.

7.   Institute leadership. The job of managers is to help people do a better job and remove barriers in the system that keep them from doing their job with pride.

Perhaps 2 million US supervisors received TWI training, which was credited with large increases in productivity and a huge drop in scrap and grievances. As the war came to an end in 1945, so did the TWI program—at least in the US. TWI training was offered in countries recovering from the war and was especially well received in Japan. As it did with Deming's ideas, Toyota brought the TWI ideas inside, added its own experiences and made it a uniquely Toyota program. To this day, supervisors at Toyota receive training based on the ideas of Charles Allen as implemented in the TWI program.[18]

## Thinking

Toyota executive Teruyuki Minoura says that the "T" in TPS stands for "thinking," and the greatest strength of Toyota's "Thinking Production System" is the way it develops people. "Under a 'push' system, there is little opportunity for workers to gain wisdom because they just produce according to the instructions they are given," he says. "In contrast, a 'pull' system asks the worker to use his or her head to come up with a manufacturing process where he or she alone must decide what needs to be made and how quickly it needs to be made."[19]

Most improvement programs put far too much emphasis on documentation and not nearly enough emphasis on encouraging every person to think every minute about how her or his work situation might be improved. Of course, most companies believe that they encourage workers to think about improvements. For years we have had suggestion systems that encourage workers to write down their good ideas and submit them to the suggestion system, and for years suggestion programs have turned in a dismal track record of improvements. In software development, we use retrospectives to generate lists of things that should change, but too often the same list seems to get generated time and again.

The problem is, most of the ideas from our suggestion programs and brainstorming sessions are turned over to someone else for evaluation and occasionally for implementation. This is a mistake. The people with ideas, working with their teams, should be the implementers of their ideas. They should not be asked to drop their ideas into a suggestion system to be implemented by others.

---

18.  See *TPS vs. Lean and the Law of Unintended Consequences*, by Art Smalley, Ibid.
19.  October 8, 2003, Public Affairs Report, Toyota Motor Corporation, www.toyota.co.jp/en/special/tps/tps.html.

They should not just add their ideas to a long list of good ideas. When good improvement ideas become someone else's problem, the originators have less personal investment in pursuing the idea, and tacit knowledge about the problem is left behind as well.

All workers, all the time, should be expected to question how their current process works and actively encouraged to use effective problem-solving techniques to try out new ideas and implement those that work. Documentation should exist as a basis for this problem-solving process. It should be developed by work teams, used by work teams, maintained by work teams, and readily changed by work teams.

If we value engaged, thinking people, we have to take a hard look at assessment programs that are based on documentation. Typically these programs measure the maturity of an organization by its conformance to documented procedures. While the objective seems innocuous enough on the surface, in practice the assessment process usually places pressure on an organization to freeze its documentation and therefore not change its processes. The result is a disturbing tendency to remove the "right to think" from front-line workers. Quite often workers are encouraged to do exactly what is documented, while the proper emphasis would be to encourage workers to constantly question what is documented. Documentation-focused assessment programs tend to value the stability of the documentation. In fact, they should view frequently changing documentation as a sign of an organization that has learned how to think.

## Measurement

Finding effective measurements for development teams has always been challenging, because results are often not apparent until some time after the development effort is finished. This has led to the proliferation of measurements based on the premise that if each piece of a process is optimized, the results of the process will also be optimized. This premise is a fundamentally flawed view of the way systems work. While it is true that optimizing every piece of a process will show benefits if you start with a totally out-of-control process, it is also true that local optimization will eventually sabotage optimization of the overall system.

Trying to improve the wrong measures creates the wrong incentives—often leading to unintended consequences. For example, project managers are often measured based on earned value. However, earned value is a measurement of adherence to plan; it ignores the question of whether or not the plan is the best way to achieve the desired results. This is how we get software delivered on time, on budget, with planned scope complete, but still have dissatisfied customers.

## Dysfunctional Measurements

A colleague whom I'll call Michelle (not her real name) took over a dysfunctional software development organization a couple of years ago. When she arrived, developer performance was measured in lines of code per hour. Tester performance was measured in number of defects found—more defects indicating better performance.

I can't think of two measurements more likely to lead to dysfunctional behavior. Measuring lines of code per hour encourages developers to produce quantity without regard for value. Measuring the number of defects found creates a huge disincentive for testers to collaborate with developers to produce defect-free code.

The first thing Michelle did was change the measurements. Lines of code were no longer measured, and teams (developers and testers together) were rewarded for *not* finding defects. Over the last two years, through these and other initiatives, Michelle has largely transformed the organization into a productive and appreciated contributor to the company's bottom line.

—Tom Poppendieck

So what measurements should we use to encourage the right behavior? We propose that instead of proliferating measurements, it is best to *reduce* the number of measurements and find system-level measurements that drive the right behavior at the subsystem level. In lean organizations, it is well known what these measurements are: cycle time, financial results, and customer satisfaction. Let's consider how they might be used in software development.

### Cycle Time

The most fundamental lean measurement is cycle time: how long—on the average—does it take to go from concept to cash or from customer "order" to deployed software? This single measurement provides a system-level gauge of your process capability. In addition, it exposes every waste in the system: Every missing skill, weak capability, and defective implementation increases cycle time. Trying to do too much at once increases cycle time, as does complexity, unnecessary dependencies, and intolerance for change.

When you measure cycle time, you should not measure the shortest time through the system. It is a bad idea to measure how good you are at expediting, because in a lean environment, expediting should be neither necessary nor acceptable. The question is not how fast *can* you deliver, but how fast *do* you *repeatedly and reliably* deliver a new capability or respond to a customer request.

The objective of a development organization is to first of all establish a repeatable, reliable cycle time for each classification of work, and then to reduce that cycle time through continuous improvement. This single measurement drives all manner of good behavior in every area of the organization, because it aligns everyone in making the right tradeoffs.

Focusing on cycle time reduction requires the full engagement of the people adding value. It drives collaboration, it drives world-class quality, and it drives standards. Almost everything else you might measure—ability to meet deadlines, quantity of work produced, speed to market, even utilization—will improve with cycle time reduction. However, the opposite is not the case; if you focus on optimizing the subsystem measurements, cycle time will probably move in the wrong direction.

**I want to see some examples of what I should measure for cycle time.**

When a defect goes on your defect list, give it a date. When it gets resolved, calculate how long it was on the list. Keep track of these numbers: average cycle time and standard deviation of resolved defects and average age of items on the defect list.

When an item goes on the product backlog, give it a date. If it is broken out into smaller pieces, each piece keeps the original date. If two items are combined, the new item gets the older date. When an item is deployed, subtract the original date from the deployment date. This is its cycle time. Compute the average cycle time and the standard deviation for the items in each release. Also compute the average waiting time of items still in the backlog.

**But I put big items on the product backlog. No one has spent any time on them, and customers don't consider them an "order."**

1.  In this case you might divide backlog items into three categories:

    A. Features customers think they have "ordered" or items that have had any measurable investment of time.

    B. Stuff you need to break out in order to think about architecture, estimate overall schedule, etc.

    C. Really big bullet product roadmap items.

    Items go into the highest category that fits—so if there are customers that are waiting for a roadmap item, it's an A.

    Date everything as it goes on the backlog. Add a new date if an item moves from C to B. Add another date when it moves to A.

> When an item is deployed, compute three categories of cycle times:
>
> 1. Elapsed time since being assigned to Category A
>
> 2. Elapsed time since being assigned to Category B
>
> 3. Elapsed time since being assigned to Category C
>
> Every release, compute the average cycle time and standard deviation for each of the three categories. See what the numbers tell you. Do you need some different categories?
>
> While you are at it, what is the average age of the A items left in the backlog? Is it within a release or two of the average cycle time of the A items in the release? If the average age of A items is significantly longer than two release cycles, you are not limiting work to capacity.

### Financial Return

Most development efforts receive funding based on a business case. Even government and nonprofit organizations make investments based on business cases. We recommend that the primary measurement of development success should be the realization of the business case. This means, of course, than only realistic business cases should be used to justify development, and that it will be necessary to *follow-up by measuring the actual results*. True, it takes time for the business case to be realized, and true, there are other factors involved. But the basic principle here is that if you measure what you really want, you are much more likely to get it.

If the ultimate goal of the development effort is to create a profitable product, then the development team should understand the profit and loss (P&L) model for the product so they can gear their work to create the most profitable product. For internal development, contracted development, or nonprofit development, the team should be challenged to realize an appropriate return on investment (ROI) or whatever other business metric (e.g., throughput) is used to justify the investment.[20]

---

20. For examples of P&L and ROI models for development teams, see our first book, *Lean Software Development: An Agile Toolkit* by Mary and Tom Poppendieck, Addison-Wesley, pp. 83–91.

We have found that most companies do not expose their development teams to the financial implications of their work. However, every development team we talk to would be delighted to understand the financial objectives of their efforts, make tradeoff decisions with those objectives in mind, and experience the sense of accomplishment that comes from having met those objectives.

Sometimes the objective will not be financial: it may be increased audience for a public radio station, number of children receiving vaccinations, etc. In any case, the first step in chartering a development team is to communicate a clear and compelling statement of what constitutes success, and the final step is to measure that success—or lack thereof—and make it visible.

### Customer Satisfaction

Great solutions delight customers. True, basic needs of customers must be met, and performance must be in line with competitors. But the goal of lean development should be to find ways to delight customers by understanding their situation deeply and solving their problem completely. In the book *The Ultimate Question*,[21] Fred Reichheld claims that companies that delight customers gain a sustainable competitive advantage, while companies that annoy customers will lose these customers the moment a more attractive alternative is available.

Reichheld proposes a single, simple measurement to find out if customers are delighted: the net promoter score. Ask customers one simple question: How likely are you to recommend our product or service? Customers respond on a scale of 0 (would not recommend) to 10 (will definitely recommend). The responses are grouped thus: Scores of 9 and 10 indicate a "promoter." Scores of 0–6 indicate a "detractor." Scores of 7 or 8 indicate a passive customer. These scores are similar to grading in school, where 90–100 is an A or B while scores below 70 are failing scores.

To calculate a net promoter score, subtract the percentage of detractors from the percentage of promoters. You will get a number between -100 percent and 100 percent. Average companies might have a score around 10 percent. Really good companies are in the 50 percent or higher range. Negative scores are cause for serious concern. Reichheld presents evidence that the net promoter score is highly correlated to both market share and profitability, making it a good high-level view of customer satisfaction in a single number.

---

21. See *The Ultimate Question: Driving Good Profits and True Growth*, by Fred Reichheld, Harvard Business School Press, 2006.

## Roadmap

A journey of a thousand miles begins with a single step.[22]

Lean development is a journey that begins where you are and takes you far into the future. As a farewell, we offer a brief roadmap for getting started on your journey:

1. **Begin where you are:** How do you create value and make a profit?

2. **Find your biggest constraint:** What is the biggest problem limiting your ability to create value and make a profit?

3. **Envision your biggest threat:** What is the biggest threat to your ability to continue creating value and making a profit over the long-term?

4. **Evaluate your culture:** Establish and reinforce a culture of deep respect for front-line workers and for partners. Remove barriers that get in the way of pride in workmanship.

5. **Train:** Train team leads, supervisors, and managers how to lead, how to teach, and how to help workers use a disciplined approach to improving work processes.

6. **Solve the biggest problem:** Turn the biggest constraint over to work teams. Expect many quick experiments that will eventually uncover a path to a solution.

7. **Remove accommodations:** Uncover the rules that made it possible to live with the constraint. Decide what the new rules should be.

8. **Measure:** See if end-to-end cycle time, true profitability, and real customer satisfaction have improved.

9. **Implement:** Adopt changes supported by results.

10. **Repeat the cycle:** With the biggest problem addressed, something else will become your biggest problem. Find it and repeat the cycle.

---

22. Lao-tzu (604 BC–531 BC), *The Way of Lao-tzu;* this has also been translated, "A journey of a thousand miles begins where you stand."

# Try This

We offer this 21-step program for implementing lean software development. Each step contains just a brief sketch of what might be done. You will find the details scattered throughout the earlier parts of this book. Consider these as suggestions—try them and see if they produce the results that you are looking for in your organization.

## Optimize the Whole

1. **Implement lean across an entire value stream and the complete product:** Appoint a value stream leader or leadership team that accepts responsibility for the entire value stream starting and ending with customers. Focus on the whole product, not just the software. Draw a value stream map and look for interruptions in flow, loop-backs or churn, and areas in the flow that are either not available when needed or not capable of delivering the needed results. Fix broken processes, and provide missing system capabilities.

2. **Restructure the measurements:** Chances are very high that there are local measurements within the value stream, and chances equally high that these measurements lead to suboptimization—or worse—dysfunction. Stop using the local measurements, and use value stream measurements instead.

3. **Reduce the cost of crossing boundaries:** If there are big delays in a value stream, they probably occur at department or company boundaries. Look at these boundaries carefully and evaluate how much they are actually costing. Anything you can do to speed the flow of value across these boundaries will almost certainly reduce the cost of crossing the boundary.

## Respect People

4. **Train team leaders/supervisors:** Instead of focusing on process leaders, give natural team leaders the training, the guidance, the charter, and the time to implement lean in their areas.

5. **Move responsibility and decision making to the lowest possible level:** Your lean initiative should be implemented by the work teams that create value under the guidance of their existing leaders. Have work teams design their own lean processes, with guidance from properly trained team leads and supervisors. Expect the work teams to ask for what they need to make the new processes work.

6.  **Foster pride in workmanship:** Many things impede pride in workmanship: individual over team rewards, sloppy workspaces and work practices, impossible deadlines, no time for proper testing or refactoring, imposed processes, routine or robot-like jobs, etc. Root out and eliminate these practices: never create conflicting incentives among team members, automate routine tasks, let workers decide the best approach to their job, never ask for sloppy work in the interest of meeting deadlines. Encourage passionate commitment and expect top-quality results. This will have a more sustained positive impact by far than individual incentives and bonuses.

## Deliver Fast

7.  **Work in small batches:** Reduce project size. Shorten release cycles. Stabilize. Repeat. Clean out every list and queue, and aggressively limit their size going forward.

8.  **Limit work to capacity:** Have teams work at a repeatable cadence to establish capacity. Expect teams to pull from queues based on their proven velocity and to completely finish the work before they start on more work. Limit queue sizes, and accept no work unless there is an empty slot in a queue.

9.  **Focus on cycle time, not utilization:** Stop worrying about resource utilization and start measuring time-to-market and/or customer response time.

## Defer Commitment

10. **Abolish the notion that it is a good practice to start development with a complete specification:** Concurrent development means allowing the specification to emerge from the development process. Concurrent development saves money, it saves time, it produces the best results, it allows you to make decisions based on the most current data. There is nothing not to like about concurrent development, so why cling to the idea that there ought to be a complete specification before getting started with development? If the answer is driven by up-front funding, then move to incremental funding. If it is driven by fixed-price contracting practices, move to another contracting model.

11. **Break dependencies:** Instead of worrying about dependencies, do everything possible to break them so that any feature can be added in any order. A divisible systems architecture is fundamental. Ruthlessly question dependencies, and tolerate them only very sparingly.

12. **Maintain options:** Develop multiple options for all irreversible decisions and never close off an option until the last responsible moment. Critical design decisions are tradeoffs. Invest enough in understanding the impact of each option to have the data and the confidence to make the best choice. For all other decisions, create change-tolerant code, keep it clean and simple, and do not hesitate to change it.

## Create Knowledge

13. **Create design-build teams:** Assure that the systems architecture allows products to be broken into logical modules that can be addressed by cross-functional teams representing the interests of all steps in the value stream. Provide each team with the appropriate leadership and incentives to maintain engagement, transparency, and intensive feedback. These teams must be encouraged to share early and often, fail fast, and learn constantly.

14. **Maintain a culture of constant improvement:** Create the time and the expectation that every team and every function will continually examine and improve its processes and test its assumptions. Hold cross-team and cross-functional events to identify accommodations and constraints in the flow of value and replace these with practices and policies that will improve overall results.

15. **Teach problem-solving methods:** Teach the PDCA cycle or the scientific method or some variation of these problem-solving methods. Expect teams to establish hypotheses, conduct many rapid experiments, create concise documentation, and implement warranted changes.

## Build Quality In

16. **Synchronize:** Aggressively reduce partially done work. Write tests first. Test code as soon as possible. Don't put defects on a list—stop and fix them the moment they are detected. Integrate code as continuously and as extensively as possible. Use nested synchronization to integrate with ever larger and more complex systems.

17. **Automate:** Accept that people make mistakes, and mistake-proof through automation. Automate every process you can as soon as early as possible. Automate testing, builds, installations, anything that is routine, but be sure to automate in a way that supports people and keeps them thinking about how to do things better.

18. **Refactor:** Keep the code base clean and simple, and the minute duplication shows up, refactor the code, the tests, and the documentation to minimize complexity.

## Eliminate Waste

19. **Provide market and technical leadership:** Assure that there is clear responsibility for developing a deep understanding of what customers value and a closely associated deep understanding of what the technology can deliver. Be sure the team builds the right thing.

20. **Create nothing but value:** Assure that all steps in all processes are focused on value-creating activities or improved capability to deliver value in so far as this is possible. Measure process cycle efficiency and keep on improving it.

21. **Write less code:** Aggressively limit the features in a system to only those that are absolutely necessary to add value. Develop an organizational intolerance for complexity.

# Bibliography

"Google Philosophy—The Things Google Has Found to Be True," available at www.google.com/corporate/tenthings.html.

"Inditex: The Future of Fast Fashion," *The Economist*, June 18, 2005.

"PC Magazine 1999 Technical Excellence Awards—Web Applications: Google," *PC Magazine*, December 14, 1999, Volume 18, Number 22, p. 104.

Allen, Charles. *The Instructor, the Man and the Job: A Handbook for Instructors of Industrial and Vocational Subjects*, J. B. Lippincott Co., Philadelphia, 1919.

*Material based on Allen's work is still used in Toyota.*

Appleton, Brad. Articles on Agile Software Configuration Management available at www.cmwiki.com/AgileSCMArticles.

Astels, David. *Test-Driven Development*, Prentice Hall, 2004.

*Award-winning book. This is the book to get if you are implementing test-driven development.*

Augustine, Sanjiv. *Managing Agile Projects*, Addison-Wesley, 2005.

*A nice summary of agile leadership practices.*

Austin, Robert D. *Measuring and Managing Performance in Organizations*, Dorset House, 1996.

*You get what you measure, but you can't measure everything, so what should you do? One of the best books on performance measurement we've seen.*

Balle, Freddy and Balle, Michael. "Lean or Six Sigma," available at www.lean.org/library/leanorsigma.pdf.

Beck, Kent (with Cynthia Andres). *Extreme Programming Explained, Second Edition.* Addison-Wesley, 2005.

*The book on XP that started it all. This second edition is a completely new book, and it's great.*

Boehm, Barry and Turner, Richard. *Balancing Agility and Discipline: A Guide for the Perplexed*, Addison-Wesley, 2004.

*The real dichotomy is learning driven vs. plan driven.*

Brin, Sergey and Page, Lawrence. "The Anatomy of a Large-Scale Hypertextual Web Search Engine," *Computer Networks and ISDN Systems*, 30(1–7):107–117, April 1998.

Brooks, Frederick. *The Mythical Man-Month, Anniversary Edition*, Addison-Wesley, 1995, originally published in 1975.

*A classic that has stood the test of time. It shows how little things have changed in 30 years.*

Carrison, Dan. *Deadline! How Premier Organizations Win the Race Against Time*, AMACOM (American Management Association), 2003.

*Stories about how several large, high-profile projects met impossible deadlines. Check out the chapter on the Boeing 777.*

Christensen, Clayton. *The Innovator's Dilemma*, Harvard Business School Press, 1997; Harper Business, 2000.

*A great book on how disruptive technologies displace market leaders almost every time.*

Christensen, Clayton, Cook, Scott, and Hall, Taddy. "Marketing Malpractice: The Cause and the Cure," *Harvard Business Review*, December 2005.

Clark, Kim B. and Fujimoto, Takahiro. *Product Development Performance: Strategy, Organization, and Management in the World Auto Industry*, Harvard Business School Press, 1991.

*Shows how the key to product integrity is information flow, from the market to the technical team and among all members of the technical team.*

Clark, Mike. *Pragmatic Project Automation: How to Build, Deploy and Monitor Java Applications*. Pragmatic Press, 2004.

*Lean mistake-proofing requires automation. This book shows you how.*

Cohn, Mike. *Agile Estimating and Planning*, Addison-Wesley, 2005.

*So you want to be agile and want to know what happens to planning? Read this!*

Cohn, Mike. *User Stories Applied*, Addison-Wesley, 2004.

*The details about how to use stories to drive your development process.*

Collins, James C. *Good to Great*, Harper Business, 2001.

*The five basics for creating great organizations. A great book.*

Constantine, Larry, and Lockwood, Lucy. *Software for Use*, Addison-Wesley, 1999.

*The authoritative book on usage-centered design.*

Cusumano, Michael A. and Selby, Richard W., *Microsoft Secrets*, paperback edition, Simon & Schuster, 1998. Originally published in 1995.

> *How Microsoft developed software in the mid-'90s: small teams, divisible architecture, daily integration, releasable code every quarter.*

de Geus, Arie. *The Living Company: Habits for Survival in a Turbulent Business Environment*, Harvard Business School Press, 1997, 2002.

Deming, W. Edwards. *Out of the Crisis*, MIT Press, 2000.

Denne, Mark and Cleland-Huang, Jane. *Software by Numbers: Low-Risk, High Return Development*, Prentice Hall, 2004.

> *This book shows how to benefit from staged deployment based on economic analysis. Provides solid financial justification for agile development.*

Drucker, Peter. *Management Challenges for the 21st Century*, Harper Business, 1999.

Evans, Eric. *Domain-Driven Design: Tackling Complexity in the Heart of Software*, Addison-Wesley, 2004.

> *An extremely important book that proposes that domain understanding is at the heart of great software design—and shows how to do it.*

Evans, Philip and Wolf, Bob. "Collaboration Rules," *Harvard Business Review*, July–August 2005.

Feathers, Michael. *Working Effectively with Legacy Code*, Prentice Hall, 2005.

> *If you are working with legacy code, get this book!*

Ferdows, Kasra, Lewis, Michael A., and Machuca, Jose A.D. "Rapid-Fire Fulfillment," *Harvard Business Review*, November 2004.

Fielding, Roy T. "Shared Leadership in the Apache Project" *Communications of the ACM*, April 1999.

Fowler, Martin. "StranglerApplication," www.martinfowler.com/bliki/StranglerApplication.html.

Fowler, Martin et al. *Refactoring*, Addison-Wesley, 1999.

> *The classic book on refactoring.*

Freedman, David H. *Corps Business: The 30 Management Principles of the US Marines*, Harper Business, 2000

> *A great book on leadership, management, and bringing out the best in front-line workers.*

George, Michael and Wilson, Stephen. *Conquering Complexity in Your Business: How Wal-Mart, Toyota, and Other Top Companies Are Breaking Through the Ceiling on Profits and Growth*, McGraw-Hill, 2004.

Gilbreth, Frank B. Jr. and Carey, Earnestine Gilbreth. *Belles on Their Toes*, T.Y. Crowell Co., 1950.

Gilbreth, Frank B. Jr. and Carey, Earnestine Gilbreth. *Cheaper by the Dozen*, T.Y. Crowell Co., 1948.

Goldratt, Eliyahu. *Beyond the Goal: Eliyahu Goldratt Speaks on the Theory of Constraints (Your Coach in a Box)*, Coach Series, Gildan Audio, 2005.

Goldratt, Eliyahu and Cox, Jeff. *The Goal*, 2nd Revised Edition, North River Press, 1992, first published in 1984.

*If you haven't read this business novel on the Theory of Constraints applied to manufacturing, you've missed a classic.*

Hamel, Gary. "Management Innovation," *Harvard Business Review*, February 2006.

Hammonds, Keith H. "How Google Grows...and Grows...and Grows," *Fast Company*, Issue 69, April 2003.

Huntzinger, Jim. "The Roots of Lean—Training within Industry: The Origin of Japanese Management and Kaizen," and other documents used for TWI are available at http://artoflean.com/documents/pdfs/ Handout_2c_Roots_of_Lean_and_TWI.pdf.

Kano, Noriaki, Seraku, Nobuhiko, Takahashi, Fumio, and Tsuji, Shinichi. "Attractive Quality and Must-Be Quality, Hinshitsu," *Quality, the Journal of the Japanese Society for Quality Control,* (April 1984), pp. 39–48.

Katzenbach, Jon R. and Smith, Douglas K. *The Wisdom of Teams*, Harvard Business School Press, 1992.

Kennedy, Michael. *Product Development for the Lean Enterprise: Why Toyota's System Is Four Times More Productive, and How You Can Implement It*, Oaklea Press, 2003.

*If you want to know how the company that invented Lean (Toyota) does product development, this is the book to read.*

Kerievsky, Joshua. *Refactoring to Patterns*, Addison-Wesley, 2005.

*The best how-to guide on refactoring.*

Liker, Jeffrey and Meier, David. *The Toyota Way Fieldbook*, McGraw Hill, 2006.

Liker, Jeffrey and Morgan, James. *The Toyota Product Development System: Integrating People, Process, and Technology*, Productivity Press, 2006.

Liker, Jeffrey. *The Toyota Way: 14 Management Principles from the World's Greatest Manufacturer*, McGraw Hill, 2004.

*Worth the price of the book just for the two chapters on the development of the Lexus and the Prius.*

Lohmeyer, Dan, Pogreb, Sofya, and Robinson, Scott. "Who's Accountable for IT?" *McKinsey Quarterly*, December 7, 2004.

MacCormack, Alan. "Product-Development Practices That Work: How Internet Companies Build Software," *MIT Sloan Management Review*, Winter 2001, Vol. 40, Number 2.

MacGibbon, Simon P., Schumacher, Jeffrey R., and Tinaikar, Ranjit S. "When IT's Customers Are External," *McKinsey Quarterly*, Q1 2006.

Marick, Brian. "Agile Testing Directions," available at www.testing.com/cgi-bin/blog/2003/08/21-agile-testing-project-1.

Marick, Brian. "Approaches to Legacy Code," available at www.testing.com/cgi%2Dbin/blog/2005/05/11.

Martin, Robert C. *Agile Software Development: Principles, Patterns, and Practices*, Prentice Hall, 2002.

*Conveys deep wisdom about leveraging object-oriented concepts.*

McAfee, Andrew. "Do You Have Too Much IT?" *MIT-Sloan Management Review*, Spring 2004.

McAfee, Andrew. "Enterprise 2.0: The Dawn of Emergent Collaboration," *MIT Sloan Management Review*, Spring 2006.

Meszaros, Gerard and Bohnet, Ralph. "Test-Driven Porting," Agile 2005 Experience Report available at http://agile2005.org/XR23.pdf.

Miller, Lynn. "Case Study of Customer Input for a Successful Product," Experience Report, Agile 2005 experience report available at http://agile2005.org/XR19.pdf.

Mira, Mattsson, Westblom, Ulf, Forssander, Stefan, Andersson, Gunnar, Medin, Mats, Ebarasi, Sari, Fahlgren,Tord, Johansson, Sven-Erik, Törnquist, Stefan, and Holmgren, Margareta. "Taxonomy of Problem Management Activities," proceedings of the 5th European Conference on Software Maintenance and Reengineering, March 2001, pp. 1–10.

Moore, Geoffrey A. *Crossing the Chasm, revised edition*, Harper Business, 2002; first published 1991.

*The classic marketing book for high-tech products. If you are trying to sell lean/agile concepts, this is a good book to read.*

Mugridge, Rich and Cunningham, Ward. *Fit for Developing Software: Framework for Integrated Tests*, Prentice Hall, 2005.

*Anyone doing automated acceptance testing, including retrofitting legacy code with acceptance tests, should read this.*

Neward, Ted and Mike Clark. *Pragmatic Project Automation for .NET*, Pragmatic Press, forthcoming.

Nonaka, Ikujiro and Takeuchi, Hirotaka. *The Knowledge Creating Company: How Japanese Companies Create the Dynamics of Innovation*, Oxford University Press, 1995.

Norwegian Computer Society. PS2000 Standard Contract—English Version, February 2006, available at http://dataforeningen.no/?module=Articles;action=ArticleFolder.publicOpenFolder;ID=1044.

O'Reilly, Charles A., III, and Pfeffer, Jeffrey. *Hidden Value: How Great Companies Achieve Extraordinary Results with Ordinary People*, Harvard Business School Press, 2000.

Ohno, Taiichi. *Toyota Production System: Beyond Large Scale Production*, Productivity Press, 1988.

*A must-read book by the father of the Toyota Production System. Easy to read, engaging, and profound.*

Poppendieck, Mary and Poppendieck, Tom. *Lean Software Development: An Agile Toolkit*, Addison-Wesley, 2003.

*If you have a lean initiative in your company and you do software development, you should read this book.*

Poppendieck, Mary. "Unjust Deserts," *Better Software Magazine*, August 2004.

*Ideas about team compensation in a lean/agile development organization.*

Public Affairs Division, Toyota Motor Corporation. *The "Thinking" Production System: TPS as a Winning Strategy for Developing People on the Global Manufacturing Environment*, available at www.toyota.co.jp/en/special/tps/tps.html.

Rapp, William V., Co-Principal Investigator. "Automobiles: Toyota Motor Corporation: Gaining and Sustaining Long-Term Advantage Through Information Technology." Case Prepared for the Columbia Project: Use of Software to Achieve Competitive Advantage by The College of International Relations Ritsumeikan University Kyoto, Japan, April 2000.

Raymond, Eric S. "The Cathedral and the Bazaar," available at www.catb.org/~esr/writings/cathedral-bazaar/cathedral-bazaar/, 2000.

Reichheld, Fred. *The Ultimate Question: Driving Good Profits and True Growth*, Harvard Business School Press, 2006.

Reinertsen, Donald G. *Managing the Design Factory*, The Free Press, New York, 1997.

*An excellent book on lean product development.*

Rogers, Paul and Blenko, Marcia. "Who Has the D? How Clear Decision Roles Enhance Organizational Performance," *Harvard Business Review*, January 2006.

Sabbagh, Karl. *21st Century Jet: The Building of the 777*, produced by Skyscraper Productions for KCTS/Seattle and Channel 4 London. 1995.

Sapolsky, Harvey. *The Polaris System Development: Bureaucratic and Programmatic Success in Government*, Harvard University Press, 1972.

Schwaber, Ken and Beedle, Mike. *Agile Software Development with SCRUM*, Prentice Hall, 2001.

*The book to read for an introduction to Scrum.*

Schwaber, Ken. *Agile Project Management with Scrum*, Microsoft Press, 2004.

*A book filled with case studies and down-to-earth tips about how to do Scrum.*

Shingo, Shigeo. *Study of Toyota Production System from an Industrial Engineering Viewpoint*, Productivity Press, 1981.

Shore, Jim. "Quality with a Name," available at www.jamesshore.com/Articles/Quality-With-a-Name.html

Smalley, Art. "TPS vs. Lean Additional Perspectives," available at http://artof-lean.com/documents/pdfs/TPS_versus_Lean_additional_perspectives_v3.pdf.

Smalley, Art. "TPS vs. Lean and the Law of Unintended Consequences," available at www.superfactory.com/articles/smalley_tps_vs_lean.htm.

Smith, Preston G. and Reinertsen, Donald G. *Developing Products in Half the Time, Second Edition*, John Wiley and Sons, 1998, originally published in 1991.

*Still the classic on rapid product development.*

Sobek, Durward Kenneth II. "Principles that Shape Product Development Systems: A Toyota-Chrysler Comparison," a dissertation submitted in partial fulfillment of the requirements for the degree of Doctor of Philosophy (Industrial and Operations Engineering) in the University of Michigan, 1997.

Spear, Stephen and Bowen, H. Kent. "Decoding the DNA of the Toyota Production System," *Harvard Business Review*, September–October 1999.

Stalk, George. "Time—The Next Source of Competitive Advantage," *Harvard Business Review*, July 1988.

Sutherland, Jeff. "Future of Scrum: Parallel Pipelining of Sprints in Complex Projects," Agile 2005 Proceedings, available at http://jeffsutherland.com/scrum/SutherlandFutureOfScrumAgile2005.pdf.

Taylor, Suzanne and Schroeder, Kathy. *Inside Intuit*, Harvard Business School Press, 2003.

Toyoda, Eiji. *Toyota: Fifty Years in Motion*, Kodansha, 1987. First published in Japanese in 1985.

Toyota Motor Corporation. October 8, 2003, Public Affairs Report, available at www.toyota.co.jp/en/special/tps/tps.html.

Ulrich, Dave, Kerr, Steve, and Ashkenas, Ron. *The GE Workout*, McGraw-Hill, 2002.

*Use this as a guide for conducting software development Kaizen Events.*

Van Schooenderwoert, Nancy. "Embedded Agile Project by the Numbers with Newbies," Proceedings, Agile 2006 Conference, Minneapolis, July 2006.

Van Schooenderwoert, Nancy and Morsicato, Ron. "Taming the Embedded Tiger—Agile Test Techniques for Embedded Software," Proceedings, Agile Development Conference, Salt Lake City, June 2004.

Vasilash, Gary S. "Engaging the ES 300," *Automotive Design and Production*, September 2001.

Vise, David A. "Google's Missing Piece," *Washington Post*, February 10, 2005.

Weick, Karl and Sutcliffe, Kathleen, *Managing the Unexpected: Assuring High Performance in the Age of Complexity,* Jossey-Bass, 2001.

*A fascinating book about what makes very dangerous places safe, including aircraft carriers, chemical plants, and emergency scenes.*

Womack, James and Jones, Daniel T. *Lean Solutions: How Companies and Customers Can Create Value and Wealth Together*, Free Press, 2005.

Womack, James, Jones, Daniel, and Roos, Daniel. *The Machine That Changed the World*, Rawson Associates, 1990.

Womack, James P. and Jones, Daniel T. *Lean Thinking*, Simon & Schuster, 1996; Second Edition, Free Press, 2003.

*For almost a decade, this was the best book on Lean. The revised edition remains a classic.*

*www.lean.org contains a wealth of resources on lean thinking.*

# Index

mass production
  *See also* lean, production
  *See also* Toyota Product Development System
  *See also* Toyota Production System
  American auto industry, 2–3
  American System of Manufacture, 1
  Ford Motor Company, 2–3
  General Motors, 2–3
  interchangeable parts, 1–2
  interchangeable people, 2–3
  Japanese auto industry, 4–7
  Japanese textiles, 3–4
  Just-in-Time manufacturing, 4–7
  and lean manufacturing, 12–13
maximizing local efficiencies, 8
McAfee, Andrew, 69
McCabe Cyclomatic Complexity Index, 194–195
Measure UP, 40–41
measurements
  customer satisfaction, 241
  cycle time, 238–240
  decreasing number of, 40–41
  dysfunctional, 238
  improving the wrong ones, 237
  Measure UP, 40–41
  net promoter score, 241
  optimize by decomposition, 40–41
  raising levels, 40–41
  reducing the number of, 238
  ROI (return on investment), 240–241
  Sloan, Alfred P., 40–41
  Sloan's metrics, 40–41
  statistical process control, 120–122
medical device interface example, 162
Meszaros, Gerard, 167
MetaScrum meeting, xvii
metrics. *See* measurements.
Microsoft, respect for people, 36
Miller, Lynn, 55, 189
mindfulness, 9
mind-meld, 50
minimum useful feature sets, 71–72
Minoura, Teruyuki, 236
mistake-proofing, 6–7, 196–198
money, as incentive, 145–146
Muda (waste), xix
Mugridge, Rick, 187
Mulally, Alan, 118, 123, 140
multitasking, causing waste, 78–80
Mura (stress), xix
Muri (bottlenecks), xix

Murphy's Law, 59–60
myths
  finishing the code, 79
  haste makes waste, 35
  one best way, 37–38
  optimize by decomposition, 40–41
  planning is commitment, 33
  predictable outcomes, 31–32
  specifications reduce waste, 24–25
  testing to find defects, 28–29

## N

National Center for Manufacturing Sciences (NCMS), 13
nested synchronization, 203–204
net promoter score, 241
New United Motor Manufacturing Incorporated (NUMMI), 226
newspaper, online subscription, 50
no partial credit, 188
no secrets, 118
Nonaka, Ikujiro, 156
nonfunctional requirements, testing, 201
nonstock production, 6
non-value-added waste, 23, 83
Norwegian Computer Society, 218–219
Norwegian University of Science and Technology (NTNU), 218–219
notebooks, keeping, 156–157
NS minivan, 56
numerical quotas, 123

## O

Ohno, Taiichi
  introduction, 5–6
  planning, 33
  value streams, 83
  waste, 23–25, 75
on the job training, 234–236
one best way, 2, 37–38
one click build, 198
Oobeya, 213
Open Source
  chief engineer approach, 54
  leadership, 54
  reviews, 196
  software example, 209–210
  Strong Project Leader, 54
operations, lean, 11–12
optimize by decomposition, 40–41
optimize the whole, principle of, 38–41

**BOOKS ONLINE**
**ENABLED**

# THIS BOOK IS SAFARI ENABLED

## INCLUDES FREE 45-DAY ACCESS TO THE ONLINE EDITION

The Safari® Enabled icon on the cover of your favorite technology book means the book is available through Safari Bookshelf. When you buy this book, you get free access to the online edition for 45 days.

Safari Bookshelf is an electronic reference library that lets you easily search thousands of technical books, find code samples, download chapters, and access technical information whenever and wherever you need it.

**TO GAIN 45-DAY SAFARI ENABLED ACCESS TO THIS BOOK:**

- Go to **http://www.awprofessional.com/safarienabled**
- Complete the brief registration form
- Enter the coupon code found in the front of this book on the "Copyright" page

If you have difficulty registering on Safari Bookshelf or accessing the online edition, please e-mail customer-service@safaribooksonline.com.

Addison
Wesley